THE
PESSIMIST'S
HANDBOOK

A COMPANION TO DESPAIR

NIALL EDWORTHY
& PETRA CRAMSIE

Illustrations by Emily Faccini

Doubleday

LONDON · TORONTO · SYDNEY · AUCKLAND · JOHANNESBURG

www.**rbooks**.co.uk

TRANSWORLD PUBLISHERS
61–63 Uxbridge Road, London W5 5SA
A Random House Group Company
www.rbooks.co.uk

First published in Great Britain
in 2008 by Doubleday
an imprint of Transworld Publishers

A CIP catalogue record for this book
is available from the British Library.

ISBN 9780385614115

Addresses for Random House Group Ltd companies outside the UK
can be found at: www.randomhouse.co.uk
The Random House Group Ltd Reg. No. 954009

The Random House Group Limited supports The Forest Stewardship
Council (FSC), the leading international forest-certification organization. All our
titles that are printed on Greenpeace-approved FSC-certified paper carry the FSC logo.

Mixed Sources
Product group from well-managed
forests and other controlled sources
www.fsc.org Cert no. TT-COC-2139
© 1996 Forest Stewardship Council
FSC

Our paper procurement policy can be found at
www.rbooks.co.uk/environment

Typeset in Minion
Printed and bound in Great Britain by
CPI Mackays, Chatham, ME5 8TD

2 4 6 8 10 9 7 5 3 1

To Cassandra and Jeremiah

Acknowledgements

The authors and publishers are grateful to the following for permission to reproduce copyright material: Winston Churchill quotations are reproduced with permission of Curtis Brown Ltd, London, on behalf of the Estate of Winston Churchill. Copyright Winston Churchill; quotation from *Vainglory* with permission of AP Watt Ltd on behalf of the Estate of Colonel Thomas Firbank; line from *The Second Sin* by Thomas Szasz (Copyright © Thomas Szasz, 1973) Reprinted by permission of AM Heath & Co. Ltd Authors' Agents; J. B. Priestley quotation is reproduced by kind permission of the Estate of J. B. Priestley; lines from Cyril Connolly are copyright © Cyril Connolly. From *The Ubu Plays*, first published in 1968, reproduced by permission of the author, c/o Rogers, Coleridge & White Ltd, 20 Powis Mews, London W11 1JN; line from *Anger in the Sky* by Susan Ertz, Hodder & Stoughton 1943; excerpt from Vladimir Nabokov's *Speak, Memory: An Autobiography Revisited* by arrangement with the Estate of Vladimir Nabokov. All rights reserved; John Mortimer quotation reproduced from an article in the *Sunday Times* by John Mortimer, 5 October 2003 (Copyright © John Mortimer 2003) by permission of PFD (www.pfd.co.uk) on behalf of John Mortimer; list of Eight Hells taken from *Dictionary of Asian Philosophies* by St Elmo Nauman, © 1978. Reproduced by permission of Taylor & Francis Books; lines from *Man and Superman* by George Bernard Shaw reprinted by permission of the Society of Authors, on behalf of the Bernard Shaw Estate; Evelyn Waugh quotation (source unknown) is Copyright © Estate of Evelyn Waugh and reproduced by permission of PFD (www.pfd.co.uk) on behalf of the Estate of Evelyn Waugh; extract from *Turtle Diary*, by Russell Hoban, published by Bloomsbury; quotations from *Afterthoughts* by Logan Pearsall Smith quoted by kind permission of the London Library; Stevie Smith quotation reproduced with kind permission of the Estate of James MacGibbon; quotation from *Nineteen Eighty Four* by George Orwell (Copyright © George Orwell, 1949) by permission of Bill Hamilton as the Literary Executor of the Estate of the Late Sonia Brownell Orwell and Secker & Warburg Ltd; J. G. Ballard quotation from Interview with Andrea Juno and V. Vale *Re/Search*, No. 8/9 (1984); 'Fire and Ice' from *The Poetry of Robert Frost* edited by Edward Connery Lathem, published by Jonathan Cape. Reprinted by permission of The Random House Group Ltd; Fran Lebowitz quotation from *Metropolitan Life*, 1978, published by Sidgwick & Jackson; extract from *Hearing Secret Harmonies* by Anthony Powell, published by Random House; line from *Shooting an Elephant and Other Essays* by George Orwell (Copyright © George Orwell, 1946); lines from *The Hitchhiker's Guide to the Galaxy*, by Douglas Adams, published by Pan Macmillan, 1979; lines from *A Writer's Notebook* by W. Somerset Maugham, published by Secker & Warburg. Reprinted by permission of The Random House Group Ltd; excerpt from *The Women's Room* by Marilyn French, published by Little, Brown; 'Thar She Blows' originally published in *Hearst's International*. Copyright © 1943 by Ogden Nash. Reprinted by permission of Curtis Brown Ltd; extract from James George Frazer's *The Golden Bough* reprinted with kind permission from the Master and Fellows of Trinity College Cambridge; line from *Incidents in the rue Laugier* by Anita Brookner (Copyright © Anita Brookner, 1995) Reprinted by permission of AM Heath & Co. Ltd Authors' Agents; 'This Be the Verse' is from *Collected Poems* by Philip Larkin, published by Faber and Faber Ltd; extract from Robert Graves's school report reproduced with kind permission of AP Watt; extract from Peter Ustinov's report is from *Ustinov* by Christopher Warwick, Sidgwick & Jackson, 1990; extract from Alan Coren's report from *Could Do Better* by Patrick Dickinson, published by Arrow Books. Reprinted by permission of The Random House Group Ltd; extract from *The Long Dark Tea-time of the Soul*, by Douglas Adams, published by William Heinemann Ltd, 1988; Al Gore quotation is copyright © 2008 by Al Gore, reprinted with permission of the Wylie Agency, Inc.; lines from 'Advice to Young Women' from *Serious Concerns* by Wendy Cope © Wendy Cope 2006; 'Be Not Too Hard' by Christopher Logue, © Christopher Logue, 1996; line from *The British Museum is Falling Down* reproduced with permission of Curtis Brown Group Ltd, London, on behalf of David Lodge. Copyright © David Lodge 1965; 'School Reports' mostly sourced from *Could Do Better* (Pocket Books, 2002) and *Could Do (Even) Better* (Pocket Books, 2004) by Catherine Hurley; extract from *Silent Spring* by Rachel Carson reproduced by permission of Pollinger Limited and the Estate of Rachel Carson; lines from *The Family, Education and Society* by F. Musgrove, 1967, Routledge and Kegan Paul, reprinted by permission of Taylor and Francis Books UK; lines from *Surprised by Joy* by C. S. Lewis copyright © C. S. Lewis Pte. Ltd. 1955, reprinted by permission; lines from chapter 14 by Joseph Alois Schumpeter, 1883-1950, in *Capitalism, Socialism and Democracy*, Routledge, 1942, reprinted by permission of Harvard University; lines from 'The Hollow Men' from *Poems: 1909-1925* by T. S. Eliot, published by Faber and Faber Ltd; 'Unfortunate Coincidence' by Dorothy Parker reproduced by permission of Gerald Duckworth & Co. Ltd.

Categories

Preface

'Not to be born is best.'

SOPHOCLES

TYPICAL, ISN'T IT? When we thought up the idea for this book, we imagined nothing more than a lazy trawl on the high seas of reference, sifting through the flotsam and jetsam of shipwrecked ideas and abandoned dreams, picking up a few miserable facts and desolate quotes to prove the point that life isn't quite as bloody marvellous as our more optimistic friends would have us believe.

We should have known it wouldn't be plain sailing.

Barely had we set out, a limp wind behind us, when quibbles and squabbles erupted among the crew. As we floated aimlessly through the doldrums and straight into a perfect storm of discontent, it was every man and woman for themselves. For a start, we hadn't realized that, lashed by an editor with a conscience, we'd have to track each quotation to its source and, worse, sometimes pay for it! To people who had died 30 years before we were born! And then, with landfall in sight, that we would suddenly be ordered to toss half of our grim haul back overboard: 'We're sinking under the weight of too many words!' our editor whined.

So here – mutiny only narrowly avoided – is *The Pessimist's Handbook*. Although its contents may afford you a certain bleak satisfaction, it's our expectation that, appalled by the absence of your own favourites, and irked by the arbitrariness of the categories, you will have as little fun reading it as we did writing it.

'I tell you, we're in a blessed drain-pipe,
and we've got to crawl along it till we die.'

H. G. WELLS

A Beginner's Guide

What's the point of weeping over parts of life? All of it calls for tears.

SENECA, c. 4 BC–AD 59

Birth, n. The first and direst of disasters.

AMBROSE BIERCE, *The Devil's Dictionary*, 1911

Nothing begins and nothing ends
That is not paid with moan;
For we are born in other's pain,
And perish in our own.

FRANCIS THOMPSON, English poet, 1859–1907, 'The Dread of Height'

Hope is nothing but the paint on the face of Existence; the least touch of truth rubs it off, and then we see what a hollow-cheeked harlot we have got hold of.

LORD BYRON, letter to Thomas Moore, 28 October 1815

The brevity of our life, the dullness of our sense, the torpor of our indifference, the futility of our occupation, suffer us to know but little: and that little is soon shaken and then torn from the mind by that traitor to learning, that hostile and faithless stepmother to memory, oblivion.

JOHN OF SALISBURY, English author, c. 1115–76

'Good morning, Little Piglet,' said Eeyore. 'If it is a good morning,' he said. 'Which I doubt,' said he. 'Not that it matters,' he said.

A. A. MILNE, *Winnie-the-Pooh*, 1926

But against the palpably sophistical proofs of Leibniz that this is the best of all possible worlds, we may even oppose seriously and honestly the proof that it is the *worst* of all possible worlds. For possible means not what we may picture in our imagination, but what can actually exist and last. Now this world is arranged as it had to be if it were to be capable of continuing with great difficulty to exist; if it were a little worse, it would be no longer capable of continuing to exist. Consequently, since a worse world could not continue to exist, it is absolutely impossible; and so this world itself is the worst of all possible worlds.

ARTHUR SCHOPENHAUER, *The World as Will and Representation*, 1818

Pessimists get a great deal of pleasure from the feeling that they are facing the worst that can be known. They exchange the bliss of ignorance for the bliss of knowledge, and they would not change back again. Pessimists as a rule live to a ripe old age. It is questionable if a despairing view of the universe even impairs the digestion as much as a single slice of new bread.

ROBERT LYND, Irish writer, 1879–1949, *The Money-box*

Stupidity is the basic building block of the universe.

FRANK ZAPPA, US musician, 1940–93

The world is disgracefully managed, one hardly knows to whom to complain.

RONALD FIRBANK, British novelist, *Vainglory*, 1915

This world is a comedy to those that think, a tragedy to those that feel.

HORACE WALPOLE, English politician, letter, 1776

A man should have the fine point of his soul taken off to become fit for this world.

JOHN KEATS, letter to J. H. Reynolds, 22 November 1817

The world is too much with us;
    late and soon,
Getting and spending, we lay waste
    our powers …

WILLIAM WORDSWORTH, 1770–1850

For the world, I count it not an inn but an hospital, and a place not to live but to die in.

SIR THOMAS BROWNE, 1605–82

Anyone happy in this age and place
Is daft or corrupt. Better to abdicate
From a material and spiritual terrain
Fit only for barbarians.

ROY FULLER, British poet, 1912–91, 'Translation'

The Pessimist's Handbook

Happiness is an imaginary condition, formerly often attributed by the living to the dead, now usually attributed by adults to children, and by children to adults.

THOMAS SZASZ, US academic, *The Second Sin*, 1973

All the things I really like to do are either illegal, immoral, or fattening.

ALEXANDER WOOLLCOTT, US author, 1887–1943

Wot's the good of Hanyfink? – Why – Nuffink!

Refrain of ALBERT CHEVALIER, music-hall entertainer, 1861–1923

A pessimist is a man who has been compelled to live with an optimist.

ELBERT HUBBARD, US writer and philosopher, 1856–1915

Nothing to do but work,
Nothing to eat but food,
Nothing to wear but clothes
To keep one from going nude.

Nothing to breathe but air,
Quick as a flash 'tis gone;
Nowhere to fall but off,
Nowhere to stand but on!

BENJAMIN FRANKLIN KING, US poet, 1857–94, 'The Pessimist'

'Blessed is the man who expects nothing, for he shall never be disappointed' was the ninth beatitude.

ALEXANDER POPE, letter, 1725

The worst is not;
So long as we can say, 'This is the worst'.

WILLIAM SHAKESPEARE, 1564–1616, *King Lear*

Nothing is so good as it seems beforehand.

GEORGE ELIOT, *Silas Marner*, 1861

Fortune's a right whore:
If she give aught, she deals it in small
     parcels,
That she may take it away all at
     one swoop.

JOHN WEBSTER, English playwright, *The White Devil*, 1612

I have always disliked myself at any given moment; the total of such moments is my life.

CYRIL CONNOLLY, *The Unquiet Grave*, 1944

Nothing matters very much; and very little matters at all.

LORD BALFOUR, British prime minister, 1848–1930

Some immutable laws

Murphy's Law *or* **Sod's Law** *or*
The Law of Universal Consciousness
If anything can go wrong, it will.

(Originally, but now not usually, known as Finagle's Law – thus proving Finagle right!)

Gumperson's Law *or*
The Law of Perverse Opposites
The probability of anything happening is in inverse ratio to its desirability.

Herblock's Law
If it's good, they'll stop making it.

Ginsberg's Theorem
- You can't win.
- You can't break even.
- You can't even quit the game.

Sturgeon's Law
Ninety-nine per cent of everything is crap.

The Second Law of Thermodynamics *or*
There's No Such Thing as a Free Lunch
In every process in the universe, entropy (disorder and a loss of usefulness) will tend to increase.

The Fatal Law of Gravity
When you are down everything falls on you.

(Attributed to SYLVIA TOWNSEND WARNER, 1893–1978)

To speak first about my temperament, I am melancholic – so much so that I have scarcely been seen to laugh more than 3 or 4 times in the last 3 or 4 years.

DUC DE LA ROCHEFOUCAULD, 1613–80

I guess I just prefer the dark side of things. The glass is half-empty – and cracked. And I just cut my lip on it. And chipped a tooth. It's a healthy cynicism and/or pragmatism.

JANEANE GAROFALO, US stand-up comedian, b. 1964

Oh! ever thus, from childhood's hour,
I've seen my fondest hopes decay;
I never loved a tree or flower,
But 'twas the first to fade away.
I never nursed a dear gazelle,
To glad me with its soft black eye,
But when it came to know me well,
And love me, it was sure to die!

THOMAS MOORE, Irish poet, *Lalla Rookh*, 1817

The dupe of friendship, and the fool of love; have I not reason to hate and to despise myself? Indeed I do; and chiefly for not having hated and despised the world enough.

WILLIAM HAZLITT, 1778–1830, *On the Pleasure of Hating*

- Nothing so good but it might have been better
- No rose without a thorn
- Great fortune brings with it great misfortune
- It never rains but it pours
- Damned if you do, damned if you don't
- Expectation is better than realization
- The grass is always greener on the other side of the fence
- All good things must come to an end

I see better things and approve;
I follow the worse.

OVID, 43 BC–AD 17

It seems my soul is like a filthy pond, wherein fish die soon, and frogs live long.

THOMAS FULLER, English churchman, 1608–61

Hence, vain deluding joys,
The brood of Folly, without father bred;
How little you bestead,
Or fill the fixed mind with all your toys.

JOHN MILTON, 'Il Penseroso', 1645

Adventure

Fools rush in where angels fear to tread.

ALEXANDER POPE, 1688–1744

At the end of January 2008 Englishman Mark Boyle set out from his hometown of Bristol on a two-and-a-half-year, 9,000-mile pilgrimage to the birthplace of Mahatma Gandhi to highlight the kindness of his fellow man. The plan was to get to India without spending any money, surviving on the kindness of people he met along the way, as a protest against commercialism. He got as far as Calais. 'People seemed to think I was some kind of refugee,' said the crestfallen adventurer, explaining the language problems that derailed his journey in optimism. 'They thought I was begging.' Boyle conceded his idiosyncratic appearance may also have been a factor in his failure to prise more than a chocolate bar and a small bag of nuts from his French cousins. Commenting on his electric yellow trousers, open sandals and blackened toenails, the organic food store manager added: 'In France, clearly they are a bit more sophisticated and they weren't impressed.'

A life without adventure is likely to be unsatisfying, but a life in which adventure is allowed to take whatever form it will is sure to be short.

BERTRAND RUSSELL, British philosopher, 1872–1970

I love the angelic in his figure, which reminds me of Shelley: the peculiarly and very mysteriously veiled, unapproachable, withdrawing, unadventurous flavour of his being, that not wanting to know, that rejection of material experience, the sublime incest of his fantastically delicate and seductive art.

THOMAS MANN, *Doctor Faustus*, 1947, of composer Frédéric Chopin

Caution is the eldest child of wisdom.

VICTOR HUGO, French poet, 1802–85

People travel to wonder at the height of mountains, at the huge waves of the sea, at the long courses of rivers, at the vast compass of the ocean, at the circular motion of the stars; and they pass by themselves without wondering.

St Augustine, 354–430

Had we lived I should have had a tale to tell of the hardihood, endurance and courage of my companions which would have stirred the heart of every Englishman. These rough notes and our dead bodies must tell the tale.

Captain Robert Falcon Scott's last message to the world, 25 March 1912

They sailed away in a Sieve, they did,
In a Sieve they sailed so fast,
With only a beautiful pea-green veil
Tied with a riband by way of a sail,
To a small tobacco-pipe mast;
And every one said, who saw them go,
'O won't they be soon upset, you
    know!
For the sky is dark, and the voyage is
    long,
And happen what may, it's extremely
    wrong
In a Sieve to sail so fast!'

Edward Lear, 1812-88, 'The Jumblies'

● It is better to be careful a hundred times than to be killed once

So many centuries after the Creation it is unlikely that anyone could find hitherto unknown lands of any value.

Committee advising Ferdinand and Isabella on Columbus's proposal for a journey of discovery, 1486

See one promontory (said Socrates of old), one mountain, one sea, one river, and see all.

Robert Burton, 1577–1640, *The Anatomy of Melancholy*

Mount Everest may be the most famous mountain in the world, but K2, the 'Mountain of Mountains', is the most infamous. So far, 77 climbers out of the 300 who have attempted its summit have been killed, with 11 of those deaths occurring in July 2008. Greg Child, the Australian who conquered K2 nearly twenty years ago, believes that, in spite of the appalling danger, people will keep being drawn to the mountain, not only because of its awesome beauty, but also because of 'the stories of what's happened to people who've tried it: how fucked up they've become and how many have died'.

Adventure is just bad planning.

Roald Amundsen, Norwegian explorer, 1872–1928

Africa

You describe our country as if it is a graveyard.

Attributed to ROBERT MUGABE, Zimbabwean president, b. 1924

The term Afro-pessimism was coined to denote all that is depressing about the state of Africa. It has been in circulation for many years now and shows no signs of going away.

The number of poor in Africa went up in the past ten years by a third, while going down in large parts of Asia (China and India). Over 300 million people in Africa still have no access to clean water and 450 million have inadequate sanitation. And nearly one African child in six dies before the age of five.

The UN has nearly 50,000 troops attempting to keep the peace across Africa. One of the most brutal conflicts of recent times in Africa was in Sierra Leone. Over the course of the lengthy war, rebels mutilated up to 20,000 people, cutting off their legs, arms, lips and even ears with knives, machetes and axes. According to Amnesty International up to another 70,000 were killed in the conflict. The International Rescue Committee Mortality Survey for the Democratic Republic of Congo estimates that 3.9 million people have died in the country since the troubles began in 1998, making it the world's deadliest conflict since the Second World War.

Small and landlocked Switzerland, with 7 million people, has a GDP on a par with the whole of Africa, with its 726 million people (BBC sources).

The AIDS epidemic is having a bigger impact on Africa than other continents. According to UN sources, Africa is home to 70 per cent of adults with AIDS and 80 per cent of children. Africa has also buried three-quarters of the 20 million people who have developed AIDS since statistics on the disease began.

The African population is projected to grow to 1.8 billion people by 2050 and this when one in three people on the continent are still deemed undernourished. Europe's share of the world population has declined dramatically in recent years from 21.7 to 12.8 per cent. Africa's share, though, has shot up from 8.9 to 12.7 per cent and will grow to 21.8 per cent. In half a century alone, West Africa, for instance, will have the same population as Europe. East Africa will have a larger population than all the countries of Latin America, Oceania and the Caribbean. Overpopulation is already leading to the overexploitation of the land. A recent report by the International Centre for Soil Fertility and Agricultural Development (IFDC) revealed that more than 80 per cent of farmland in sub-Saharan Africa is hit by severe degradation.

In Africa, 340 million people, or half the population, live on less than US$1 per day. The mortality rate of children under five years of age is 140 per 1,000, and life expectancy at birth is only 54 years. Just 58 per cent of the population have access to safe water. The rate of illiteracy for people over 15 is 41 per cent. There are only 18 mainline telephones per 1,000 people in Africa, compared with 146 for the rest of the world as a whole and 567 for high-income countries. Under a quarter of people in sub-Saharan Africa have access to electricity.

The Association of African Universities believes up to 30 per cent of Africa's university-trained professionals and up to 50,000 Africans with PhDs live and work outside the continent. The problem is especially acute in sub-Saharan Africa where many countries lost precious members of their skilled workforce during the 1970s and 1980s. It is believed that Africa lost more than $1.2 billion worth of investment on the 60,000 professionals who left the continent between 1985 and 1990.

Although Africa suffers from some of the world's most virulent and dangerous diseases, access to adequate and up-to-date medication remains limited compared to industrialized countries. The World Health Organization (WHO) estimates that prompt diagnosis and treatment with appropriate medicines could save millions of lives a year in Africa.

Corruption continues to drain Africa of vital income. It has been suggested that it accounts for a quarter of the GDP of African states – nearly $150 billion.

Afterlife

The eternal silence of these infinite spaces (the heavens) terrifies me.

BLAISE PASCAL, 1623–62, *Pensées*

Millions long for immortality who don't know what to do with themselves on a rainy Sunday afternoon.

SUSAN ERTZ, Anglo-American novelist, 1894–1985, *Anger in the Sky*

The cradle rocks above an abyss, and commonsense tells us that our existence is but a brief crack of light between two eternities of darkness. Although the two are identical twins, man, as a rule, views the prenatal abyss with more calm than the one he is heading for (at forty-five hundred heartbeats an hour).

VLADIMIR NABOKOV, 1899–1977, *Speak, Memory: An Autobiography Revisited*

But the children of the kingdom shall be cast out into outer darkness: there shall be weeping and gnashing of teeth.

The Bible, Matthew 8:12

 _____

To die, to sleep!
To sleep, perchance to dream,
  ay there's the rub,
For in that sleep of death what dreams
  may come
When we have shuffled off this
  mortal coil
Must give us pause –

WILLIAM SHAKESPEARE, *Hamlet*

_____

Hell in Scotland: A Survey of Where the Nation's Clergy Think Some Might Be Heading

A survey of 750 Scottish clergy of many different denominations found that, while ministers rarely preach fire and brimstone any more, more than a third still believe in the existence of Hell as a real place where wicked souls will suffer eternal mental anguish, with hardline churchmen, mostly in the Highlands and the Western Isles, *believing that the sinful will suffer endless physical torment to boot. Dr Eric Stoddart, a lecturer in practical theology at St Andrews University, also revealed that more than half of those that he surveyed believed in an actual Day of Judgement on which souls will be divided up into the saved and the damned. You have been warned.*

Hell is an all-male black-tie dinner of chartered accountants which goes on for eternity.

JOHN MORTIMER, *Sunday Times*, 2003

That's what Hell will be like, small chat to the babbling of Lethe about the good old days when we wished we were dead.

SAMUEL BECKETT, 1906–89, *Embers*

I'm definitely not going to heaven. I'm sure it's very white and cold, sparsely furnished with maybe a bit of shining chrome here and there.

JEFFREY BERNARD, legendary English journalist, 1932–97

It's a curious thing that every creed promises a paradise which will be absolutely uninhabitable for anyone of civilised taste.

EVELYN WAUGH, 1903–66

Eight hells await sinners after death and prior to re-birth, according to Buddhism:

1 Hell of Repetition (*Samjiva*), for those who kill, lasting 500 years;

2 Black Rope Hell (*Kala-Sutra*), for those who steal, lasting 1,000 years;

3 Crowded Hell (*Samghata*), for those who abuse sex, lasting 2,000 years;

4 Screaming Hell (*Raurava*), for drunks, lasting 4,000 years;

5 Great Screaming Hell (*Maharaurava*), for those who lie, lasting 8,000 years;

6 Hell of Burning Heat (*Tapana*), for those who hold false views (such as not believing in *Tapana*), lasting 16,000 years;

7 Hell of Great Burning Heat (*Pratapana*), for those guilty of sexual defilement of religious people, lasting half a medium *kalpa* (a *kalpa*, according to one account, is the length of time it would take an angel who polished a cube-shaped rock measuring eighty leagues just once in every hundred years to completely wear out the rock); and

8 Hell of No Interval (*Avici*), for murderers, lasting a medium *kalpa*.

ST ELMO NAUMAN, JR, *Dictionary of Asian Philosophies*, 1978

The website www.near-death.com gathers together stories of people who have been through near-death experiences. Many were declared clinically dead before coming back to life, and some have been so deeply affected by their horrific visions of the Afterlife that they have never fully recovered. Bryan Melvin, who 'died' in Arizona in 1980, recalls leaving his body and seeing a figure resembling Jesus, before being sucked towards a place of foul smells where dreadful creatures were held captive in small gelatinous and mirrored cubes. Tony Lawrence, senior lecturer in psychology at the University of Coventry, is currently studying negative near-death experiences, intrigued as to why people from such different backgrounds and religious beliefs, and with no particular profile for vice or drug-taking, seem to share similarly terrifying visions of hell and eternal darkness.

The terrible meditation of hell fire and eternal punishment much torments a sinful silly soul. What's a thousand year to eternity? … a finger burnt by chance we may not endure, the pain is so grievous, we may not abide an hour, a night is intolerable; and what shall this unspeakable fire then be that burns for ever, innumerable infinite millions of years … O eternity!

ROBERT BURTON, 1577–1640, *The Anatomy of Melancholy*

Abandon hope, all ye who enter here

In Dante's Inferno, depending on which particular sin has led you to eternal damnation (and it's hard to think that many of us would escape, since the list includes pagans, fortune tellers, the lustful, gluttons, hoarders, the avaricious and the prodigal, the wrathful and the gloomy, heretics, suicides, blasphemers, sodomites, hypocrites, flatterers, thieves, false counsellors and traitors), souls are placed in one of the nine hierarchies of Hell. Here's a mere taste of the punishments on offer:

- *Level 2*: Along with Cleopatra and Helen of Troy, lustful souls spend eternity being buffeted and molested by a cruel whirlwind of unquenchable desire
- *Level 5*: The wrathful tear at each other with their teeth, naked and raging, while the gloomy lie gurgling in the River Styx, trying to speak but unable to because their mouths are full of turgid mud
- *Level 7*: Here, the violent suffer for ever in a river of boiling blood, while naked blasphemers lie on scorching sand and are showered with fiery flakes
- *Level 8 (the Malebolge or Evil Pouches)*: A pit of despair with ten vile ditches each with its own speciality, such as Number 2 where flatterers wallow in human excrement, and Number 5, where corrupt politicians swelter in boiling pitch

- *Level 9 (Cocytus):* The last circle of Hell is reserved for traitors, deep frozen, eyes and mouths iced shut, with the worst traitors of all time, including Judas, being chewed on by Satan himself

Ah well, there is just this world and then the next, and then all our troubles will be over with.

OLD LADY, quoted by L. O. Asquith

Let me complete my friend Lucifer's similitude of the classical concert. At every one of those concerts in England you will find rows of weary people who are there, not because they really like classical music, but because they think they ought to like it. Well, there is the same thing in heaven. A number of people sit there in glory, not because they are happy, but because they think they owe it to their position to be in heaven. They are almost all English.

GEORGE BERNARD SHAW, 1856–1950, *Man and Superman*

F. W. H. Myers, whom spiritualism had converted to belief in a future life, questioned a woman who had lately lost her daughter as to what she supposed had become of her soul. The mother replied, 'Oh well, I suppose she is enjoying eternal bliss, but I wish you wouldn't talk about such unpleasant subjects.'

BERTRAND RUSSELL, *Unpopular Essays*, 1950

A dungeon horrible, on all
    sides round
As one great furnace flamed, yet from
    those flames
No light, but rather darkness visible
Served only to discover sights of woe,
Regions of sorrow, doleful shades,
    where peace
And rest can never dwell, hope
    never comes
That comes to all; but torture
    without end
Still urges, and a fiery deluge, fed
With ever-burning sulphur
    unconsumed …

JOHN MILTON, 1608–74, *Paradise Lost*

We have no reliable guarantee that the afterlife will be any less exasperating than this one, have we?

NOËL COWARD, 1899–1973, *Blithe Spirit*

There is a dreadful Hell,
And everlasting pains;
There sinners must with devils dwell
In darkness, fire, and chains.

ISAAC WATTS, 1674-1748, *Divine Songs for Children*

Animals

I confess freely to you, I never could look long upon a monkey, without very mortifying reflections.

WILLIAM CONGREVE, 1670–1729

I loathe people who keep dogs. They're cowards who have not got the guts to bite people themselves.

AUGUST STRINDBERG, Swedish dramatist, 1849–1912

That indefatigable and unsavoury engine of pollution, the dog.

JOHN SPARROW, English academic, letter to *The Times*, 1975

A man who carries a cat by the tail learns something he can learn in no other way.

MARK TWAIN, 1835–1910

Cat, n. A soft, indestructible automaton provided by nature to be kicked when things go wrong in the domestic circle.

AMBROSE BIERCE, *The Devil's Dictionary*, 1911

Nothing to be done really about animals. Anything you do looks foolish. The answer isn't in us. It's almost as if we're put here on earth to show how silly they aren't.

RUSSELL HOBAN, *Turtle Diary*, 1975

It was a spring without voices. On the mornings that had once throbbed with the dawn chorus of robins, catbirds, doves, jays, wrens, and scores of other bird voices there was now no sound; only silence lay over the fields and woods and marsh …

No witchcraft, no enemy action had silenced the rebirth of new life in this stricken world. The people had done it themselves.

RACHEL CARSON, *Silent Spring*, 1962

- He who lies down with dogs, rises with fleas
- Don't count your chickens before they hatch
- Curiosity killed the cat

Living Species

The irreversible loss of species, which by 2100 may reach one third of all species now living, is especially serious. We are losing the potential they hold for providing medicinal and other benefits, and the contribution that genetic diversity of life forms gives to the robustness of the world's biological systems and to the astonishing beauty of the earth itself. Much of this damage is irreversible on a scale of centuries or permanent … Our massive tampering with the world's interdependent web of life – coupled with the environmental damage inflicted by deforestation, species loss, and climate change – could trigger widespread adverse effects, including unpredictable collapses of critical biological systems whose interactions and dynamics we only imperfectly understand.

From 'The World Scientists' Warning to Humanity', 1992

The Holocene Extinction Event

– that is, the first manmade mass extinction, is now well under way, with the rate of extinctions estimated at 100 to 1,000 times the usual, natural extinction rate. One terrible story, the life and death of the Passenger Pigeon, highlights mankind's wretched shortsightedness. Once the most common bird in North America, this pigeon would migrate in stupendously enormous flocks of about a billion birds, a mile wide and three hundred miles long, which took several days to pass. This proved such a temptation to the men with guns that, by the 1870s, the species was declining catastrophically. Martha, the last pathetic survivor out of five billion, died on 1 September 1914, in Cincinnati, Ohio.

Two Questions, from *Ishmael* by Daniel Quinn, 1998:

> WITH MAN GONE,
> WILL THERE
> BE HOPE
> FOR GORILLA?

and:

> WITH GORILLA GONE,
> WILL THERE
> BE HOPE
> FOR MAN?

Read 'Em and Weep

Sebastian Brooke, a stone-carver from Monmouth, is proposing to create a Mass Extinction Memorial Observatory (MEMO) on the island of Portland, off Dorset. The plan is for a massive stone monument open to the sky, with a single arched entrance, and each of the structure's stones bearing the image and name of a single extinct creature. Roofless, this unique structure will be perpetually unfinished as more species perish (so far, according to the IUCN Red List, the number of known extinctions since the Dodo now stands at around 850 species). For more, see www.memoproject.org.

I fell also to think, what advantage these innocent animals had of man, who as soon as nature cast them into the world, find their meat dressed, the cloth laid, and the table covered; they find their drink brewed, and the buttery open, their beds made, and their clothes ready; and though man hath the faculty of reason to make him a compensation for the want of those advantages, yet this reason brings with it a thousand perturbations of mind and perplexities of spirit, griping cares and anguishes of thought, which those harmless silly creatures were exempted from.

JAMES HOWELL, British writer, 1594–1666

Colony Collapse

In 2007, in the USA, 25 per cent of the honeybees in commercial hives simply disappeared. No dead bodies were found, just hives, mysteriously empty. In fact, in an unprecedented die-off, bee populations are starting to collapse worldwide and we don't know why. Is it because of GM, pesticides, radiation from mobile phone networks, climate change, or something else? It's not just our honey that's in danger; a third of the world's food supply – an estimated 130,000 plants, from apples to zucchini – needs bees for pollination, while another third is indirectly supported by the hive of industry (cows need hay, hay needs bees). The workers from just one hive can visit a million flowers in a day. Who will do this if they disappear for ever? Will the sound of a lazy summer's day in the future be not the hum of bees but the roar of giant blowers as desperate farmers attempt to pollinate their own crops?

———

From the fact that there are 400,000 species of beetles on this planet, but only 8,000 species of mammals, Haldane concluded that the Creator, if He exists, has a special preference for beetles.

From a report of a lecture by J. B. S. HALDANE, 7 April 1951

It's unlucky to see:

- Three seagulls flying directly overhead – it's a warning of impending death.

- An albatross, when you're out at sea, because it's a harbinger of bad weather. But don't kill it. Remember what happened to the Ancient Mariner.

- A lone magpie – unless, of course, you tip your hat and say 'Good morning, Mr Magpie' three times.

You must not love animals, they don't last long enough. You must not love humans, they last too long.

ANON

All animals, except man, know that the principal business of life is to enjoy it – and they do enjoy it as much as man and other circumstances will allow.

SAMUEL BUTLER, *The Way of All Flesh*, 1903

It is well known that, worldwide, more people die every year by being kicked to death by donkeys than in plane crashes. In Africa, hippos allegedly kill more people per year than crocodiles, buffalo and lions put together. In other animal-related news, it's useful to know that you're far more likely to be bitten to death by a dog than a spider. Other animals to run/swim a mile from (or lie down and play dead from) are:

Bears (roughly 5 human fatalities per year worldwide)

Sharks (30)

Jellyfish (100)

Bees (400)

Elephants (500)

Scorpions (5,000)

Snakes (100,000)

Mosquitos (2,000,000)

Architecture

For it seems that long before the first enterprising man bent some twigs into a leaky roof, many animals were already accomplished builders.

BERNARD RUDOFSKY, *Architecture without Architects*, 1964

Very few architects know anything about architecture. For 500 years architecture has been a phoney.

Attributed to FRANK LLOYD WRIGHT, 1867–1959

At the moment it looks as though London seems to be turning into an absurdist picnic table – we already have a giant gherkin, now it looks as if we are going to have an enormous salt cellar.

PRINCE CHARLES, on the design for Renzo Piano's 1,000ft 'Shard of Glass', 2003

Architecture is the art of how to waste space.

ARATA ISOZAKI, Japanese architect, b. 1931

The Carbuncles competition was established in 2000 to stimulate debate on the miserable quality of development blighting many of Scotland's towns and cities. It now causes quite a stir when announced. The Plook on the Plinth Award for the Most Dismal Town in Scotland first went to Airdrie in North Lanarkshire. The following year the award was handed to Cumbernauld. See www.thecarbuncles.co.uk.

———

The Ryugyong Hotel in Pyongyang, North Korea, is reckoned by many to be the most unsightly and worst-built monument in the world. It is 105 storeys high and dominates Pyongyang's skyline like a titanic hydra. The place is such a carbuncle that official photos of the North Korean capital sometimes airbrush out the hotel. Inside are 3,000 totally cheerless rooms. The hotel relies on 328-foot-long wings which shape it into a concrete pyramid. It stands 1,083 feet high and is lovingly called the Hotel of Doom by the citizens of Pyongyang.

Art

What do these so-called artists mean when they preach the discovery of the 'new'? Is there anything new? Everything has been done, everything has been discovered.

JEAN AUGUSTE DOMINIQUE INGRES, 1780–1867

Painting: The art of protecting flat surfaces from the weather and exposing them to the critic.

AMBROSE BIERCE, *The Devil's Dictionary*, 1911

I thought it would be my one and only exhibition, so I decided to call it My Major Retrospective.

TRACEY EMIN, b. 1963

Sculpture is the art of the hole and the lump.

AUGUSTE RODIN, 1840–1917

Every time I paint a portrait I lose a friend.

JOHN SINGER SARGENT, US painter, 1856–1925

Look, it's my misery that I have to paint this kind of painting, it's your misery that you have to love it, and the price of the misery is thirteen hundred and fifty dollars.

MARK ROTHKO, abstract expressionist, 1903–70

For all their labelling of much of modern art as degenerate, and their persecution of well-known artists such as Otto Dix and Oskar Kokoschka, the Nazis were also keen on plundering Old Masters. Over the course of the Second World War, everything from disused mines to museum vaults were used to stock hundreds of thousands of looted works of art, many stolen from murdered Jewish collectors. www.lostart.de is a database set up by the German government to register and trace lost artworks.

The canvas was always saying no to me.

ROMARE BEARDEN, US painter, 1914–88

Baldness

Good to see a lot of bald men here tonight. Did you first notice it, sir, when it took longer and longer to wash your face? Flannels not quite lasting as long as they should?

HARRY HILL, English stand-up comedian, b. 1964

And he [Elisha] went up from thence unto Beth-el: and as he was going up by the way, there came forth little children out of the city, and mocked him, and said unto him, Go up, thou bald head; go up, thou bald head. And he turned back, and looked on them, and cursed them in the name of the Lord. And there came forth two she-bears out of the wood, and tare [ripped apart] forty and two children of them.

The Bible, II Kings 2:23–4

A man is usually bald four or five years before he knows it.

EDGAR WATSON HOWE, US novelist, 1853–1937

Attention All Slapheads: if you want to keep your head, get a hat!

If you must go out for a walk in the countryside, make sure you go bewigged or behatted – or risk suffering the fate of Aeschylus. On a sunny day in 456 BC, according to legend, the bald-pated playwright went for an innocent stroll in Sicily. A great eagle-like vulture, the lammergeier, mistook his shiny bonce for a rock, and dropped a tortoise on it to smash it – the tortoise, that is. In the event, Aeschylus' head was broken open; the tortoise got away with minor injuries.

An Egyptian papyrus scroll dating back to at least 1000 BC prescribes a crocodile-fat-and-hippopotamus-dung ointment for hair loss, which may be the reason that the Pharaohs were never seen out in public without wigs on. Meanwhile, Hippocrates, the Father of Medicine, and not known for being a quack, recommended an application of cumin, pigeon droppings, nettles and horseradish.

Beauty

A beautiful face is a dumb commendation.

SYRUS PUBLILIUS, 1st century BC

What is beauty, but a well-dressed skull that loses colour with the slightest illness, and, before death robs it of everything, the grace of its external and apparent surface is mortified by the years in such a way that, if eyes could penetrate within beauty, they could watch it only full of horror?

ANTONIO VIEIRA, Portuguese missionary, 'Sermon of the Silent Devil', 1666

When a woman isn't beautiful, people always say, 'You have lovely eyes, you have lovely hair.'

ANTON CHEKHOV, Uncle Vanya, 1897

Nothing is beautiful from every point of view.

CHARLES HORACE MAYO, 1865–1939

Beauty is but a flower
Which wrinkles will devour.

THOMAS NASHE, 'A Litany in Time of Plague', 1592

One evening, I sat Beauty on my knees. – And I found her bitter. – And I hurt her.

ARTHUR RIMBAUD, Une Saison en enfer, 1873

Piobbico is a small town in the Marche region of Italy and it is home to Italy's one and only Club dei Brutti (Ugly Club). Every year, on the first Sunday of September, the small town throngs with ugly people who have come to celebrate the annual festival of ugliness. There is a top prize and for several years now it has been awarded to a certain Telesforo Iacobelli.

US bumper stickers

- Beauty is in the eye of the beer holder.
- Beauty is only skin deep. Ugly goes straight to the bone.

Love built on beauty, soon as beauty, dies.

JOHN DONNE, 1572–1631

Gurning is the high art of pulling extremely ugly and completely repellent grimaces. It is generally done by sucking in one's cheeks, twisting the lips and popping out one's eyes as much as possible without causing damage to the face. Cumbria has been holding an annual gurning fair since 1267! See www.egremontcrabfair.org.uk.

In the last decade, there has been an almost 800 per cent increase in the number of non-surgical cosmetic procedures. People are increasingly acting to stop their cheeks sagging, their lips thinning and their brow creasing, with the most popular 'lunch-break procedures' being regular injections with hyaluronic acid or Botulinum toxin (Botox, to its friends). So, if you've got £200 to spare, why don't you pop out for a bit of youthful plumping-up instead of a sandwich?

People don't very much like things that are beautiful – they are so far from their nasty little minds.

CLAUDE DEBUSSY, 1862–1918

What a terrifying reflection it is, by the way, that nearly all our deep love for women who are not our kindred depends – at any rate, in the first instance – upon their personal appearances.

SIR RIDER HAGGARD, *She*, 1887

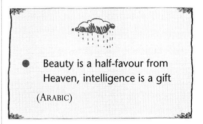

- Beauty is a half-favour from Heaven, intelligence is a gift
  (ARABIC)

The demand for cosmetic surgery is rising every year, with around 11.5 million cosmetic procedures in the US alone in 2006. Generally, the top five procedures requested are: liposuction, breast augmentation, eyelid surgery, breast reduction and rhinoplasty. Among the potential complications, however, are: gangrene, body asymmetry, numbness and, of course, death.

Doctor Faustus, of Helen of Troy:

Was this the face that launch'd a
    thousand ships,
And burnt the topless towers of Ilium?

CHRISTOPHER MARLOWE, 1564–93,
Doctor Faustus

Books and Reading

With a goose quill and a few sheets of paper I mock the universe.

PIETRO ARETINO, 1492–1557

The more books one reads, the more stupid one becomes.

MAO TSE-TUNG, 1893–1976

And what is the use of a book, thought Alice, without pictures or conversations?

LEWIS CARROLL, *Alice's Adventures in Wonderland*, 1865

I have the conviction that excessive literary production is a social offence.

GEORGE ELIOT, 1819–80

Books, like men their authors, have no more than one way of coming into the world, but there are ten thousand to go out of it, and return no more.

JONATHAN SWIFT, *A Tale of a Tub*, Epistle Dedicatory, 1704

Times are bad. Children no longer obey their parents, and everyone is writing a book.

MARCUS TULLIUS CICERO, 106–43 BC

Writing a book of poetry is like dropping a rose petal down the Grand Canyon and waiting for the echo.

DON MARQUIS, US author, 1878–1937

Bees are sometimes drowned in the honey which they collect – so some writers are lost in their collected learning.

NATHANIEL HAWTHORNE, *The American Notebooks*, 1842

What is a modern poet's fate?
To write his thoughts upon a slate;
The critic spits on what is done,
Gives it a wipe – and all is gone.

THOMAS HOOD, 1799–1845, 'A Joke'

A report released by the National Endowment for the Arts entitled 'Reading at Risk: A Survey of Literary Reading in America' points to a dramatic decline in the number of US adults reading literary fiction. The biggest drop in readers was in the youngest age groups, where a 28 per cent decline was noticed between 1982 and 2002.

All poets are mad.

ROBERT BURTON

No place affords a more striking conviction of the vanity of human hopes, than a public library.

SAMUEL JOHNSON, *The Rambler*, 1750–2

Everything has been said. After seven thousand years of human thought, we have come too late.

JEAN DE LA BRUYÈRE, 1688

Lies and literature have always been friends.

JEAN DE LA FONTAINE, *Fables*, 1668

I like to write when I feel spiteful; it's like having a good sneeze.

D. H. LAWRENCE, letter to Lady Asquith, November 1913

The Infinite Monkey Theory in popular culture is that if you get a million monkeys and give them a million typewriters, one or several of them would eventually come up with a Shakespeare play. They might also come up with Madame Bovary, War and Peace or The Descent of Man while they were at it.

Boredom

Dear World, I am leaving because I am bored. I am leaving you with your worries in this sweet cesspool.

GEORGE SANDERS, actor, 1906–72, said to be the opening line of his suicide note

If only people had the gift of knowing when they were bored and the courage to admit the fact openly when it was discovered, how many novelists, poets, playwrights, musicians and entertainers would be compelled to join the ranks of the unemployed?

ARNOLD BENNETT, *Journals*, 1932

Look for pleasure and you'll find boredom.

HONORÉ DE BALZAC, 1799–1850, *La Fille aux yeux d'or*

Since boredom advances and boredom is the root of all evil, no wonder, then, that the world goes backwards, that evil spreads. This can be traced back to the very beginning of the world. The gods were bored; therefore they created human beings.

SØREN KIERKEGAARD, 1813–55

The effect of boredom on a large scale has been underestimated. It is a main cause of revolutions and would soon bring to an end all static Utopias and the farmyard civilization of the Fabians.

WILLIAM RALPH INGE, the 'gloomy dean', *The End of an Age*, 1948

Symmetry is boredom and boredom is the basis of grief. Despair yawns.

VICTOR HUGO, *Les Misérables*, 1862

The camel's hump is an ugly lump
Which well you may see at the Zoo;
But uglier yet is the hump we get
From having too little to do.

RUDYARD KIPLING, *Just So Stories*, 1902

British Empire

I get angry when I hear that word 'empire'; it reminds me of slavery, it reminds me of thousands of years of brutality, it reminds me of how my foremothers were raped and my forefathers brutalized. It is because of this concept of empire that my British education led me to believe that the history of black people started with slavery and that we were born slaves, and should therefore be grateful that we were given freedom by our caring white masters. It is because of this idea of empire that black people like myself don't even know our true names or our true historical culture.

BENJAMIN ZEPHANIAH, poet, on why he turned down an OBE from Tony Blair's government, *Guardian*, 27 November 2003

We scorn you like the drippings of a privy; rage, you English thieves, white swine, burst if you want ... You English are liars, thieves, drunkards, idlers who drain away the money of the black folk.

SEMAKULA MULUMBA of Uganda, telegram to PM Clement Attlee, 1950

The idea of defending, as integral parts of our Empire, countries 10,000 miles off, like Australia, which neither pay a shilling to our revenue ... nor afford us any exclusive trade ... is about as quixotic a specimen of national folly as was ever exhibited.

RICHARD COBDEN, British statesman, 1804–65

It was just robbery with violence, aggravated murder on a great scale, and men going at it blind – as is very proper for those who tackle a darkness. The conquest of the earth, which mostly means the taking it away from those who have a different complexion or slightly flatter noses than ourselves, is not a pretty thing when you look into it.

JOSEPH CONRAD, British novelist, 1857–1924

These wretched colonies are a millstone around our neck.

BENJAMIN DISRAELI in 1852, before his conversion to imperialism

Onward Christian Soldiers, on to
    heathen lands,
Prayer books in your pockets, rifles in
    your hands.
Take the glorious tidings where trade
    can be done,
Spread the peaceful gospel – with a
    Maxim gun.

Liberal MP HENRY LABOUCHÈRE'S
send-up of the Empire hymn 'Onward
Christian Soldiers'

And the end of the fight is a
    tombstone white
With the name of the late deceased,
And the epitaph drear: 'A Fool
    lies here
Who tried to hustle the East.'

RUDYARD KIPLING, 1865–1936

Wherever the European has trod,
death seems to pursue the aboriginal.
We may look to the wide extent of
the Americas, Polynesia, the Cape of
Good Hope and Australia, and we
find the same result.

CHARLES DARWIN, *Voyage of the
Beagle*, 1839

Under the present system of
management, therefore, Great
Britain derives nothing but loss
from the dominion which she
assumes over her colonies … A
great empire has been established
for the sole purpose of raising up a
nation of customers who should be
obliged to buy from the shops of
our different producers all the
goods with which these could
supply them. For the sake of that
little enhancement of price which
this monopoly might afford our
producers, the home-consumers
have been burdened with the whole
expence [*sic*] of maintaining and
defending that empire …

… It is not very probable that they
[American colonists] will ever
voluntarily submit to us; and we
ought to consider that the blood
which must be shed in forcing them
to do so is, every drop of it, blood
either of those who are, or of those
whom we wish to have for our
fellow-citizens. They are very weak
who flatter themselves that, in the
state to which things have come,
our colonies will be easily
conquered by force alone.

ADAM SMITH, *Wealth of Nations*, 1776

I went to a restaurant the other day
called A Taste of the Raj. The waiter
hit me with a stick and got me to
build a complicated railway system.

HARRY HILL

Change

There is a certain relief in change, even though it be from bad to worse … I have often found in travelling in a stagecoach, that it is often a comfort to shift one's position and be bruised in a new place.

WASHINGTON IRVING, *Tales of a Traveller*, 'To the Reader', 1824

Progress would be wonderful – if only it would stop.

ROBERT MUSIL, 1880–1942

Change doth unknit the tranquil
    strength of men.
Love tends life a little grace,
A few sad smiles; and then,
Both are laid in one cold place,
    In the grave.

MATTHEW ARNOLD, English poet, 1822–88

I believe we are on an irreversible trend toward more freedom and democracy – but that could change.

DAN QUAYLE, US vice president, b. 1947

● Plus ça change, plus c'est la meme chose
(Everything always stays the same)
(FRANCE)

● A leopard does not change its spots

By the time a person has achieved years adequate for choosing a direction, the die is cast and the moment has long since passed which determined the future.

ZELDA FITZGERALD, 1900–48

The lapse of ages changes all things – time – language – the earth – the bounds of the sea – the stars of the sky, and everything 'about, around and underneath' man, except man himself, who has always been and always will be, an unlucky rascal.

LORD BYRON, *Diary*, 9 January 1821

What we call progress is the exchange of one nuisance for another nuisance.

HENRY HAVELOCK ELLIS, 1859–1939

What can be more palpably absurd than the prospect held out of locomotives travelling twice as fast as stagecoaches?

Quarterly Review, March 1825

The one thing constant in a changing world is the avant-garde.

LOUIS JOUVET, French actor, 1887–1951

Progress might have been all right once, but it has gone on too long.

OGDEN NASH, 1902–71

Everyone thinks of changing the world, but no one thinks of changing himself.

LEO TOLSTOY, 1828–1910

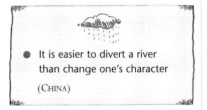

- It is easier to divert a river than change one's character

(CHINA)

All changes, even the most longed for, have their melancholy; for what we leave behind us is a part of ourselves; we must die to one life before we can enter another.

ANATOLE FRANCE, 1844–1924

- He who reforms also deforms
- Happy the man who forgets what he cannot change

(GERMANY)

Full fathom five thy father lies;
Of his bones are coral made:
Those are pearls that were his eyes:
Nothing of him that doth fade,
But doth suffer a sea-change
Into something rich and strange.
Sea-nymphs hourly ring his knell:
    Ding-dong,
Hark! now I hear them, – ding-
    dong, bell.

WILLIAM SHAKESPEARE, *The Tempest*, 1623

In August 2008, Andrew Simms, the policy director at the New Economics Foundation, announced that, if we carry on as usual, we will reach the tipping point for the beginnings of runaway climate change within 100 months. Will we change our ways and habits in time? See www.onehundredmonths.org.

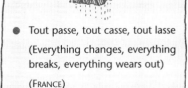

- Tout passe, tout casse, tout lasse
(Everything changes, everything breaks, everything wears out)

(FRANCE)

Civilization

No society can survive, no civilization can survive, with 12-year-olds having babies, with 15-year-olds killing each other, with 17-year-olds dying of AIDS, with 18-year-olds getting diplomas they can't read.

NEWT GINGRICH, US politician, after the Republican election victory, December 1994

Every civilization that has ever existed has ultimately collapsed.

HENRY KISSINGER, *New York Times*, 1974

According to many, oil production has either already peaked, is peaking, or will peak very soon. We can only guess at what this will mean for a civilization addicted to cheap oil. According to the US Department of Energy's Hirsch Report of 2005, peak oil presents the world with 'an unprecedented risk management problem'. It seems we do need to start doing something about the situation to avoid catastrophic upheaval, but so far the message from governments is: business as usual.

A short history of Easter Island

When Europeans arrived on this tiny scrap of land in the middle of the Pacific, 1,300 miles from anywhere, in 1722, it was clear that the few degraded cannibals who lived there were the descendants of a great civilization that had built the extraordinary 80-ton stone statues that look out to sea from the cliffs. What had happened? In a nutshell, the islanders had committed ecological suicide. They chopped down all their trees to act as rollers and levers for their statues, thereby deforesting their island to the extent that soil erosion killed off agriculture; over 40 kinds of seabird could no longer nest there and so became extinct; palm fruits no longer grew; canoes could not be built for fishing; and there could be no more firewood. Does this all sound familiar? For 80-ton statues, read global economy; for 10,000 people with axes, read 6 billion with bulldozers; for the most remote habitable island in the world, read Planet Earth, alone in the galaxy ...

Why, as civilization spreads, do exceptional men become fewer?

ALEXIS DE TOCQUEVILLE, 1805–59

As it will be in the future, it was at the birth of Man –
There are only four things certain since Social Progress began –
That the Dog returns to his Vomit and the Sow returns to her Mire,
And the burnt Fool's bandaged finger goes wabbling back to the Fire.

RUDYARD KIPLING, 'The Gods of the Copybook Headings', 1919

When asked, c. 1930, what his view of Western civilization was, Mahatma Gandhi reportedly said, 'I think it would be a good thing.'

You can't say civilization don't advance, however, for in every war they kill you in a new way.

WILL ROGERS, New York Times, 1929

When machines and computers, profit motives and property rights, are considered more important than people, the giant triplets of racism, extreme materialism, and militarism are incapable of being conquered.

MARTIN LUTHER KING JR, 1929–68

In 2007, the number of people visiting social networking sites such as MySpace, Facebook and Bebo was into the hundreds of millions. Indeed, according to a recent report by Ofcom, 40 per cent of adults in the UK regularly visit these sites to meet 'like-minded' people. Although some psychiatrists believe that these kinds of contacts are seriously contributing to the 'atomization' of society, and should therefore be kept to a minimum, the numbers are increasing daily. Cyber-civilization is here to stay.

From time to time, in the towns, I open a newspaper. Things seem to be going at a dizzy rate. We are dancing not on a volcano, but on the rotten seat of a latrine.

GUSTAVE FLAUBERT, letter to Louis Bouilhet, 14 November 1850

Après moi, le déluge.
(After me, come the floods.)

LOUIS XIV of France, 1638–1715

Clock

The Eleventh Hour

In 1947, shortly after the US dropped its A-bombs on Japan, the Doomsday Clock was conceived. This symbolic clockface, in which midnight stands for 'catastrophic destruction', has appeared on every cover of the Chicago-based Bulletin of the Atomic Scientists since, with the hands never further away than 17 minutes to midnight, and never closer, except during the Cold War, than they are now, at five minutes to midnight. This reflects expert opinion that the world is in grave danger from:

- nuclear ambitions in 'rogue' states
- nuclear material unaccounted for in Russia and elsewhere
- the 'launch-ready' status of 2,000 of the 25,000 weapons held by Russia and the US
- problems with climate change leading to more nuclear power stations and associated risks of proliferation
- ever-increasing terrorism.

Countryside

It is my belief, Watson, founded upon my experience, that the lowest and vilest alleys of London do not present a more dreadful record of sin than does the smiling and beautiful countryside.

SIR ARTHUR CONAN DOYLE, British writer, 1859–1930

Rural life can offer great advantages and I have seen many examples of real community spirit and creative solutions to problems. But I have also witnessed people in real hardship and struggling to get by. There are over 928,000 rural households (i.e., 32 per cent of all rural households) living below the official government poverty threshold of £16,492 household income per annum. But because rural disadvantage is scattered it is hidden through the averaging of official statistics and a perception of the countryside as affluent and idyllic.

DR STUART BURGESS, the government's Rural Advocate, March 2008

I have no relish for the country; it is a kind of healthy grave.

SYDNEY SMITH, 1771–1845

———

Today there are 400,000 fewer young people aged 15–29 in rural areas than there were 20 years ago, a drop from 21 to 15 per cent. The average age of rural inhabitants is getting three months older every year.

———

Over 60 per cent of British orchards have been dug up in the last 30 years and today over 70 per cent of the apples eaten in the UK are imported. In East Anglia, where the countryside was once covered in apple trees, 80 per cent of the orchards have been grubbed up.

———

It will be said of this generation that it found England a land of beauty and left it a land of 'beauty spots'.

C. E. M. JOAD, *The Horrors of the Countryside*, 1931

If what is called development is allowed to multiply at the present rate, then by the end of the century Great Britain will consist of isolated oases of preserved monuments in a desert of wire, concrete roads, cosy plots and bungalows ... Upon this new Britain the *Review* bestows a name in the hope that it will stick – SUBTOPIA.

IAN NAIRN, *Architectural Review*, 1955

———

Hedgerows are a defining feature of the countryside, vital to our wildlife, but half of them, roughly 200,000 miles, have disappeared since 1947.

———

Lovers of the town have been content, for the most part, to say they loved it. They do not brag about its uplifting qualities. They have none of the smugness which makes the lover of the countryside insupportable.

AGNES REPPLIER, *Times and Tendencies*, 1931

———

The suicide rate among British farmers and farm workers is twice the average rate for all workers in the UK.

———

In 1959, there were over 28,000 dairy farms in England and Wales. Today there are 13,000, as farmers are forced out of business by rising costs and less money from supermarkets. The figures have raised fears that soon Britain may have to start importing milk for the first time in her history. A total of 81,500 farmers and farm workers left the land between 1995 and 2004.

———

Noise and light pollution in England from cities, towns, infrastructure and industry have doubled since the late 1960s. Over 50 per cent of England is now classified as suffering from such pollution, compared to 41 per cent in the early 1990s and 26 per cent in the early 1960s. The proportion of England enjoying truly dark skies at night fell from 15 to 11 per cent between 1993 and 2000.

———

I have no idea why anybody agreed to go on being rustic after about 1400.

SIR KINGSLEY AMIS, English novelist, 1922–95, *The Green Man*

Death

When you look on my grave,
And behold how they wave,
The cypress, the yew, and the willow,
You think tis the breeze,
That gives motion to these –
Tis the laughter that's shaking
   my pillow.
I must laugh when I see
A poor insect like thee
Dare to pity the fate thou must own,
Let a few moments slide,
We shall lie side by side,
And crumble to dust bone for bone.
Go, weep thine own doom,
Thou wert born for the tomb –
Thou has lived, like myself, but to die.
Whilst thou pity'st my lot,
Secure fool, thou'st forgot
Thou art no more immortal than I.

H. J. LOARING, *Curious Records*, 1872

A single death is a tragedy, a
million deaths is a statistic.

JOSEPH STALIN, 1879–1953

> ● There is hope from the mouth
> of the sea, but none from the
> mouth of the grave

There is ... no death ... There is
only ... *me* ... *me* ... *who is going to
die* ...

ANDRÉ MALRAUX, French author,
1901–76, *The Royal Way*

Dying is a very dull, dreary affair.
And my advice to you is to have
nothing whatever to do with it.

W. SOMERSET MAUGHAM, shortly before
his death in 1965

I am not so much afraid of death, as
ashamed thereof: 'tis the very
disgrace and ignominy of our
natures, that in a moment can so
disfigure us that our nearest
friends, wife, and children, stand
afraid and start at us.

SIR THOMAS BROWNE, 1605–82,
Religio Medici

Any man's death diminishes me, because I am involved in mankind; and therefore never send to know for whom the bell tolls; it tolls for thee.

JOHN DONNE, 'Meditation XVII'

Futility

Move him into the sun –
Gently its touch awoke him once,
At home, whispering of fields
    half-sown.
Always it woke him, even in France,
Until this morning and this snow.
If anything might rouse him now
The kind old sun will know.

Think how it wakes the seeds –
Woke once the clays of a cold star.
Are limbs, so dear achieved, are sides
Full-nerved, still warm, too hard
    to stir?
Was it for this the clay grew tall?
– O what made fatuous sunbeams toil
To break earth's sleep at all?

WILFRED OWEN, 1893–1918

Strange how sternly I am possessed of the idea that I shall not live much longer. Not a personal thought but is coloured with this conviction. I never look forward more than a year at the utmost; it is the habit of my mind, in utter sincerity, to expect no longer tenure of life than that. I don't know how this has come about; perhaps my absolute loneliness has something to do with it. Then I am haunted with the idea that I am consumptive. I never cough without putting a finger to my tongue, to see if there be a sign of blood. Morbidness – is it? I only know that these forecasts are the most essential feature of my mental and moral life at present. Death, if it came now, would rob me of not one hope, for hopes I simply have not.

GEORGE GISSING, English novelist, *Diary*, 3 June 1888

I paint as a means to make life bearable. Don't weep. What I have done is best for all of us. No use, I shall never be rid of this depression.

VINCENT VAN GOGH, words left behind before his suicide, 1890

But in this world, nothing can be said to be certain, except death and taxes.

BENJAMIN FRANKLIN, 1706–90

The graveyards are full of indispensable men.

CHARLES DE GAULLE, French president, 1890–1970

The only choice then to be made is the most aesthetically satisfying form of suicide: marriage, and a forty-hour week; or a revolver.

ALBERT CAMUS, 1913–60, *Notebooks*

Ay, but to die, and go we know not
   where,
To lie in cold obstruction and to rot;
This sensible warm motion to become
A kneaded clod … 'tis too horrible!
The weariest and most loathed
   worldly life
That age, ache, penury, and
   imprisonment
Can lay on nature is a paradise
To what we fear of death.

WILLIAM SHAKESPEARE, *Measure for Measure*

To the Editor of the *Daily Chronicle*, 14 August 1893

(This letter appeared in the newspaper on 16 August, under the heading 'Tired of Life')

Sir,

When you receive this, I shall have put an end to my existence by the aid of a bullet. This act is thoroughly premeditated, being planned six months ago. My best and most serious thoughts have been given to it, and my sanity, if ever man was sane, can be acknowledged by the friends I have spent the last fortnight with.

I resolved long ago that life is a sequence of shams. That men have had to create utopias and heavens to make it bearable; and that all the wisest men have been disgusted with life as it is … Only the transcendental and aesthetic in life are worth our thought. Only a life following beauty and creating it approaches any degree of joyousness, but the ugliness and vile monotony in my life have crowded beauty out …

Three weeks ago I bought a revolver. On going to spend my holiday in Cambridgeshire I left it at the cloak-room, Liverpool-street, until this evening … I consider this explanation due to my fellows, to those who care. I was not consulted when I became a sentient being. Having reached maturity I object to life. Will not have it. Hate and despise it. That there should be no doubt in my own mind I have been at least three months with the certainty of my end before my eyes.

This is the only writing concerning my death.

Graffito

- God is dead – *Nietzsche*.
- Nietzsche is dead – *God*.

—————————

 —————————

Rich men, trust not in wealth,
Gold cannot buy you health;
Physic himself must fade;
All things to end are made;
The plague full swift goes by:
I am sick, I must die –
   Lord, have mercy on us!

THOMAS NASHE, 1567–1601, 'Adieu!
Farewell Earth's Bliss!'

—————————————————

Alas! what is man? whether he be
deprived of that light which is from
on high, or whether he discard it; a
frail and trembling creature, standing
on time, that bleak and narrow
isthmus between two eternities, he
sees nothing but impenetrable
darkness on the one hand, and doubt,
distrust, and conjecture still more
perplexing on the other. Most gladly
would he take an observation as to
whence he has come, or whither he is
going. Alas, he has not the means; his
telescope is too dim, his compass too
wavering, his plummet too short.
Nor is that little spot, his present
state, one whit more intelligible, since
it may prove a quicksand that may
sink in a moment from his feet; it can
afford him no certain reckoning as to
that immeasurable ocean that he may
have traversed, or that still more
formidable one that he must.

CHARLES CALEB COLTON, English
clergyman, c. 1780–1832

Oh the sad Day,
When friends shall shake their heads and
   say
Of miserable Me,
Hark how he groans, look how he pants
   for breath,
See how he struggles with the pangs of
   Death!
When they shall say of these poor eyes,
How hollow, and how dim they be!
Mark how his breast does swell and rise,
Against his potent enemy!
When some old Friend shall step to my
   bed-side,
Touch my chill face, and thence shall
   gently slide,
And when his next companions say,
How does he do? what hopes? shall turn
   away,
Answering only with a lift-up hand,
Who can his fate withstand?
Then shall a gasp or two, do more
Than e'er my Rhetoric could before,
Persuade the peevish World to trouble
   me no more!

THOMAS FLATMAN, English poet, 1637–88

—————————————————

If there wasn't death, I think you
couldn't go on.

STEVIE SMITH, British poet, *Observer*,
1969

Dreams

We live as we dream – alone.

JOSEPH CONRAD, *Heart of Darkness*, 1902

All men dream, but not equally. Those who dream by night in the dusty recesses of their mind wake in the day to find that it was vanity; but the dreamers of the day are dangerous men, for they may act their dream with open eyes, to make it possible.

T. E. LAWRENCE, *Seven Pillars of Wisdom*, introduction, 1926

- One can but dream
- Dream on
- To believe in one's dreams is to spend all of one's life asleep

(CHINA)

What dreamest thou, drunkard,
  drowsy pate?
Thy lust and liking is from thee gone.
Thou blinkard blowboll, thou wakest
  too late.

JOHN SKELTON, 'Lullay, Lullay, Like a Child', 1527

Who so regardeth dreams is like him that catcheth at a shadow, and followeth after the wind.

The Bible, Ecclesiastes 34:2

The hope I dreamed of was a dream,
Was but a dream; and now I wake,
Exceeding comfortless, and worn, and
  old,
For a dream's sake.

CHRISTINA ROSSETTI, 'Mirage', 1862

Drink and Drinking

'Harris, I am not well, pray get me a glass of brandy.' These were the words of the Prince of Wales (later George IV) on first seeing his future wife, Caroline of Brunswick, in 1795. The prince was so appalled by Caroline, whom he thought unattractive and unhygienic, that he went on a three-day drinking binge and had to be held up by his groomsmen at the wedding ceremony. The prince's letters show that the couple had sexual intercourse on three occasions, including twice on the first night, after which the future king, still stupefied with drink, slept in the bedroom fireplace. The third occasion took place the following night. Princess Charlotte, George's only legitimate child, was born from one of those presumably awkward unions, on 7 January 1796, after which the couple began to live separate lives and were never seen together in public again.

- Let but the drunkard alone, and he will fall of himself
- You cannot make people sober by Act of Parliament
- Wine makes old wives wenches

It was early last December,
As near as I remember,
I was walking down the street in tipsy pride;
No one was I disturbing,
As I lay down by the curbing,
And a pig came up and lay down by my side.
As I lay there in the gutter
Thinking thoughts I shall not utter,
A lady passing by was heard to say:
'You can tell a man who boozes
By the company he chooses';
And the pig got up and slowly walked away.

ANON, 'The Drunkard and the Pig'

Wine hath drowned more men than the sea.

THOMAS FULLER, writer and physician, 1608–61

A man who exposes himself when he is intoxicated, has not the art of getting drunk.

SAMUEL JOHNSON, 1709–84

Drunkenness is nothing but voluntary madness.

SENECA, Roman philosopher

'Mid pleasures and palaces, though we
    may roam,
Be it ever so humble, there's no place
    like home.
But there is the father lies drunk on
    the floor,
The table is empty, the wolf's at the
    door,
And mother sobs loud in her broken-
    back'd chair

ANON, 'Ruined by Drink'

A recent survey showed that 34 per cent of 18–25-year-olds have had unprotected sex when drunk, and 23 per cent have had sex with someone they didn't want to.

Famous alcoholics

Richard Burton
Calamity Jane
Bonnie Prince Charlie
Edward VIII
Douglas Fairbanks
W. C. Fields
Errol Flynn
Judy Garland
Edgar Allan Poe
Jackson Pollock
Joseph Stalin
Boris Yeltsin

Alcohol causes nearly 10 per cent of all ill-health and premature deaths in Europe, according to the World Health Organization's Global Burden of Disease Study published in 2008. It found that alcohol is the third most important risk factor, after smoking and raised blood pressure.

Drunkenness is temporary suicide.

BERTRAND RUSSELL

Best while you have it use your
    breath,
There is no drinking after death.

JOHN FLETCHER, 1579–1625, *The Bloody Brother*

Drugs

Drugs are a waste of time. They destroy your memory and your self-respect and everything that goes along with your self-esteem.

KURT COBAIN, musician, 1967–94

—

Eighty per cent of British banknotes – and 99 per cent in London – are contaminated with cocaine or heroin and over £15 million of the most dangerously contaminated notes have to be destroyed each year. Roughly 5 per cent of cocaine users are thought to be infected with hepatitis C and leave traces of blood on the banknotes through which they snort the drug. Eight out of 10 hepatitis C carriers are unaware they have the blood-carried virus, raising fears that infection rates will soar. Untreated, hepatitis C can lead to chronic liver disease.

—

Taking LSD is like going to Stratford-on-Avon: you only need to go there once.

JOHN PEEL, radio presenter, 1939–2004

There are estimated to be 280,000 problematic drug users in the UK, mostly heroin and crack cocaine users. Three-quarters of crack and heroin users claim they commit crime to feed their habit. An average of 2,500 mainly young adults die every year as a result of drug abuse.

—

Coca is a plant that the devil invented for the total destruction of the natives.

DON DIEGO DE ROBLES, 16th-century Orthodox Catholic artist

—

A hugely complicating element in the West's policy towards Afghanistan is the fact that the country is the world's biggest producer of opium, the main ingredient of heroin. Between 80 and 90 per cent of Europe's heroin can be traced back to Afghanistan; according to the CIA World Factbook, if its entire poppy crop were processed, 'it is estimated that 526 metric tons of heroin could be produced'.

A study of 450 people published in 2008 by the National Institute of Drug Abuse in the United States found that smoking marijuana posed significant health risks to users. A study comparing 173 cancer patients and 176 healthy individuals produced evidence that smoking marijuana doubled or tripled the risk of developing cancer of the head or neck. Marijuana abuse also has the potential to promote cancer of the lungs and other parts of the respiratory tract because it produces 50–70 per cent more carcinogenic hydrocarbons than tobacco smoke. Marijuana users usually inhale more deeply and hold their breath longer than tobacco smokers do, which increases the lungs' exposure to carcinogenic smoke.

1   Heroin
2   Cocaine
3   Barbiturates
4   Street methadone
5   Alcohol
6   Ketamine
7   Benzodiazepines
8   Amphetamine
9   Tobacco
10   Buprenorphine
11   Cannabis
12   Solvents
13   4-MTA
14   LSD
15   Methylphenidate
16   Anabolic steroids
17   GHB
18   Ecstasy
19   Alkyl nitrates
20   Khat

In 2007, Professor David Nutt of Bristol University proposed a new framework for classifying harmful substances, using three combined factors: the harm to the user, the addictive potential of the drug, and the resulting impact on society as a whole. It reveals that our existing laws, in which alcohol and tobacco are legal while dealers of cannabis and Ecstasy can expect to be imprisoned, are both arbitrary and dangerous. The research, which was published in the Lancet, rated the twenty most dangerous drugs (starting with the worst) as:

The United Nations' 2005 World Drug Report found that the global trade in illegal drugs generates more than $320 billion a year in revenues, which is higher than the GDP of 88 per cent of the countries in the world.

I seemed every night to descend, not metaphorically, but literally to descend, into chasms and sunless abysses, depths below depths, from which it seemed hopeless that I could ever reascend.

THOMAS DE QUINCEY, *Confessions of an English Opium Eater*, 1822

Education

Tedium is the worst disease in schools, the corrupting tedium that comes equally from monotony, work or leisure.

RAUL D'AVILA POMPEIA, Brazilian writer, 1863–95

It is the business of education to eliminate the influence of parents on the life-chances of the young.

FRANK MUSGROVE, *The Family, Education and Society*, 1966

A real, honest, old-fashioned Boarding-school, where a reasonable quantity of accomplishments were sold at a reasonable price, and where girls might be sent to be out of the way and scramble themselves into a little education, without any danger of coming back prodigies.

JANE AUSTEN, *Emma*, 1816

You teach a child to read, and he or her will be able to pass a literacy test.

GEORGE W. BUSH, b. 1946

But, good gracious, you've got to educate him first. You can't expect a boy to be vicious till he's been to a good school.

SAKI, British writer, 'Reginald in Russia', 1910

Education consists mainly in what we have unlearned.

MARK TWAIN

In early 2008 a New Jersey librarian placed a sign in her computer room saying 'Just say No to Wikipedia'. Her campaign was picked up by other libraries who decided to block access to the online encyclopedia on their computers. The criticism of Wikipedia and search engines is that students are no longer studying anything, merely copying and pasting the first thing that pops up on their screens, without verifying sources or finding out the facts. What happened to students reading and studying till the small hours of the morning?

Nothing in this world can take the place of persistence. Talent will not; nothing is more common than unsuccessful people with talent. Genius will not; unrewarded genius is almost a proverb. Education will not; the world is full of educated derelicts.

CALVIN COOLIDGE, 1872–1933

Democracy means government by the uneducated, while aristocracy means government by the badly educated.

G. K. CHESTERTON, *New York Times*, 1931

———

Children in England are being tested within an inch of their lives with national tests at 7, 11 and 14. A report in the Cambridge Primary Review *noted that English kids face more pressures than their peers in other countries. England is alone in using testing to the degree it does.*

———

Teaching is not a lost art, but the regard for it is a lost tradition.

JACQUES BARZUN, *Newsweek*, 1955

———

The 1990 World Conference on Education for All in Jomtien, Thailand, called for an end to what it dubbed 'business as usual' in education. It was no longer enough to cram children into already overcrowded factory schools with outdated teaching techniques and ill-adapted subjects and expect them to come out with an education. What was needed were new and innovative approaches to education and clear action on classroom overcrowding. Where has all this got us? In 2008, the UK National Union of Teachers voiced concern on overcrowding in schools and demanded legislation to limit classroom size! Nearly two thirds of local education authorities in England have reported an increase in the level of overcrowding in the last five years. Pupil/teacher ratios in the developing world are even more alarming.

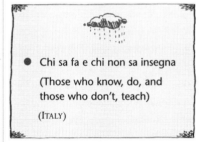

- Chi sa fa e chi non sa insegna
(Those who know, do, and those who don't, teach)
(ITALY)

———

With the advent of the internet, bullying in schools has taken a nastier turn, with pupils targeting each other through the web or cyber-stalking. Websites attacking and teasing children are becoming commonplace. For advice on how to deal with this, see www.bullying.co.uk/schools.

Environment

The Earth is one, but the world is not.

Opening words of the Brundtland Report, 'Our Common Future', 1987

Nice Gaias Finish Last

According to the renowned scientist and originator of Gaia theory James Lovelock, 'We are on the edge of the greatest die-off humanity has ever seen. We will be lucky if 20 per cent of us survive what is coming. We should be scared stiff ... What we have lived through, the 20th century, has been like a great party. Adults now have had the best time humanity has ever had. Now the party is over and the Earth is reckoning up.'

Lovelock, who was instrumental in discovering that CFCs were destroying the ozone layer, has not often been wrong. In The Revenge of Gaia, he asserts that the planet, which is a self-regulating and complex but single organism, is suffering from an illness – mankind – and that a tipping point has almost certainly been reached. The Earth will restabilize, but not in a way that favours civilization. Billions will die, and eventually a few breeding pairs of humans will migrate to the only places where the climate remains tolerable: Canada, Siberia, and the Arctic basin – if we're lucky, and not in the grip of runaway global warming, which could lead to the Earth ending up as hot as Venus (average temperature: 900 degrees F). Scorning the concept of 'sustainable development', Lovelock suggests that 'sustainable retreat' is now the only sensible option, if, indeed, we still have an option.

Only when the last tree has been cut down
Only after the last river has been poisoned
Only after the last fish has been caught
Only then will you find that money cannot be eaten.

Cree Indian prophecy

As temperatures rise, mountain glaciers all around the world are vanishing, threatening an unprecedented environmental and humanitarian catastrophe. According to a UN climate report, the glaciers could disappear by 2030, leading to devastating floods and then water shortage problems for about two billion people. Meanwhile, a 2008 EU report highlighted fears of 'water wars' in the Middle East, where two thirds of the Arab world relies on external supplies, and pointed out the very real risk of climate change sparking global conflict as countries fight over increasingly threatened energy and other natural resources.

God forbid that India should ever take to industrialism after the manner of the west ... keeping the world in chains. If our nation took to similar economic exploitation, it would strip the world bare like locusts.

MAHATMA GANDHI, 1869–1948

India's middle class has grown to about 250 million in the last decade, and is now one of the fastest growing car markets, with about a million being sold every year. Luxury cars, particularly, are selling like hot cakes.

At any minute the Yellowstone National Park Super-volcano could erupt

Last time this volcano erupted, about 640,000 years ago, it covered North America in a layer of dust several feet deep. It is known to erupt every 600,000 to 700,000 years, so we're bang on schedule – and, according to some scientists, global warming only makes an eruption more likely. Apparently, the caldera underneath the volcano is filling up with magma, preparing for an almighty explosion whose force, it's estimated, could be similar to 1,000 Hiroshima-style atomic bombs per second, bringing on an interminable winter in which nothing grows and most life is extinguished.

Not Waving, but Drowning

As the world warms (and it has been warmer than this but it has never, since life began, warmed at such a headlong pace), we enter uncharted territory, where positive feedback mechanisms – 'positive' as in more and more, not 'better' – start to kick in. A very few years ago, scientists assumed that the Earth's ice would take thousands of years to melt; now, it appears that the Arctic will be completely free of sea ice in summer within five or six years. So, what can we expect? The geological record shows that, 3 million years ago, when the temperature was five degrees higher than it is now, sea levels were at least 80 feet higher.

Of the long, and lengthening, list of the stupid things we're doing to our planet, the rapacious destruction of tropical rainforests ranks highly. Some 90 per cent of all species on Earth live there, but it's being cut down at such a phenomenal rate, it will have vanished for ever in 40 years. Do we really believe that we will be far behind? Besides losing 137 plant and animal species per day, we are hacking out the lungs of the planet, for the rainforest absorbs a massive amount of carbon, as well as generating most of the world's rainfall. And, since most of the trees are cleared by burning, phenomenal amounts of greenhouse gas are generated: yesterday's deforestation alone released as much CO_2 into the atmosphere as 8 million people flying from New York to London.

We're finally going to get the bill for the Industrial Age. If the projections are right, it's going to be a big one: the ecological collapse of the planet.

JEREMY RIFKIN, US economist, *World Press Review*, December 1989

As we watch the sun go down, evening after evening, through the smog across the poisoned waters of our native earth, we must ask ourselves seriously whether we really wish some future universal historian on another planet to say about us: 'With all their genius and with all their skill, they ran out of foresight and air and food and water and ideas,' or 'They went on playing politics until their world collapsed around them.'

U THANT, Secretary-General of the United Nations, speech, 1970

Only about 4 per cent of the world's oceans remain undamaged by human activity. The UN Environment Programme estimates that every square mile of ocean contains 46,000 pieces of floating plastic – syringes, condoms, cigarette lighters, etc. – causing the deaths of more than a million seabirds and 100,000 marine mammals every year. There is now a ten-million-square-mile continent of plastic rubbish in the North Pacific Tropical Gyre, held in place by swirling underwater currents; this 'Great Pacific Garbage Patch' is just one of seven major tropical oceanic gyres where more and more Barbies and Kens, among other products of our consume-then-throw-away culture, gyrate for ever.

Whoops, excuse me

Millions of acres of Siberian permafrost are starting to melt, releasing vast quantities of methane, a greenhouse gas 25 times more potent than CO_2, into the atmosphere. And methane may have another surprise for us: as the temperature of the oceans rises, the icy clathrates in the seabed may vent their methane in a series of monstrous burps, each with the violence of an atomic bomb.

———

The UN's International Panel on Climate Change is the most respected body reporting on the climate crisis, but, with the facts changing from day to day, its admirably conservative, consensual approach means that the conclusions in its last report, in 2007, were out of date before they were published. Its next report is not due until 2012; meanwhile, be aware that, regardless of how dreadful the 'facts' seem, the real situation is almost certainly far worse.

———

Colin Mason's 2006 book, A Short History of the Future, focuses on six powerful 'drivers' which, converging in about 20 years' time, could plunge the world into a new Dark Age. The drivers are: peak oil; massive population growth; global climate change; poverty; famine and water shortages; and the breakdown of international law and order.

How can you buy or sell the sky, the warmth of the land? The idea is strange to us. What is man without the beasts? If all the beasts were gone, man would die from a great loneliness of spirit. For whatever happens to the beasts, soon happens to man. All things are connected.

If men spit upon the ground, they spit upon themselves. This we know: the earth does not belong to man; man belongs to the earth. This we know.

Contaminate your own bed, and you will one night suffocate in your own waste.

Where is the thicket? Gone.

Where is the eagle? Gone.

The end of living and the beginning of survival.

CHIEF SEATTLE, letter to the President of the US, 1854

And God said, Let us make man in our image, after our likeness: and let them have dominion over the fish of the sea, and over the fowl of the air, and over the cattle, and over all the earth, and over every creeping thing that creepeth upon the earth.

The Bible, Genesis 1

Fame

Being a celebrity is like being raped, and there's absolutely nothing a player can do about it.

JOHN MCENROE, b. 1949

A *survey, carried out in schools and on the web by Luton First for National Kids' Day, found that being a celebrity for no specific reason was voted the best thing in the world by children.*

Fame is a food that dead men eat,
I have no stomach for such meat.

HENRY DOBSON, 1906

Throughout my life, I have seen narrow-shouldered men, without a single exception, committing innumerable stupid acts, brutalizing their fellows and perverting souls by all means. They call the motive for their actions fame.

COMTE DE LAUTRÉAMONT, 1846–70

What I'd really like to say about stardom is that it gave me everything I never wanted.

AVA GARDNER, *My Story*, 1990

If you can't be famous, at least you can be notorious.

MOHAMAD MAHATHIR, Malaysia's longest-serving prime minister, b. 1925

Fame and tranquillity are two things that cannot stay under the same roof.

MICHEL DE MONTAIGNE, *Essais*, 1580

I want to be alone.

GRETA GARBO, 1905–90

For a soldier I listed, to grow great in fame,
And be shot at for sixpence a day.

CHARLES DIBDIN, 1745–1814

There is not in the world so toilsome a trade as the pursuit of fame; life concludes before you have so much as sketched your work.

JEAN DE LA BRUYÈRE, 1645–96

John Lennon's killer, Mark Chapman, reportedly shot the singer because he wanted to steal his fame from him. To a certain degree, he did.

Once you become famous you get completely dehumanized. I think people forget there is a person in there trying to deal with it … Partly the way you deal with it is by not reading, not looking and seeing any of it and burying your head in the sand. It is the only path to sanity.

KEIRA KNIGHTLEY, b. 1985, BBC web interview

Fame has also this great drawback, that if we pursue it, we must direct our lives so as to please the fancy of men.

BARUCH SPINOZA, 1632–77

Folly loves the martyrdom of fame.

LORD BYRON, 1788–1824

Why stir the wasps that rim Fame's luscious pot?

EDGELL RICKWORD, English poet, 1931

Fame is a bee.
It has a song –
It has a sting –
Ah, too, it has a wing.

EMILY DICKINSON, 1830–86

Fame for fame's sake is fast becoming an international rallying cry. Versions of Big Brother exist across the world. It is an example of how the notion of celebrity doesn't actually have to mean achievement other than getting on to TV. In a recent survey of teenagers in Britain, run by the Learning and Skills Council (LSC), 16 per cent of 777 teenagers, aged 16–19, said they would be famous one day and one in ten said they thought celebrity was a good way to earn money without any skills or qualifications. This when the odds of being famous are very slim – and when you're famous, it's not for very long nowadays.

I stopped believing in Santa Claus when my mother took me to see him in a department store, and he asked for my autograph.

SHIRLEY TEMPLE, b. 1928

Famous Last Words

Doctor, do you think it could have been the sausage?

PAUL CLAUDEL, French poet and playwright, 1868–1955

I should never have switched from Scotch to Martinis.

HUMPHREY BOGART, 1899–1957

Everything has gone wrong, my girl.

ARNOLD BENNETT, English novelist, 1867–1931

Maria, don't let me die!

D. H. LAWRENCE, 1885–1930

It wasn't worth it.

LOUIS B. MAYER, film producer, 1882–1957

To his confessor:
What the devil are you trying to sing, monsieur le curé? Your voice is out of tune.

JEAN-PHILIPPE RAMEAU, French composer, 1683–1764

I'm bored with it all.

WINSTON CHURCHILL, 1874–1965

Suicide note:
And so I leave this world, where the heart must either break or turn to lead.

NICOLAS CHAMFORT, 1741–94

I am a Queen, but I have not the power to move my arms.

LOUISE, QUEEN OF PRUSSIA, 1776–1810

I knew it. I knew it. Born in a hotel room – and God damn it – died in a hotel room.

EUGENE O'NEILL, US playwright, 1888–1953

I have spent a lot of time searching through the Bible for loopholes.

W. C. FIELDS, US actor, 1879–1946

This is absurd! This is absurd!

SIGMUND FREUD, 1856–1939

Elegy for Himself

*(written in the Tower on the eve
of his execution)*

My prime of youth is but a frost
   of cares,
My feast of joy is but a dish of pain;
My crop of corn is but a field of tares;
And all my good is but vain hope
   of gain:
The day is past, and yet I saw no sun;
And now I live, and now my life
   is done.

My tale was heard, and yet it was
   not told;
My fruit is fall'n, and yet my leaves
   are green;
My youth is spent, and yet I am
   not old;
I saw the world, and yet I was
   not seen:
The thread is cut, and yet it is
   not spun;
And now I live, and now my life
   is done.

I sought my death, and found it in my
   womb;
I looked for life, and saw it was
   a shade;
I trod the earth, and knew it
   was my tomb;
And now I die, and now I was
   but made;
My glass is full, and now my glass
   is run;
And now I live, and now my life
   is done.

CHIDIOCK TICHBORNE, 1558–86

As the lamp by his bed flared up:
What? The flames already?

VOLTAIRE, French essayist, 1694–1778

Only one man ever understood me
… And he didn't understand me.

GEORG WILHELM FRIEDRICH HEGEL,
German philosopher, 1770–1831

Light! More light!

JOHANN WOLFGANG VON GOETHE,
1749–1832

Let down the curtain, the farce
is over.

FRANÇOIS RABELAIS, French humanist,
1494–1553

All is lost. Monks, Monks, Monks!

HENRY VIII, 1491–1547

All my possessions for a moment
of time.

ELIZABETH I, 1533–1603

Die, my dear doctor? That's the last
thing I shall do.

LORD PALMERSTON, British prime
minister, 1784–1865

Go on, get out! Last words are for
fools who haven't said enough!

KARL MARX, 1818–83

Fashion

Beware all enterprises that require new clothes.

HENRY DAVID THOREAU, *Walden*, 'Economy', 1854

All this buttoning and unbuttoning!

ANON, 18th-century suicide note

Fashion is more tyrannical at Paris than in any other place in the world; it governs even more absolutely than their king, which is saying a great deal. The least revolt against it is punished by proscription. You must observe and conform to all the minutiae of it, if you will be in fashion there yourself; and if you are not in fashion, you are nobody.

4TH EARL OF CHESTERFIELD, letter to son, 1750

Fashion constantly begins and ends in the two things it abhors most, singularity and vulgarity.

WILLIAM HAZLITT

Proposals to ban saggy trousers that reveal too much underwear are being considered in some American cities. The fashion began as a way of mimicking the style of dress in prison, where the absence of belts and braces (in case of hanging, self-harm or violence) means that clothes often hang loose. It seems the process has come full circle as many lawmakers are proposing that citizens revealing too much buttock in the street can now be fined or end up in jail.

Fashion condemns us to many follies; the greatest is to make ourselves its slave.

NAPOLEON BONAPARTE, 1769–1821

When seen in the perspective of half-a-dozen years or more, the best of our fashions strike us as grotesque, if not unsightly.

THORSTEIN VEBLEN, *Theory of the Leisure Class*, 1899

Fashion victims are not just people who want to wear the latest styles. According to the organization PETA, 85 per cent of the fur industry's skins come from animals brought up in captivity. The most farmed fur animals are minks and foxes. Rabbits, chinchillas and lynxes are also used. Killing methods vary, but the ultimate aim is to keep the animals' pelts unblemished. This means that poisoning, genital electrocution, gassing, decompression chambers and neck-breaking are all used on a regular basis. For animals captured in the wild the process can be even more brutal.

I hold that gentleman to be the best dressed whose dress no one observes.

ANTHONY TROLLOPE, *Thackeray*, 1879

Sweatshop and child labour scandals regularly tear through the fashion industry. While much is being done to stamp out child labour, can fashion houses really say that none of their clothes have been made by children or vastly underpaid adults? To be on the safe side, check the ethical ratings of your clothes: www.ethicalproducts.org.uk.

And it is a wonder what will be the fashion after the plague is done as to periwigs, for nobody will dare to buy any hair for fear of the infection – that it had been cut off the heads of people dead of the plague.

SAMUEL PEPYS, *Diary*, 3 September 1665

Tight clothes are a risk you may have underestimated, and it's not just corsets. They can cause what has been described as heat castration. Medics, in fact, recommend that men avoid wearing tight pants as they overheat the testicles, which, in turn, damages the sperm-forming process and reduces the vital quality of semen. It is not only men who are at risk. Tight legwear also restricts the access of air to the female genital area. This can generate higher humidity as well as harmful heat and increase the risk of infectious diseases.

Fashion, n. A despot whom the wise ridicule and obey.

AMBROSE BIERCE, *The Devil's Dictionary*, 1911

Fashion, though Folly's child, and
    guide of fools,
Rules e'en the wisest, and in learning
    rules.

GEORGE CRABBE, *The Library*, 1781

Fishing

Give a man a fish and you feed him for a day. Teach him how to fish and he will sit in a boat and drink beer all day.

GEORGE CARLIN, US comedian, b. 1937

Give a man a fish, and he can eat for a day. But teach a man how to fish, and he'll be dead of mercury poisoning inside of three years.

CHARLES HAAS, US screenwriter, b. 1952

The fishers also shall mourn, and all they that cast angle into the brooks shall lament, and they that spread nets upon the waters shall languish.

The Bible, Isaiah 19:8

Angling or float fishing I can only compare to a stick and a string, with a worm at one end and a fool at the other.

SAMUEL JOHNSON

For Cod's Sake!

1497: the explorer John Cabot and his crew brought back to Bristol tales of an Atlantic so teeming with codfish that they hindered the ships and made them go slowly. There were so many fish that one could practically walk to shore on their backs, and the sailors had seen bears swimming out to sea and catching cod in their claws. Another explorer reported catching 67 cod in less than two hours.

2000: the Worldwide Fund for Nature placed cod on the list of endangered species. It reported that, if we continued to act without the most basic regard for sustainability, the world's cod stocks would disappear in 15 years. And it's not the only species that has been criminally overfished. By-catch is a nasty word; like collateral damage, it's a euphemism for laziness and cruelty. Greenpeace has estimated that, for every 186 million fish caught in 2006, UK fishermen threw away 17 million. That's not just wanton, it's stupid: these discarded, dead and dying fish, turtles and other creatures float belly-up as a testimony to our greed, and a reminder of how we'll be looking in a few years' time.

F... the art of angling, the cruellest, the coldest, and the stupidest of pretended sports.

LORD BYRON

In response to the news that fish stocks are in steep decline, how did the international community react? Did it call for restraint, so that little fish could get bigger and make more little fish? Did it hell. Instead, humanity began to use ever more extreme fishing methods to catch those that still remain. Step forward 'bottom-trawling', the results of which can be seen from space. Worldwide, there are tens of thousands of trawlers, dragging heavy metal nets with mouths as wide as the length of a rugby field, crushing and killing everything in their wake as they create scars on the seabed up to 4 km long, in the search for a few edible fish for our plates. Scientists predict that, if this wholesale devastation of marine ecosystems continues, fisheries worldwide will collapse by 2050.

Like most fathers of a certain kind Moominpappa liked fishing. He had got his fishing-rod on his birthday a couple of years before and it was a very fine one. But

sometimes it stood in its corner in a slightly unpleasant way, as though reminding him that it was for catching fish.

TOVE JANSSON, Finnish author, 1914–2001

Fishing is a delusion entirely surrounded by liars in old clothes.

DON MARQUIS

A Whale of a Time

In spite of the 1986 moratorium on whaling, Norway and Iceland continue to flout the will of the International Whaling Commission, with Norway catching 545 whales in the 2006–7 season alone. Japan, which keeps to the letter of the moratorium, if not the spirit of it, caught 866 whales in the same period, for 'scientific research'. Indeed, since 1986, 30,000 whales have been killed, and the number is increasing year on year, with several of the species known to be severely endangered. Presumably, however, all whaling will stop once there are no more whales.

We ask a simple question
And that is all we wish:
Are fishermen all liars?
Or do only liars fish?

ANON

Food

- He who eats alone chokes alone

You are offered a piece of bread and butter that feels like a damp handkerchief and sometimes, when cucumber is added to it, like a wet one.

SIR COMPTON MACKENZIE, British writer, 1883–1972, on an English tea party

Over a billion people worldwide are overweight and at least 300 million obese.

World Health Organization

Vegetarians have wicked, shifty eyes, and laugh in a cold calculating manner. They pinch little children, steal stamps, drink water, favour beards.

J.B. MORTON, 1893–1979, writing as 'Beachcomber', *Daily Express*

The term 'superfoods' is at best meaningless and at worst harmful. There are so many wrong ideas about superfoods that I don't know where to begin to dismantle the concept … On a restricted budget, it is even more important to ignore dubious, expensive products in the belief you can take shortcuts to a good diet. Rather than buying some ridiculous African algae, with all the emissions associated with travel, eating a cheap British apple would be better for the environment too.

CATHERINE COLLINS, chief dietician at St George's Hospital, London, 2007

Slow-baked cheese-and-onion tart – snot in a box. Grilled kipper – smoked postman's Odour Eater. Battered saveloy, a thing that only specialist medical staff handle, with rubber gloves. Now, I haven't actually been sick for 20 years, but it's amazing how fresh and strong the memory was. Who would have thought a simple motherless mongrel sausage could do that? … Coq au vin was thick-skinned chicken knuckles soaked in tepid Brylcreem and aftershave. Sherry trifle: unspeakable. Black forest gateau and apple pie: both would have worried gypsy caterers at a Troggs concert in Norwich. Congratulations ... for managing to come up with quite the peerlessly worst restaurant so far this millennium.

A. A. GILL on a well-known London restaurant, 2000

I'm frightened of eggs; worse than frightened, they revolt me. That white round thing without any holes – have you ever seen anything more revolting than an egg yolk breaking and spilling its yellow liquid? Blood is jolly, red. But egg yolk is yellow, revolting. I've never tasted it.

ALFRED HITCHCOCK, film director, 1899–1980

If only it was as easy to banish hunger by rubbing the belly as it is to masturbate.

DIOGENES THE CYNIC, Greek philosopher, c. 412–323 BC

Boiled cabbage à l'anglaise is something compared with which steamed coarse newsprint bought from bankrupt Finnish salvage dealers and heated over smoky oil stoves is an exquisite delicacy.

SIR WILLIAM NEIL CONNOR, 1909–67, writing as 'Cassandra', Daily Mirror

While millions around the world die of starvation and malnutrition, with riots on the streets due to food prices, the notorious European food mountains and lakes of the 1980s are starting to re-emerge. Government figures in 2007 showed that 265 million bottles of wine and more than 13 million tonnes of cereal, rice, sugar and dairy products were being stored. The EU's 12,187,741 tonnes of cereals is enough to fill the new Wembley Stadium 12 times over; the 1,112,651 tonnes of sugar, enough to sweeten 445 billion cups of tea; the 117,831 tonnes of butter would spread 79 billion sandwiches; and the 61,589 tonnes of rice would provide for 615 million curries.

———

The English who eat their meat red and bloody, show the savagery that goes with such food.

J. O. DE LA METTRIE, French physician, 1709–51

What we should be talking about is food security, not food production ... and if [gigantic multinationals] think it's somehow going to work because they are going to have one form of clever genetic engineering after another then again count me out, because that will be guaranteed to cause the biggest disaster environmentally of all time.

PRINCE CHARLES, Daily Telegraph, August 2008

France and the French

I love France and Belgium, but we must not allow ourselves to be pulled down to that level.

WINSTON CHURCHILL to his doctor, January 1952, after the Treaty of Paris set Europe on the road to integration

COMTE D'ORSAY: I was born French, I have lived French and I will die French.

BENJAMIN DISRAELI: Have you no ambition, man?

I have tried to lift France out of the mud. But she will return to her errors and vomitings. I cannot prevent the French from being French.

CHARLES DE GAULLE

I fear the French are so fickle, corrupt and ignorant, so conceited and foolish that it is hopeless to think of their being sensibly governed ... I fear they are incurable as a nation though so charming as individuals.

QUEEN VICTORIA, 1819–1901

You must hate a Frenchman as you do the devil.

LORD NELSON, 1758–1805

It is unthinkable for a Frenchman to arrive at middle age without having syphilis and the Cross of the Legion of Honour.

ANDRÉ GIDE, 1869–1951

The general stereotype of the French ... is of a voluble, excessively excitable, often slightly bearded and somewhat lecherous personality.

'MASS-OBSERVATION' Public Opinion Survey, 1941

The English consider us talkative, arrogant, dirty, smelling of sweat and garlic, flighty, cheating and corrupt ... The English love France but not the French.

Le Point, 1999

How can you govern a country which has 246 varieties of cheese?

CHARLES DE GAULLE

Friendship

No one ever really minds seeing a friend fall from a high roof.

CONFUCIUS, Chinese philosopher, 551–479 BC

Friendship, n. A ship big enough to carry two in fair weather, but only one in foul.

AMBROSE BIERCE, *The Devil's Dictionary*, 1911

My life is spent in a perpetual alternation between two rhythms, the rhythm of attracting people for fear I may be lonely and the rhythm of trying to get rid of them because I know that I am bored.

C. E. M. JOAD, British philosopher, 1891–1953

Few friendships would endure if each party knew what his friend said about him in his absence, even when speaking sincerely and dispassionately.

BLAISE PASCAL

But of all plagues, good Heaven, thy wrath can send,
Save me, oh save me, from the candid friend.

GEORGE CANNING, British prime minister, 1770–1827

How few of his friends' houses would a man choose to be at when sick!

SAMUEL JOHNSON, 1709–1784

One friend in a lifetime is much; two are many; three are hardly possible.

HENRY BROOKS ADAMS, US historian, 1838–1918

Old friendships are, like meats served up repeatedly, cold, comfortless and distasteful. The stomach turns against them.

WILLIAM HAZLITT, *Table Talk*, 'On the Pleasure of Hating', 1822

Whenever a friend succeeds, a little something inside me dies.

GORE VIDAL, US writer, b. 1925

The Future

Why should I care about posterity?
What's posterity ever done for me?

GROUCHO MARX, 1890–1977

And Then You'll Be Sorry

Cassandra, a princess of Troy, was so
beautiful that Apollo fell in love with
her and gave her the gift of prophecy.
But when she didn't return his love,
he cursed her so that no one would
ever believe her predictions. Her
words, as given by Aeschylus in his
play Agamemnon, *must resonate*
with gloom-mongers everywhere:

What does it matter now if men
    believe or no?
What is to come will come. And soon
    you too will stand aside,
To murmur in pity that my words
    were true.

The future ain't what it used to be.

ANON

I would sum up my fear about the
future in one word: boring. And
that's my one fear: that everything
has happened; nothing exciting or
new or interesting is ever going to
happen again … the future is just
going to be a vast, conforming
suburb of the soul.

J. G. BALLARD, British author, b. 1930

Merlin's prophecies weren't much
more optimistic:
Luxury shall overspread the land,
and fornication shall not cease to
debauch mankind. Famine shall
then return, and the inhabitants
shall grieve for the destruction of
their cities … The Severn sea shall
discharge itself through seven
mouths, and the river Usk burn for
seven months! Fishes shall die in the
heat thereof, and from them
serpents will be born … The monks
in the cowls shall be forced to
marry, and their cry shall be heard
upon the mountains of the Alps.

GEOFFREY OF MONMOUTH, *The History*
of the Kings of Britain, 1136

Apocalypse Now

Traditionally, the four horsemen who will herald the Apocalypse (when God will intervene on behalf of the righteous, cast the wicked into outer darkness, and establish a new order) are named after the powers they represent:

White Horse	=	Conquest (and persecution)
Red Horse	=	War (slaughter and violence)
Black Horse	=	Pestilence (famine, plague, corruption and economic meltdown)
Pale/Green Horse	=	Death by all of the above and other means

A volcano collapse could trigger a mega-tsunami

The western flank of the Cumbre Vieja volcano on the island of La Palma in the Canaries is starting to slide seawards. Research suggests that eventually a gigantic mass of rock, with a volume of up to 500km³, will plunge into the ocean. This monstrous landslide will, we hope, give us warning that it's about to occur, but in any case the event will be catastrophic, producing waves of around one kilometre in height and striking the entire Atlantic seaboard a few hours after the Splash. Ate a vista, Rio de Janeiro, So long, New York.

If you want a picture of the future, imagine a boot stamping on a human face – forever.

GEORGE ORWELL, *Nineteen Eighty-Four*, 1948

More than any other time in history, mankind faces a crossroads. One path leads to despair and utter hopelessness. The other, to total extinction. Let us pray we have the wisdom to choose correctly.

WOODY ALLEN, *Side Effects*, 'My Speech to the Graduates', 1980

Boast not thyself of tomorrow; for thou knowest not what a day may bring forth.

The Bible, Proverbs 27:1

An Eschatological Taxonomy

What are we actually talking about when we say 'the world's going to end'? Do we mean the end of our civilization, or the death of all humanity, or the Earth itself becoming a cold, lifeless planet? Just so that we know where we are (or will be), here is a synopsis of the ethical futurist Jamais Cascio's hierarchy of scenarios (you can get the full picture at www.openthefuture.com):

0 REGIONAL CATASTROPHE
(e.g. minor asteroid impact)
Millions to hundreds of millions dead.

1 HUMAN DIE-BACK
(e.g. global thermonuclear war)
Global civilization set back to pre-industrial conditions; several billion dead, but humans as a whole survive.

2 CIVILIZATION EXTINCTION
(e.g. worst-case global warming)
Global civilization destroyed, chance of human recovery slim; chance of biosphere recovery good.

3a HUMAN EXTINCTION – ENGINEERED
(e.g. targeted nano-plague)
All humans dead. Chance of biosphere recovery excellent.

3b HUMAN EXTINCTION – NATURAL
(e.g. major asteroid impact, methane clathrates melt)
All humans dead. Chance of biosphere recovery moderate.

4 BIOSPHERE EXTINCTION
(e.g. 'iceball Earth' re-emergence, late-era molecular nanotech warfare)
All humans dead; chance of biosphere recovery slim. Chance of eventual re-emergence of organic life good.

5 PLANETARY EXTINCTION
(e.g. dwarf-planet-scale asteroid impact)
All humans dead, all species extinct. Chance of eventual re-emergence of organic life slim.

X PLANETARY ELIMINATION
(e.g. post-Singularity* beings disassemble planet for their own purposes)

Global civilization destroyed; all humans dead. Ecosystem destroyed; all species extinct. Planet itself destroyed.

* With technological change growing exponentially, the Singularity is the point at which artificial intelligence will outstrip human intelligence, leading to a change so profound that we can't even imagine it.

Fire and Ice

Some say the world will end in fire,
Some say in ice.
From what I've tasted of desire
I hold with those who favor fire,
But if I had to perish twice,
I think I know enough of hate
To say that for destruction ice
Is also great
And would suffice.

ROBERT FROST, 1874–1963

Goodbye, Sun

Theories about how the universe will end include 'The Big Crunch', where it stops expanding and shrinks into a black hole, and 'The Big Rip', where it's torn apart by its own continued expansion, with galaxies separating from each other, the solar system falling apart, stars and planets being ripped asunder and, finally, in the last instant, atoms being destroyed. But, no matter – it will all be over for life on Earth long before any of these scenarios are played out. In about 5 billion years, the sun will exhaust its supply of hydrogen and evolve into a Red Giant, becoming hugely bigger than it is now. The extra heat will almost certainly boil the Earth's oceans, causing all our water to evaporate; and the atmosphere will disintegrate shortly before the rock begins to melt. In the unlikely event of us surviving this heatstroke, we will die of cold when the sun eventually turns into a White Dwarf, and gives off no heat at all.

This is the way the world ends
Not with a bang but a whimper.

T. S. ELIOT, 'The Hollow Men', 1925

Genius

I hate everything approaching temperamental inspiration, 'sacred fire' and all those attributes of genius which serve only as cloaks for untidy minds.

PIET MONDRIAN, Dutch artist, 1872–1944

There is in every madman a misunderstood genius whose idea, shining in his head, frightened people, and for whom delirium was the only solution to the strangulation that life had prepared for him.

ANTONIN ARTAUD, French playwright, 1896–1948

Art is a jealous mistress, and if a man have a genius for painting, poetry, music, architecture, or philosophy, he makes a bad husband and an ill provider.

RALPH WALDO EMERSON, *The Conduct of Life*, 'Wealth', 1860

Every positive value has its price in negative terms ... The genius of Einstein leads to Hiroshima.

Attributed to PABLO PICASSO, 1881–1973

Savant syndrome is a rare condition in which people display serious mental or physical disability as well as spectacular talent or genius. People with this condition have been disparagingly described as 'idiot savants'. Sufferers typically might have difficulty tying their shoelaces but can provide an accurate drawing of a complex building from memory.

Genius is sorrow's child.

JOHN ADAMS, US president, 1735–1826

There are two paths in life: one is the regular one, direct, honest. The other is bad, it leads through death – that is the way of genius!

THOMAS MANN, *The Magic Mountain*, 1924

Genius is only a greater aptitude for patience.

GEORGES-LOUIS LECLERC, Comte de Buffon, 1707–88

The difference between stupidity and genius is that genius has its limits.

Attributed to ALBERT EINSTEIN, 1879–1955

John Forbes Nash, born 1928, was a Cold War strategist and winner of the 1994 Nobel Prize for economics. Recognized as a mathematical genius, he spiralled downwards into paranoid schizophrenia at the age of 30. His remarkable powers were brought to life in an award-winning book by Sylvia Nasar and in the 2001 film A Beautiful Mind, directed by Ron Howard and starring Russell Crowe.

A FEW PENNILESS GENIUSES

- Paul Gauguin
- Vincent van Gogh
- Wolfgang Amadeus Mozart
- Edgar Allan Poe
- Arthur Rimbaud
- Nikola Tesla

Genius is one per cent inspiration and ninety-nine per cent perspiration.

THOMAS ALVA EDISON, Harper's Monthly, 1932

It takes a lot of time to be a genius, you have to sit around so much doing nothing, really doing nothing.

GERTRUDE STEIN, Everybody's Autobiography, 1937

The public is wonderfully tolerant. It forgives everything except genius.

OSCAR WILDE, 1854–1900

History is littered with child prodigies who failed to go on and achieve in later life. Is too much expected of them by their peers or can they simply not carry their genius into adult life? Be very careful before pronouncing your child a genius, or seek professional advice. Check out the National Association for Gifted Children: www.nagcbritain.org.uk.

We know that the nature of genius is to provide idiots with ideas twenty years later.

LOUIS ARAGON, French writer, 1897-1982

Health

- St Luke was a saint and a physician and yet he died

Most of the time we think we're sick, it's all in the mind.

THOMAS CLAYTON WOLFE, *Look Homeward, Angel*, 1929

A child dies of malaria every 30 seconds. Malaria kills well over a million people each year and is second only to tuberculosis in its impact on world health. The disease, spread by mosquitoes, is endemic in 90 countries and every year roughly 600 million people, or one person in every 10 on the planet, become severely ill with malaria. Malaria is both preventable and curable.

Be careful about reading health books. You may die of a misprint.

MARK TWAIN

It may seem a strange principle to enunciate as the very first requirement of a Hospital that it should do the sick no harm.

FLORENCE NIGHTINGALE, *Notes on Hospitals*, 1863

The number of people living with HIV/AIDS has risen from around 8 million in 1990 to more than 33 million today, and continues to grow. Africa has 12 million AIDS orphans, and people under 25 years old account for half of all new HIV infections worldwide. In 2007, AIDS claimed the lives of an estimated 2 million people, including 330,000 children; more than 25 million people have died of it since 1981.

The men who really believe in themselves are all in lunatic asylums.

G. K. CHESTERTON, *Orthodoxy*, 1908

It is a most extraordinary thing, but I never read a patent medicine advertisement without being impelled to the conclusion that I am suffering from the particular disease therein dealt with in its most virulent form.

JEROME K. JEROME, *Three Men in a Boat*, 1889

The abdomen, the chest, and the brain will forever be shut from the intrusion of the wise and humane surgeon.

SIR JOHN ERICKSEN, Surgeon-Extraordinary to Queen Victoria, 1873

———

The number of people in the UK living with dementia (Alzheimer's disease) is forecast to more than double to 1.5 million within a generation as longevity rates continue to increase. But, for every £25 spent on cancer research in the UK, only one is spent on Alzheimer's.

A few bumper stickers to keep your mind on the road

- I used to be mental, but we're OK now.
- Out of my mind. Back in five minutes.
- Are the voices in my head bothering you?

Louis Pasteur's theory of germs is ridiculous fiction.

PIERRE PACHET, Professor of Physiology at Toulouse, 1872

———

Tuberculosis, the 'greatest killer of humans throughout all of history', according to the World Health Organization, is raging throughout the developing world. In 2008, three million people will die from the disease. In Britain, where an average of 7,000 new cases of TB have been diagnosed every year over the last 10 years, it is staging an alarming comeback. One third of the world's population is already infected by the TB bacillus. Like the common cold, TB spreads through the air and relatively casual contact. Twenty-five people have died of TB while you have been reading this.

———

A recent report shows that, within 15 years, nine out of ten men will be overweight; in 25 years, over half of the UK's population will be obese. Rates of limb amputations, diabetes, heart disease, bowel and breast cancer will soar, and there will also be a huge increase in the numbers of children dying before their parents do.

———

Eat right, exercise regularly, die anyway.

ANON

Humankind

We . . .

are born between shit and piss.

Sᴛ Aᴜɢᴜsᴛɪɴᴇ ᴏғ Hɪᴘᴘᴏ

are born crying, live complaining and die disappointed.

Dʀ Tʜᴏᴍᴀs Fᴜʟʟᴇʀ, *Gnomologia*, 1732

are just statistics, born to consume resources.

Hᴏʀᴀᴄᴇ, 65–8 ʙᴄ, *Epistles*

are all of us sentenced to solitary confinement inside our own skins, for life.

Tᴇɴɴᴇssᴇᴇ Wɪʟʟɪᴀᴍs, *Orpheus Descending*, 1957

There is no such thing as inner peace. There is only nervousness or death.

Fʀᴀɴ Lᴇʙᴏᴡɪᴛᴢ, *Metropolitan Life*, 1978

Man is the only animal that blushes. Or needs to.

Mᴀʀᴋ Tᴡᴀɪɴ, *Following the Equator*, 1897

How did I get into the world? Why was I not asked about it and why was I not informed of the rules and regulations but just thrust into the ranks as if I had been bought by a peddling shanghaier of human beings? How did I get involved in this big enterprise called actuality? Why should I be involved?

Søʀᴇɴ Kɪᴇʀᴋᴇɢᴀᴀʀᴅ, *Repetition*, 1843

Anyone informed that the universe is expanding and contracting in pulsations of eighty billion years has a right to ask, 'What's in it for me?'

PETER DE VRIES, *The Glory of the Hummingbird*, 1974

Vanity of Vanities, saith the Preacher, vanity of vanities: all is vanity. What profit hath a man of all his labour which he taketh under the sun? One generation passeth away, and another generation cometh.

The Bible, Ecclesiastes 1:2

Ah, love, let us be true
To one another! For the world,
    which seems
To lie before us like a land of dreams,
So various, so beautiful, so new,
Hath really neither joy, nor love,
    nor light,
Nor certitude, nor peace, nor help
    for pain;
And we are here as on a darkling
    plain
Swept with confused alarms of
    struggle and flight,
Where ignorant armies clash by night.

MATTHEW ARNOLD, 'Dover Beach', 1867

Human existence must be a kind of error. It may be said of it, 'It is bad today and every day it will get worse, until the worst of all happens.'

ARTHUR SCHOPENHAUER, German philosopher, 1788–1860

I don't believe in the infinite importance of man. I see no reason to believe that a shudder would go through the sky if the whole ant-heap were kerosened.

F. R. LEAVIS, British literary critic, 1895–1978

MAN:

- a vessel that the slightest shaking, the slightest toss will break ... A body weak and fragile, naked, in its natural state defenceless, dependent upon another's help and exposed to all the affronts of Fortune.

  SENECA, Stoic philosopher

- on this earth is an unforeseen accident which does not stand close investigation.

  JOSEPH CONRAD, *Victory*, 1915

- is born unto trouble, as the sparks fly upward.

  The Bible, Job 3:7

He who despairs over an event is a coward, but he who holds hopes for the human condition is a fool.

ALBERT CAMUS, *Notebooks*

Sic Vita

Like to the falling of a star,
Or as the flights of eagles are,
Or like the fresh spring's gaudy hue,
Or silver drops of morning dew,
Or like a wind that chafes the flood,
Or bubbles which on water stood:
Even such is man, whose
   borrowed light
Is straight called in, and paid to night.

The wind blows out, the bubble dies;
The spring entombed in autumn lies;
The dew dries up, the star is shot;
The flight is past: and man forgot.

HENRY KING, Bishop of Chichester, 1592–1669

No arts; no letters; no society; and which is worst of all, continual fear and danger of violent death; and the life of man, solitary, poor, nasty, brutish, and short.

THOMAS HOBBES, *Leviathan*, 1651

Humanity is a pigsty where liars, hypocrites and the obscene in spirit congregate.

GEORGE MOORE, *Confessions of a Young Man*, 1888

It is really very disheartening how we depend on other people in this life.

ROBERT LOUIS STEVENSON, 1850–94

One of the worst things about life is not how nasty the nasty people are. You know that already. It is how nasty the nice people can be.

ANTHONY POWELL, *Hearing Secret Harmonies*, 1975

To see others suffer does one good, to make others suffer even more: this is a hard saying but an ancient, mighty, human, all-too-human principle to which even the apes might subscribe; for it has been said that in devising bizarre cruelties they anticipate man and are, as it were, his 'prelude'. Without cruelty there is no festival …

FRIEDRICH NIETZSCHE, *The Genealogy of Morals*, 1887

Gruesome historical devices such as the Iron Maiden, the thumb screw, the rack and the wheel may be seen in museums today, bearing testimony to the vile cruelty as well as the imagination of men – but torture itself is still at large. One infamous, modern, CIA-approved technique is that of 'water boarding', which involves cellophane being wrapped over the face and then water being poured over the victim, who is tied to a board with his feet lower than

his head, to produce a feeling of drowning – a punishment that is apparently unbearable after around 14 seconds. Don't expect to see this in a museum any time soon ...

Do you think, said Candide, that men have always massacred each other, as they do today, that they have always been false, cozening, faithless, ungrateful, thieving, weak, inconstant, mean-spirited, envious, greedy, drunken, miserly, ambitious, bloody, slanderous, debauched, fanatic, hypocritical, and stupid?

VOLTAIRE, *Candide, or Optimism*, 1759

The people only anxiously desire two things: bread and the Circus games.

JUVENAL, Roman poet, late 1st–early 2nd century AD, *Satires*

When were not the majority wicked, silly and pigheaded?

ARTHUR HUGH CLOUGH, English poet, 1819–61

Obedience to Authority
In the 1960s, Stanley Milgram carried out a notorious experiment in New Haven, Connecticut. Volunteers were told that they were taking part in a psychological study of the effects of learning. A 'learner' (actually an actor) was wired up with electrodes, and the volunteer was told to keep increasing the voltage every time the learner made a mistake. As the voltage increased, through 30 positions ending with 'severe shock/XXX450 volts', many of the volunteers grew stressed and asked if they had to continue, but, on being told that they should, carried on even though the 'learner' was screaming in agony and begging them to stop. Indeed, of the 40 volunteers, 26 continued all the way to the last shock on the generator.

In nature a repulsive caterpillar turns into a lovely butterfly. But with human beings it is the other way round: a lovely butterfly turns into a repulsive caterpillar.

ANTON CHEKHOV, 1860–1904

Cruelty has a human heart,
And Jealousy a human face;
Terror the human form divine,
And Secrecy the human dress.

WILLIAM BLAKE, 1757–1827,
'A Divine Image'

It is not contrary to reason to prefer the destruction of the whole world to the scratching of my finger.

DAVID HUME, *A Treatise upon Human Nature*, 1739

If some great catastrophe is not announced every morning, we feel a certain void. 'Nothing in the paper today', we sigh.

PAUL VALÉRY, French poet, 1871–1945

The heart is a small thing, but desireth great matters. It is not sufficient for a kite's dinner, yet the whole world is not sufficient for it.

FRANCIS QUARLES, 1592–1644, 'Emblems'

Out of the crooked timber of humanity no straight thing can ever be made.

IMMANUEL KANT, 1724–1804

The Stanford Prison Experiment
In 1971, Philip Zimbardo, of Stanford University, wanted to do a psychological study of the behavioural effects of captivity on prisoners and prison guards. Undergraduates volunteered to play the role of both guards and prisoners and to live for two weeks in a mock prison in the Stanford psychology building basement. However, the experiment went well beyond what had been predicted, and, with the guards becoming increasingly sadistic, had to be brought to an end after a mere six days. See www.LuciferEffect.com for more on this classic exposé of the dark side of human nature and how good people turn evil.

The Seven Deadly (or Capital) Sins:
Lust • Gluttony • Avarice • Sloth • Anger • Envy • Pride

Mahatma Gandhi's list of seven deadly modern sins:
Wealth without work • Pleasure without conscience • Science without humanity • Knowledge without character • Politics without principle • Commerce without morality • Worship without sacrifice

But when the sun is shining in a sapphire sky, when a happy wind is singing among the leaves and softly rocking the branches, when the whole world is intoxicated with perfume, fresh air, light, and love, why does this shabby creature still continue his disconsolate wail? Why is his capacity for happiness so short-lived that it cannot last through one week of pleasant weather?

GEORGE SAND, diary, 6 June 1837

Shower upon him every blessing, drown him in a sea of happiness, give him economic prosperity, such that he should have nothing else to do but sleep, eat cakes, and busy himself with the continuation of his species, and even then, out of sheer ingratitude, sheer spite, man would play you some nasty trick.

FYODOR DOSTOEVSKY, *Notes from the Underground*, 1864

Have you ever thought what a fine world this would be if it weren't for the people in it?

EDEN PHILPOTTS, English novelist, 1862–1960

We live and learn, but not the wiser grow.

JOHN POMFRET, 'Reason', 1700

Man is an exception, whatever else he is. If it is not true that a divine being fell, then we can only say that one of the animals went entirely off its head.

G. K. CHESTERTON, 1874–1936

If one looks with a cold eye at the mess man has made of his history, it is difficult to avoid the conclusion that he has been afflicted by some built-in mental disorder which drives him towards self-destruction.

ARTHUR KOESTLER, *Observer*, 1968

If all the good people were clever, And all clever people were good, The world would be nicer than ever We thought that it possibly could. But somehow, 'tis seldom or never The two hit it off as they should, The good are so harsh to the clever, The clever so rude to the good!

ELIZABETH WORDSWORTH, British author and educator, 1840–1932

Drinking when we are not thirsty and making love all year round, madam; that is all there is to distinguish us from other animals.

PIERRE-AUGUSTIN CARON DE BEAUMARCHAIS, *Le Mariage de Figaro*, 1785

The Voluntary Human Extinction Movement believes that Earth would be better off without humans, to which end a gradual dying out is desirable. If you agree with the motto 'Live long and die out!', go to www.vhemt.org (pronounced 'vehement').

If the whole human race lay in one grave, the epitaph on the headstone might well be, 'It seemed a good idea at the time.'

REBECCA WEST, Irish writer, 1892–1983

Law and Lawyers

Dice are small polka-dotted cubes of ivory, constructed like a lawyer to lie on any side.

AMBROSE BIERCE, *The Devil's Dictionary*, 1911

A learned gentleman who rescues your estate from your enemies ... and keeps it for himself.

LORD BROUGHAM, British writer and statesman, of a lawyer

The law doth punish man or woman
That steals the goose from the
    common,
But lets the greater felon loose
That steals the common from
    the goose.

ANON

The first thing we do, let's kill all the lawyers.

WILLIAM SHAKESPEARE, *King Henry VI, Part II*

We all know here that the law is the most powerful of schools for the imagination. No poet ever interpreted nature as freely as a lawyer interprets the truth.

JEAN GIRAUDOUX, *Tiger at the Gates*, 1935

Old saying

- 'Home is home' as the Devil said when he entered the Court of Session

It usually takes a hundred years to make a law; and then, after it has done its work, takes a hundred to get rid of it.

HENRY WARD BEECHER, *Life Thoughts*, 1858

A jury is composed of twelve men of average ignorance.

HERBERT SPENCER, English philosopher, 1820–1903

A man may as well open an oyster without a knife as a lawyer's mouth without a fee.

BARTEN HOLYDAY, English clergyman and poet, 1593–1661

The Pessimist's Handbook

- A man who is his own lawyer has a fool for his client
- The devil makes his Christmas pies of lawyers' tongues and clerks' fingers
- It is better to be a mouse in a cat's mouth than a man in a lawyer's hands

A man without money need no more fear a crowd of lawyers than a crowd of pickpockets.

WILLIAM WYCHERLEY, *The Plain Dealer*, 1674

Bad laws are the worst sort of tyranny.

EDMUND BURKE, 1729–97

Some Jokes About Lawyers

- What do you call a lawyer with an IQ of 70?
  - Your Honour.

- How can you tell when a lawyer is lying?
  - His lips are moving.

- How do you get a group of lawyers to smile for the camera?
  - Just say 'Fees!'

The Latest Decalogue

I)   Thou shalt have one God only; who
     Would be at the expense of two?

II) No graven images may be
     Worshipp'd, except the currency:

III) Swear not at all; for, for thy curse
     Thine enemy is none the worse:

IV) At church on Sunday to attend
     Will serve to keep the world thy friend:

V)   Honour thy parents; that is, all
     From whom advancement may befall:

VI) Thou shalt not kill; but need'st not strive
     Officiously to keep alive:

VII) Do not adultery commit;
     Advantage rarely comes of it:

VIII) Thou shalt not steal; an empty feat,
     When it's so lucrative to cheat:

XI) Bear not false witness; let the lie
     Have time on its own wings to fly:

X)   Thou shalt not covet; but tradition
     Approves all forms of competition.

ARTHUR HUGH CLOUGH, 1819–61

The one great principle of the English law is to make business for itself.

CHARLES DICKENS, *Bleak House*, 1852–3

Life

You fall out of your mother's womb, you crawl across open country under fire, and you drop into your grave.

QUENTIN CRISP, 1908–99, *An Evening with Quentin Crisp*

There are only three events in a man's life; birth, life and death; he is unaware of being born, he dies in pain, and he forgets to live.

JEAN DE LA BRUYÈRE

In the small hours when the acrid stench of existence rises like sewer gas from everything created, the emptiness of life seems more terrible than its misery.

CYRIL CONNOLLY, British writer, 1903–74

What do baths bring to your mind? Oil, sweat, dirt, greasy water and everything that is disgusting. Such, then, is life in all its parts and such is every material thing in it.

MARCUS AURELIUS, Roman emperor, 121–80, *Meditations*

The world is a grindstone and life is your nose.

FRED ALLEN, US comedian, 1894–1956

Macbeth regrets the way life has turned out:
Life's but a walking shadow, a poor
    player,
That struts and frets his hour upon
    the stage,
And then is heard no more; it is a tale
Told by an idiot, full of sound
    and fury,
Signifying nothing.

WILLIAM SHAKESPEARE

Most people get a fair amount of fun out of their lives, but on balance life is suffering and only the very young or the very foolish imagine otherwise.

GEORGE ORWELL, *Shooting an Elephant*, 1950

There is only one inborn error, and that is the notion that we exist in order to be happy ... So long as we persist in this ... the world seems to us full of contradictions. For at every step, in great things and small, we are bound to experience that the world and life are certainly not arranged for the purpose of maintaining a happy existence ... hence the countenances of almost all elderly persons wear the expression of what is called *disappointment*.

ARTHUR SCHOPENHAUER

When you don't have any money, the problem is food. When you have money, it's sex. When you have both it's health.

J. P. DONLEAVY, *The Ginger Man*, 1955

Ah! que la vie est quotidienne.
Oh, what a day-to-day business life is.

JULES LAFORGUE, French symbolist poet, 1860–87

What is life? A frenzy. What is life? An illusion, a shadow, a fiction. And the greatest good is of slight worth, as all life is a dream, and dreams are dreams.

PEDRO CALDERÓN DE LA BARCA, Spanish playwright, *La Vida es Sueno*, 1636

As our life is very short, so it is very miserable, and therefore it is well it is short.

BISHOP JEREMY TAYLOR, *The Rule and Exercise of Holy Dying*, 1651

Time is a great teacher, they say. Unfortunately, it kills all its pupils.

HECTOR BERLIOZ, French composer, 1803–69

All day, every day, we breathe in a highly toxic substance which leads to the production of free radicals in our systems. These, in turn, sometimes cause damage to our DNA which may, occasionally, result in the formation of a tumour. This chain of events is statistically likely to happen over a long period of time, so, as we live for longer and longer, more and more of us will get cancer. Already it's one in three. But it's no use trying to avoid inhaling the noxious stuff that will get us in the end: it's called oxygen.

And the Days Are Not Full Enough
And the days are not full enough
And the nights are not full enough
And life slips by like a field mouse
 Not shaking the grass.

EZRA POUND, US poet, 1885–1972

LIFE IS . . .

... a cheap table d'hôte in a rather dirty restaurant, with time changing the plates before you've had enough of anything.

THOMAS KETTLE, Irish poet, 1880–1916

... everywhere a state in which much is to be endured, and little to be enjoyed.

SAMUEL JOHNSON, *Rasselas*, 1759

... one long process of getting tired.

SAMUEL BUTLER, 1835–1902

... just one damned thing after another.

ELBERT HUBBARD, US writer and philosopher, 1856–1915

It is not true that life is one damn thing after another – it is one damn thing over and over.

EDNA ST VINCENT MILLAY, US poet, 1892–1950

What is it all but a trouble of ants in the gleam of a million million of suns?

ALFRED, LORD TENNYSON, 'Vastness'

A medical friend once took Samuel Beckett for a walk in the Dublin hills, hoping to cheer him up. 'It's a beautiful day,' said the friend. 'Oh, it's all right,' grunted the writer. 'It's the sort of day that makes you glad to be alive,' insisted the medic, to which Beckett snapped, 'I wouldn't go that far.'

DECLAN KIBBERD, 'Murphy and the World of Samuel Beckett', *Samuel Beckett 100 Years*, 2006

Life can then little else supply
But a few good fucks and then we die.

JOHN WILKES and THOMAS POTTER, 'An Essay on Woman', 1755

Love

I can understand companionship.
I can understand bought sex in the
afternoon. What I cannot
understand is the love affair.

GORE VIDAL, *Sunday Times*, 1973

I shall say what inordinate love is:
The furiosity and wodness of mind,
An instingible burning,
    faulting bliss,
A great hunger, insatiate to find,
A dulcet ill, an evil sweetness blind,
A right wonderful sugared sweet
    error,
Without labour rest, contrary to kind,
Or without quiet, to have huge labour.

ANON, 15th century

Love's pleasure lasts but a moment,
love's sorrow lasts all through life.

JEAN-PIERRE CLARIS DE FLORIAN,
French writer, 1755–94

Unfortunate Coincidence
By the time you swear you're his
Shivering and sighing
And he vows his passion is
Infinite, undying –
Lady, make a note of this:
One of you is lying.

DOROTHY PARKER, 1893–1967

Love, love, love – all the wretched
cant of it, masking egotism, lust,
masochism, fantasy under a
mythology of sentimental postures,
a welter of self-induced miseries
and joys, blinding and masking the
essential personalities in the frozen
gestures of courtship, in the kissing
and the dating and the desire, the
compliments and the quarrels
which vivify its barrenness.

GERMAINE GREER, *The Female Eunuch*,
1970

What is love, anyway?

... the delightful interval between meeting a beautiful girl and discovering that she looks like a haddock.

JOHN BARRYMORE, US actor, 1882–1922

... a spaniel that prefers even punishment from one hand to caresses from another.

CHARLES CALEB COLTON, English clergyman, c. 1780–1832

... the desire to prostitute oneself. There is, indeed, no exalted pleasure that cannot be related to prostitution.

CHARLES BAUDELAIRE, *Intimate Journals*, 1887

... the desire of satisfying a voracious appetite with a certain quantity of delicate white human flesh.

HENRY FIELDING, *Tom Jones*, 1729

... a sin in theology, a forbidden intercourse in jurisprudence, a mechanical insult in medicine, and a subject philosophy has no time for.

KARL KRAUS, Austrian satirist, 1874–1936

... like any other luxury. You have no right to it unless you can afford it.

ANTHONY TROLLOPE, *The Way We Live Now*, 1875

We all know that romantic, passionate love doesn't last, but surely the 'companionate' love it turns into is the real thing – a long-term emotion that only grows as couples stay together through thick and thin? Not so, according to psychology professor Elaine Hatfield at the University of Hawaii. After a series of interviews with nearly 1,000 couples, she and her fellow social psychologist Jane Traupmann presented their findings that, contrary to prevailing wisdom, companionate love declines as precipitously as romantic love, and never stops declining.

The love that lasts longest is the love that is never returned.

W. S. MAUGHAM, *A Writer's Notebook*, 1949

Love is the fart
Of every heart:
It pains a man when 'tis kept close,
And others doth offend, when 'tis
    let loose.

JOHN SUCKLING, 1609–42, 'Love's Offence'

Oh, when I was in love with you,
Then I was clean and brave,
And miles around the wonder grew
How well I did behave.

And now the fancy passes by,
And nothing will remain,
And miles around they'll say that I
Am quite myself again.

A. E. HOUSMAN, 'A Shropshire Lad', 1896

Love seeketh only Self to please,
To bind another to its delight,
Joys in another's loss of ease,
And builds a Hell in Heaven's despite.

WILLIAM BLAKE, 'The Clod and the Pebble', 1794

Ten Country-and-Western Songs

- I Liked You Better Before I Got to Know You So Well

- How Can I Miss You If You Won't Go Away?

- It's Hard To Kiss The Lips At Night That Chewed Your Ass Out All Day Long

- She Got The Ring And I Got The Finger

- You're The Reason Our Kids Are Ugly

- If I Can't Be Number One In Your Life, Then Number Two On You

- I'm So Miserable Without You, It's Like You're Still Here

- If The Phone Don't Ring, You'll Know It's Me

- I Still Miss You Baby, But My Aim's Gettin' Better

- If I Had Shot You When I First Wanted To, I'd Be Out Of Prison By Now

Being loved can never be a patch on being murdered. That's when someone gives their all for you.

QUENTIN CRISP, 1908–99, *An Evening with Quentin Crisp*

Greeting an ex-lover after several years:
I thought I told you to wait in the car.

TALLULAH BANKHEAD, Hollywood actress, 1902–68

Marriage

Nearly half of the marriages in Britain are likely to end in divorce. The Office for National Statistics (ONS) has come to the conclusion that 45 per cent of marriages will end in divorce (prior to a 50th anniversary, and most before ten years) if trends continue as they are today.

Waking this morning out of my sleep of a sudden, I did with my elbow hit my wife a great blow over her face and nose, which waked her with pain, at which I was sorry, and to sleep again.

SAMUEL PEPYS, *Diary*, 1 January 1662

Vienna has a phenomenally high divorce rate: 69 per cent. The city, therefore, decided to hold a Divorce Fair to enable people to meet the right lawyers, estate agents, travel agents, counsellors, etc. Sunday's fair was open to women and Saturday's to men.

The most happy marriage I can picture or imagine to myself would be the union of a deaf man to a blind woman.

SAMUEL TAYLOR COLERIDGE, 1772–1834

LADY ASTOR: If you were my husband, I'd poison your coffee.

WINSTON CHURCHILL: If you were my wife I'd drink it.

A pity that this is thought to be apocryphal

Many a good hanging prevents a bad marriage.

WILLIAM SHAKESPEARE, *Twelfth Night*

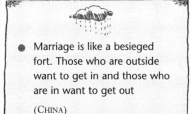

- Marriage is like a besieged fort. Those who are outside want to get in and those who are in want to get out

(CHINA)

Bumper stickers in the USA

- I never knew what real happiness was until I got married; and then it was too late.
- Love may be blind, but marriage is a real eye-opener.
- My other wife is beautiful.
- No husband has ever been shot while doing the dishes.

1 out of 7 married women worldwide are raped by their spouse, and marital rape accounts for 25 per cent of all rapes.

WESLEY CENTER FOR WOMEN, Texas

70 per cent of men and women interviewed in a Kenyan survey, published by the Kenyan Women's Rights Awareness programme in 1997, said they knew neighbours who beat their wives. Almost 60 per cent said the women were to blame for their beatings. Only 51 per cent said the husbands should be penalized for their actions.

When a man opens the car door for his wife, it's either a new car or a new wife.

Attributed to PRINCE PHILIP, Duke of Edinburgh, b. 1921

In marriage, a man becomes slack and selfish, and undergoes a fatty degeneration of his moral being.

ROBERT LOUIS STEVENSON

What it was in him he did not know, but the thought of love, marriage, and children, and a life lived together, in the horrible privacy of domestic and connubial satisfaction, was repulsive.

D. H. LAWRENCE, *Women in Love*

According to Charles L. Nunn of the Department of Biology at the University of Virginia, mammals that are monogamous or have small harem groups are more prone to extinction. Several duiker species which are monogamous died out around ten years after reserves had been set up for them in Ghana. The African Buffalo, however, which has harems of about fifteen females, is still thriving in those reserves. 'The most sexually active species ... may have evolved elevated immune systems as a defence mechanism against disease ... We looked at animal species with a range of mating behaviours and found a strong relationship between high white blood cell counts and high promiscuity in healthy animals.'

I know nothing about sex because I was always married.

ZSA ZSA GABOR, b. 1917

- Needles and pins, needles and pins: when a man marries, his trouble begins
- It is hard to wive and thrive both in a year
- Honest men marry soon, wise men not at all
- He that has a wife, has strife
- A dead wife's the best goods in a man's house

Matrimony hath many children; Repentance, Discord, Poverty, Jealousy, Sickness, Spleen, Loathing.

JONATHAN SWIFT, 1677–1745

Are men and women really equal partners in marriage? Professor Stefan Felder of Magdeburg University, Germany, has revealed that, in a study of more than 50,000 couples across Europe, while marriage lengthens the lifespan of the male by 1.7 years, it knocks 1.4 years off the life of the average wife. One factor is that women tend to imitate their husbands' unhealthy lifestyles (such as smoking, drinking, etc.), and another decisive element might be the stress of balancing the roles of housewife and career woman. A further suggestion is that regular sex could be detrimental to the longevity of the wife, while benefiting the husband, thanks to hormonal changes.

But for the funeral train which the
    bridegroom sees in the distance,
Would he so joyfully, think you, fall in
    with the marriage procession?

ARTHUR HUGH CLOUGH

I wonder, among all the tangles of this mortal coil, which one contains tighter knots to undo, and consequently suggests more tugging, and pain, and diversified elements of misery, than the marriage tie.

EDITH WHARTON, 1862–1937

- Marriage is the tomb of love
- Matrimony is a school in which one learns too late
- Keep your eyes wide open before marriage, and half shut afterwards
- Marry in haste, and repent at leisure
- Never marry for money, ye'll borrow it cheaper

Advice to persons about to marry – Don't.

PUNCH

Men

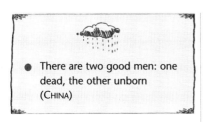

- There are two good men: one dead, the other unborn
(CHINA)

Men first feel necessity, then look for utility, next attend to comfort, still later amuse themselves with pleasure, thence grow dissolute in luxury, and finally go mad and waste their substance.

GIAMBATTISTA VICO, Italian philosopher, 1668–1744

Man that is born of a woman hath but a short time to live, and is full of misery.

Book of Common Prayer

What is man, when you come to think upon him, but a minutely set, ingenious machine for turning, with infinite artfulness, the red wine of Shiraz into urine?

ISAK DINESEN, Danish writer, *The Dreamers*, 1935

Men, my dear, are very queer animals – a mixture of horse-nervousness, ass-stubbornness and camel-malice.

T. H. HUXLEY, English scientist, 1825–95

A single sentence will suffice for modern man: he fornicated and read the papers.

ALBERT CAMUS

Probably the only place where a man can feel really secure is in a maximum security prison, except for the imminent threat of release.

GERMAINE GREER, *The Female Eunuch*, 1970

A man is two people, himself and his cock. A man always takes his friend to the party. Of the two, the friend is the nicer, being more able to show his feelings.

BERYL BAINBRIDGE, British author, b. 1934

Between the ages of 15 and 24, with the onset of the 'testosterone storm', males are nearly five times more likely to die than females. It comes as no surprise to find that most of these deaths are from car accidents; followed by homicide, suicide, cancer and death by drowning. The difference between men and women then narrows until after 55 when, again, more men than women die, thanks to heart disease (five in a thousand), suicide, car accidents, and smoking and drinking. And, finally, when male and female get old, men will, on average, die five years younger than women do. Is that all? No. The gods have more direct means still: men are about five times more likely than women to be struck by lightning. (Could this be a judgement on the sex that plays golf?)

There is, of course, no reason for the existence of the male sex except that one sometimes needs help with moving the piano.

REBECCA WEST, *Sunday Telegraph*, 1970

The man who has cured himself of BO and halitosis, has learned French to surprise the waiter, and the saxophone to amuse the company, may find that people still avoid him because they do not like him.

HEYWOOD BROUN, US journalist, 1888–1939

The mass of men lead lives of quiet desperation. What is called resignation is confirmed desperation.

HENRY DAVID THOREAU, *Walden*, 1854

Sometimes it's hard to be a man
In 1987, Eisler and Skidmore of Virginia Polytechnic Institute and State University found four typical mechanisms of masculinity that often result in Masculine Gender Role Stress:

- the emphasis on prevailing in situations requiring fitness and strength
- the need to feel conquering in regard to sexual matters and work
- the need, as is the traditional masculine custom, to repress tender emotions
- the fear of being perceived as emotional and thereby feminine.

He is the most ridiculous beast on earth and the reason is his mind and his pudendum.

EDWARD DAHLBERG, US novelist, 1900–77

All men are rapists, and that's all they are. They rape us with their eyes, their laws, and their codes.

MARILYN FRENCH, *The Women's Room*, 1977

No man is a hero to his valet.

MME CORNUEL, 17th-century Parisian hostess

In the new code of laws which I suppose it will be necessary for you to make I desire you would remember the ladies, and be more generous and favourable to them than your ancestors. Do not put such unlimited power into the hands of the husbands. Remember all men would be tyrants if they could.

ABIGAIL ADAMS, First Lady 1797–1801, letter to her husband, John Adams, 1776

Most men devote the greater part of their lives to making their remaining years unhappy.

JEAN DE LA BRUYÈRE

Men plant the seeds of their own obsolescence
Until recently, men (not just male scientists) were the only ones who could make spermatozoa. But, in 2007, scientists discovered a way of making sperm cells from bone marrow, thereby opening up the possibility of a woman making sperm from her own bone marrow and fertilizing another woman's egg – and leaving men neatly out of the equation. Redundancy beckons, and probably no severance package.

The more I see of men, the more I like dogs.

Attributed to various French women of the 18th century

Monstrous Men

NERO, 37–68, the mad, matricidal Roman emperor, persecuted thousands of Christians, hoping to wipe them off the face of the earth. He enjoyed dipping Christians in wax, impaling them on poles and lighting them like lamps.

VLAD THE IMPALER, 1431–76, the original Count Dracula, inflicted extraordinary horrors on his victims. In one notorious incident, he impaled 20,000 prisoners on sharpened tree trunks – men, women and children.

GENGHIS KHAN, 1162–1227, once rounded up 70,000 men, women and children and shot them with arrows.

IDI AMIN, c. 1925–2003, murdered more than a quarter of a million people, allegedly sometimes licking the blood of his victims.

POL POT, 1925–98, the leader of the Khmer Rouge, tortured and starved over 1 million people to death (over a quarter of the Cambodian population).

ADOLF HITLER, 1889–1945, was responsible for the deaths of up to 11 million people in the Holocaust.

JOSEPH STALIN, 1878–1953, killed around 20 million through purges and forced famine.

MAO ZEDONG, 1893–1976, caused the deaths of up to 70 million Chinese people with his policies such as the 'Cultural Revolution' and the 'Great Leap Forward'.

Middle Age

Fair, fat and forty.

SIR WALTER SCOTT, *St Ronan's Well*, 1823

In the middle of the journey of our
    life
I found myself in a dark wood
Where the straight path was lost.

DANTE ALIGHIERI, *La Divina Commedia, Inferno*, c. 1320

To live beyond 40 is bad taste.

FYODOR DOSTOYEVSKY, 1821–81

Following the collapse of his marriage, a 44-year-old Australian from Perth auctioned his life (his house, his job, his clothes, his friends) on eBay. By throwing out everything, from his car to his friends, Ian Usher says he got rid of the chaos and the midlife blues and started again. You can help him on his way at www.100goals100weeks.com.

Everybody has a talent at twenty-five. The difficult thing is to have it at fifty.

EDGAR DEGAS, 1834–1917

Forty is a terrible age. It is the age in which we become what we are.

CHARLES PÉGUY, French writer, 1873–1914

Nature gives you the face you have when you are twenty. Life shapes the face you have at thirty. But it is up to you to earn the face you have at fifty.

Attributed to COCO CHANEL, 1883–1971

The man who views the world at 50 the same as he did at 20 has wasted 30 years of his life.

MUHAMMAD ALI, b. 1942

The man who is a pessimist before 48 knows too much; if he is an optimist after it, he knows too little.

MARK TWAIN, *Notebook*, December 1902

Monarchy

Monarchy is as absurd as an hereditary mathematician.

TOM PAINE, English revolutionary, 1791

It has been said, not truly, but with a possible approximation to truth 'That in 1802 every hereditary monarch [in Europe] was insane.'

WALTER BAGEHOT, English essayist 1826–77

There, I guess King George will be able to read that.

JOHN HANCOCK on signing American Declaration of Independence, 1776

 ──────────

Here lies a great and mighty King, Whose promise none relied on; He never said a foolish thing, Nor ever did a wise one.

JOHN WILMOT, EARL OF ROCHESTER, 1647–80, of Charles II

──────────

A crown is no more than a hat that lets in rain.

FREDERICK THE GREAT of Prussia, 1740

Tell me, Alvanley, who is your fat friend?

BEAU BRUMMELL, English dandy, of the Prince Regent, 1813

Upon the highest throne in the world, we are seated, still, upon our arses.

MICHEL DE MONTAIGNE, French writer, 1533–92

The metaphor of the king as the shepherd of his people goes back to ancient Egypt. Perhaps the use of this particular convention is due to the fact that, being stupid, affectionate, gregarious and easily stampeded, the societies formed by sheep are most like human ones.

NORTHROP FRYE, Canadian literary critic, 1957

I tell you we will cut off his head with the crown upon it.

OLIVER CROMWELL, 1599–1658, on the execution of Charles I

Strip your Louis XIV of his king-gear, and there is nothing left but a poor forked radish with a head fantastically carved.

THOMAS CARLYLE, 1840

How is it that the British, the first modern industrial society, should have such a blatant anachronism at their centre? Isn't this a huge example of a failure of self-analysis? An inability to see ourselves as others see us?

REPUBLICAN ALLIANCE, 2000

The king must die so that the country can live.

MAXIMILIEN ROBESPIERRE, French revolutionary leader, 1758–94

Certainly that people needs be mad or strangely infatuated that build the chief hope of their common happiness or safety on a single person; who, if he happen to be good, can do no more than another man; if he happen to be bad, hath in his hands to do more evil without check than millions of other men.

JOHN MILTON, 1660

Here lies Fred,
Who was alive and is dead.
Had it been his father,
I had much rather.
Had it been his brother,
Still better than another.
Had it been his sister,
No one would have missed her.
Had it been the whole generation,
The better for the nation.
But since 'tis only Fred,
Who was alive, and is dead,
There's no more to be said.

ANON, on the death of Frederick, Prince of Wales, 1751

An old, mad, blind, despised and dying king.

PERCY BYSSHE SHELLEY, 1792–1822, on George III

There never was an individual less regretted by his fellow creatures than this deceased King. What eye has wept for him? What heart has heaved one sob of unmercenary sorrow?

The Times, on the death of George IV, 1830

I believe that it's Elizabeth the Last.

PROFESSOR STEPHEN HASELER, chairman of anti-monarchist group Republic

Months

January, month of empty pockets! let us endure this evil month, anxious as a theatrical producer's forehead.

COLETTE, French writer, 1873–1954

February, fill the dyke with what thou dost like.

THOMAS TUSSER, English writer and farmer, 1524–80

Indoors or out, no-one relaxes
In **March**, that month of wind and
    taxes,
The wind will presently disappear,
The taxes last us all the year.

OGDEN NASH, US poet, 1902–71

April is the cruellest month, breeding
Lilacs out of the dead land, mixing
Memory and desire, stirring
Dull roots with spring rain.

T. S. ELIOT, 'The Waste Land', 1922

May is a pious fraud of the almanac.

JAMES RUSSELL LOWELL, US poet, 'Under the Willows', 1869

June *is usually the peak month of the year for sufferers of allergic rhinitis or 'hay fever', because it's when grasses release their pollen. Hay fever is a modern disease: two hundred years ago, it was largely unknown; today, 20 per cent of the UK's population is affected, and this proportion continues to rise, as it does for eczema and asthma. What's to blame for this escalation? Theories include pollution, over-hygienic childhoods, vaccinations and global warming, or a combination of all four.*

Don't worry, the fans don't start booing until **July**.

EARL WEAVER, American baseball player, b. 1930

The English winter – ending in July,
To recommence in **August**.

LORD BYRON

Not every man has gentians in his
    house
in soft **September**, at slow, sad
    Michaelmas.
Bavarian gentians, big and dark,
    only dark
darkening the daytime, torch-like,
with the smoking blueness of Pluto's
    gloom,
ribbed and torch-like, with their blaze
    of darkness spread blue
down flattening into points, flattened
    under the sweep of white day
torch-flower of the blue-smoking
    darkness, Pluto's dark-blue daze,
black lamps from the halls of Dis,
    burning dark blue,
giving off darkness, blue darkness, as
    Demeter's pale lamps give off light,
        lead me then, lead the way.

D. H. LAWRENCE, 'Bavarian Gentians'

October. This is one of the
peculiarly dangerous months to
speculate in stocks. The others are
July, January, September, April,
November, May, March, June,
December, August, and February.

MARK TWAIN

No warmth, no cheerfulness, no
    healthful ease,
No comfortable feel in any member –
No shade, no shine, no butterflies, no
    bees –
No fruits, no flowers, no leaves, no
    birds –
November!

THOMAS HOOD, English poet,
1789–1845

Glad Tidings of Comfort and Joy

*On 14 December 2007 Reuters
reported that the government was
promising action to help address
domestic violence over Christmas,
when the number of incidents was
expected to rocket. Police say that
there are about a third more incidents
of domestic assault on Christmas Day
than the daily average.*

Music

Music is no different from opium. Music affects the human mind in a way that makes people think of nothing but music and sensual matters ... Music is a treason to the country, a treason to our youth, and we should cut out all this music and replace it with something instructive.

AYATOLLAH KHOMEINI, Ramadan speech, 23 July 1979

Music was invented to deceive and delude mankind.

EPHORUS OF CUMAE, 400–330 BC

We need silence to be able to touch souls.

MOTHER THERESA, *A Gift for God*, 1975

Music was invented to confirm human loneliness.

Attributed to LAWRENCE DURRELL, 1912–90

Accordion, n. An instrument in harmony with the sentiments of an assassin.

Piano, n. A parlour utensil for subduing the impenitent visitor. It is operated by depressing the keys of the machine and the spirits of the audience.

AMBROSE BIERCE, *The Devil's Dictionary*, 1911

The music industry is currently in the doldrums. It is increasingly hard for new talent to emerge given the massive range of channels available to everyone to promote themselves and their music on the web. TV shows like X Factor give everyone the chance to be somebody in music, but few make it through to a lasting position. Meanwhile sales of music are in steep decline. Forced to compete with illegal downloading, file-sharing, home printing and suchlike, sales of compact discs have plummeted.

Music helps not the toothache.

GEORGE HERBERT, *Jacula Prudentum*, 1651

I must confess that I live a miserable life … I live entirely in my music.

LUDWIG VAN BEETHOVEN, 1801

You can't mess with people's heads, that's for sure. But that's what music's all about, messing with people's heads.

JIMI HENDRIX, 1942–70

———

So-called muzak, elevator music, canned music and piped music is fast becoming a form of pollution. It is part of the background in everything from supermarkets to restaurants and normally what is played to a phone-in customer when they are put on hold. The organization to stop muzak, Pipedown, managed to persuade Gatwick airport to discontinue the use of piped music when the results of a survey revealed that most people were not in favour of it. To find out more about Pipedown's campaigns against wall-to-wall muzak, see www.pipedown.info.

———

Today, what is not worth speaking is sung.

PIERRE BEAUMARCHAIS, writer of *The Barber of Seville* and *The Marriage of Figaro*, 1775

Three farts and a raspberry, orchestrated.

Attributed to SIR JOHN BARBIROLLI, 1899–1970, on modern music

I know two kinds of audience only – one coughing and one not coughing.

ARTUR SCHNABEL, *My Life and Music*, 1961

———

At the time of the Third Reich only three composers were really approved of: Richard Wagner, Beethoven and Anton Bruckner.

———

Today musicians listen to see what makes the most money on a style, and then they set to copying him. And they don't copy the ones that are beautiful, creative and good.

Attributed to CHARLES MINGUS, 1922–79

Brass bands are all very well in their place – outdoors and several miles away.

SIR THOMAS BEECHAM, 1879–1961

Newspapers and Other Media

CHARLES: Anything interesting in *The Times?*

RUTH: Don't be silly, Charles.

NOËL COWARD, *Blithe Spirit*, 1941

Television? No good will come of this device. The word is half Greek and half Latin.

C. P. SCOTT, English editor, 1846–1932

Anyone here been raped and speak English?

EDWARD BEHR book title, 1975, inspired by an incident at an airport in Congo when a British reporter approached Belgian refugees fleeing from rebel troops

There's a lot to be said for not being known to the readers of the *Daily Mirror.*

ANTHONY BURGESS, English writer, 1917–93

My work is being destroyed almost as soon as it is printed. One day it is being read; the next day someone's wrapping fish in it.

AL CAPP, US cartoonist, 1909–79

The cinema is little more than a fad. It's canned drama. What audiences really want to see is flesh and blood on the stage.

CHARLIE CHAPLIN, 1916

The wireless music box has no imaginable commercial value. Who would pay for a message sent to nobody in particular?

Response of colleagues to a call from DAVID SARNOFF, US pioneer of broadcast media, to invest in commercial radio in the 1920s

There is practically no chance communications space satellites will be used to provide better telephone, telegraph, television, or radio service inside the United States.

T. CRAVEN, US Federal Communications Commissioner, in 1961. The first commercial communications satellite went into service in 1965.

———

It's estimated that about 1.4 blogs are created every second of every day.

Since online sources of information, on every subject under the sun, can be constantly updated, our daily papers risk being out of date in more ways than one. Will newsprint survive the onslaught of the digital age?

Instead of being arrested, as we stated, for kicking his wife down a flight of stairs and hurling a lighted kerosene lamp after her, the Rev. James P. Wellman died unmarried four years ago.

Correction in a US newspaper, quoted in a letter by SIR EDWARD BURNE JONES, 1833–98

In 2008, it was reported by Childwise that nearly 80 per cent of 5–16-year-olds now have TV sets in their bedrooms and spend 2 1/2 hours a day watching TV (and another 3 hours or so looking at computer screens). Too much TV is, apparently, responsible for inhibiting language development, social development and brain development (the ability to concentrate and process information); it's also implicated in creating poor sleep patterns and obesity. As in so many things, it seems that the UK is hot on the heels of the US, where 43 per cent of three-month-olds watch TV regularly.

I am unable to understand how a man of honour could take a newspaper in his hands without a shudder of disgust.

CHARLES BAUDELAIRE, 1821–67

Electronic mail has made everybody's life much easier, with communication possible at the mere touch of a button. But, with around two million emails being sent every second (nearly three quarters of them spam), the shine is beginning to wear off. Bill Gates may have staff to deal with his four million daily unsolicited emails, but recent reports suggest that a third of workers are feeling stressed by the sheer number of emails in their inbox.

Newspapers always excite curiosity. No one ever lays one down without a feeling of disappointment.

CHARLES LAMB, English essayist, 1775–1834

If one morning I walked on top of the water across the Potomac River, the headline that afternoon would read: President Can't Swim.

LYNDON B. JOHNSON, US president, 1908–73

Great Satan Sits Down with the Axis of Evil

Headline, *The Times*, on US–Iran talks, 29 May 2007

Old Age

Every man desires to live long; but no man would be old.

JONATHAN SWIFT, *Thoughts on Various Subjects*, 1727

- You can't teach an old dog new tricks
- No fool like an old fool

To speak humanely, death has a useful function: it puts an end to old age.

JEAN DE LA BRUYÈRE, *Les Caractères ou les moeurs de ce siècle*

You have to live old, even very old, even excessively old. Then you have the pleasure, as years pass by, of burying the people who mocked you.

JEAN DUTOURD, French writer, b. 1920

Old age is the most unexpected of things that can happen to a man.

LEON TROTSKY, *Diary in Exile*, 1959

Incontinence can be the blight of old age. Studies in Canada have concluded that it affects up to 44 per cent of otherwise healthy elderly ladies in the country and 24 per cent of elderly men.

Too often, the idea that people die from old age means that they are not receiving the care and support they need, says Paul Cann from Help the Aged UK. The Commission for Social Care Inspection, in fact, estimates that more than 700,000 elderly people in England struggle with the basic routines of their daily lives, from washing and eating to cleaning their homes.

A study by the National Centre for Social Research and King's College London, reported in the Guardian, suggested that 342,000 older people living in private households are subject to some form of mistreatment every year in the UK.

Age is deformed, youth unkind
We scorn their bodies, they our mind.

THOMAS BASTARD, *Chrestoleros*, 1598

In 2000, there were 600 million people in the world aged 60 and over. There will be 1.2 billion by 2025 and 2 billion by 2050. Today, about two thirds of all elderly people are living in the developing world. By 2025, it will be 75 per cent. In the developed world, the very old (that is, people aged 80 and over) are the most rapidly growing population group. The mechanisms for dealing with this boom in grey-haired humans have yet to be thought out. In China alone, the elderly population is set to double between 2000 and 2027. The World Health Organization is warning that such rapid rises throughout the world are going to have a massive and disruptive impact on the way we live, from an increase in diseases, dementia and nursing care to the way we run our pension systems, homes and workplaces.

Do I enjoy getting older? No, I'm thrilled and delighted for those people who enjoy the experience. I just don't happen to be one of them.

CHER, *Scotsman*, 11 May 2004

Habits which speed up the ageing process

White refined foods are barely beneficial in nutritional terms. Eating them causes weight gain and lessens your chances of achieving longevity. No more white sugar, white flour or white bread then. Processed food is high in additives, artificial sweeteners and fat and should be avoided for the same reason. Smoking and pollution, we know, destroy cells. Lack of sleep means the skin has less time to repair and look youthful. Not taking enough exercise weakens bones, increases the risk of heart disease, arthritis, obesity, etc. Above all, stress and anxiety destroy the body and accelerate the ageing process so you mustn't think about it too much.

Youth is a blunder: Manhood a struggle; Old Age a regret.

BENJAMIN DISRAELI, *Coningsby*, 1844

I prayed to rediscover my childhood and it returned, and I feel that it is as difficult as it was then, and that growing old has had no purpose at all.

RAINER MARIA RILKE, *Die Aufzeichnungen des Malte Laurids Brigge*, 1910

Age discrimination or ageism is regularly practised by employers the world over, despite many governments signing up to conventions and laws condemning it.

But the longer I live on this
    Crumpetty Tree
The plainer than ever it seems to me
That very few people come this way
And that life on the whole is far from
    gay!
Said the Quangle-Wangle Quee

EDWARD LEAR, 'The Quangle Wangle's Hat', 1871

Help the Aged reckons that hundreds of thousands of elderly people are having their homes, state benefits and savings abused by members of their own families. The total sums from this kind of abuse could run into tens of millions.

According to the World Health Organization, the highest rates of suicide in almost every country in the world are among those aged 75 and over. More young people attempt suicide but greater numbers of elderly men and women die this way. The reasons are many, but illness, loneliness and depression are high on the list.

Bodily decay is gloomy in prospect, but of all human contemplations the most abhorrent is body without mind.

THOMAS JEFFERSON, 1743–1826

Thou shouldst not have been old till thou hadst been wise.

WILLIAM SHAKESPEARE, King Lear, 1605

All decrepit is this body, diseases' nest and frail; this foul mass is broken up for life does end in death.

The Dhammapada, Chapter 11, verse 148

The failure of the mind in old age is often less the results of natural decay, than of disuse. Ambition has ceased to operate; contentment brings indolence, and indolence decay of mental power, ennui, and sometimes death. Men have been known to die, literally speaking, of disease induced by intellectual vacancy.

SIR BENJAMIN COLLINS BRODIE, surgeon, 1783–1862

Old age is a shipwreck.

CHARLES DE GAULLE

Order

Chaos often breeds life, when order breeds habit.

HENRY BROOKS ADAMS, *The Education of Henry Adams*, 1907

The rich man in his castle,
The poor man at his gate,
God made them, high or lowly,
And ordered their estate.

CECIL FRANCES ALEXANDER, 'All Things Bright And Beautiful', 1848

In any country there must be people who have to die. They are the sacrifices any nation has to make to achieve law and order.

IDI AMIN, president of Uganda, 1976

Chaos, a rough unordered mass.

OVID, *Metamorphoses*

Obsessive Compulsive Disorder can be an extremely debilitating condition in which sufferers, among other things, yearn for exactness in the way things are ordered or arranged. Listed by the World Health Organization as one of the most crippling illnesses for its pernicious effect on work, life and income, it is believed to affect up to 3 per cent of the UK population. It is, by its very nature, an illness that forces sufferers to keep silent about their pain, but professional help should be sought: see www.ocduk.org.

Life creates order, but order does not create life.

ANTOINE DE SAINT-EXUPÉRY, *Lettre à un otage*, 1943

Collapse of social and economic order can lead to chaos. The following are the top most unstable places in the world (source: Jane's Country Risk Ratings): Gaza and West Bank, Somalia, Sudan, Afghanistan and Côte d'Ivoire.

Parenthood

Children begin by loving their parents; after a time they judge them; rarely, if ever, do they forgive them.

OSCAR WILDE, *The Importance of Being Earnest*, 1895

How sharper than a serpent's
   tooth it is
To have a thankless child!

WILLIAM SHAKESPEARE, *King Lear*, c. 1603

What you say of the pride of giving life to an immortal soul is very fine, dear, but I own I cannot enter into that; I think much more of our being like a cow or a dog at such moments; when our poor nature becomes so very animal and unecstatic.

QUEEN VICTORIA, letter to the Princess Royal, 15 June 1858

Literature is mostly about having sex and not much about having children. Life is the other way around.

DAVID LODGE, *The British Museum Is Falling Down*, 1965

He that hath wife and children hath given hostages to fortune; for they are impediments to great enterprises, either of virtue or mischief.

FRANCIS BACON, 1561–1626

My father was frightened of his mother; I was frightened of my father, and I am damned well going to see to it that my children are frightened of me.

Attributed to KING GEORGE V, 1865–1936

There is no good father, that's the rule. Don't lay the blame on men but on the bond of paternity, which is rotten. To beget children, nothing better; to *have* them, what iniquity!

JEAN-PAUL SARTRE, 'Lire', *Les Mots*, 1964

There was an old woman who lived in a shoe,
She had so many children she didn't know what to do;
She gave them some broth without any bread;
She whipped them all soundly and put them to bed.

This Be the Verse

They fuck you up, your mum and dad.
They may not mean to, but they do.
They fill you with the faults they had
And add some extra, just for you.

But they were fucked up in their turn
By fools in old-style hats and coats,
Who half the time were soppy-stern
And half at one another's throats.

Man hands on misery to man.
It deepens like a coastal shelf.
Get out as early as you can,
And don't have any kids yourself.

PHILIP LARKIN, 1922–85

The awe and dread with which the untutored savage contemplates his mother-in-law are amongst the most familiar facts of anthropology.

JAMES GEORGE FRAZER, *The Golden Bough*, 1890

I have reached the age when a woman begins to perceive that she is growing into the person she least plans to resemble: her mother.

ANITA BROOKNER, English novelist, *Incidents in the Rue Laugier*, 1995

If you desire to drain to the dregs the fullest cup of scorn and hatred that a human fellow creature can pour out for you, let a young mother hear you call her baby 'it'.

JEROME K. JEROME, *Idle Thoughts of an Idle Fellow*, 1886

A mother loves the child more than the father does, for she knows it's her own, while he only thinks it is.

MENANDER, Greek playwright, 342–293 BC

The Stern Parent

Father heard his Children scream,
So he threw them in the stream,
Saying, as he drowned the third,
'Children should be seen, *not* heard!'

HARRY GRAHAM, English verse-writer, 1874–1936

The fathers have eaten sour grapes, and the children's teeth are set on edge.

The Bible, Ezekiel 18:2

As fathers go, it is seldom a misfortune to be fatherless; and considering the general run of sons, as seldom a misfortune to be childless.

LORD CHESTERFIELD, *Letters to His Son*, 1774

My son – and what's a son? A thing
    begot
Within a pair of minutes, thereabout,
A lump bred up in darkness.

THOMAS KYD, English playwright, 1558–94, *The Spanish Tragedy*

I have found the best way to give advice to your children is to find out what they want and then advise them to do it.

HARRY S. TRUMAN, US president, 1884–1972

Are they worth it?

In 2006, research from Liverpool Victoria, the financial services provider, showed that the average cost of bringing up baby – from birth to 21 – is £180,137 – that's about £23.50 a day. But don't fool yourself that, just because your child has 'come of age', they'll cease to be a drain on your resources. Children aren't always

leaving home in the way they used to, and it's estimated that, in the UK, there are now nearly 7 million 'KIPPERS' (Kids In Parents' Pockets Eroding Retirement Savings).

Their eldest son was such a disappointment to them; they wanted him to be a linguist, and spent no end of money on having him taught to speak – oh, dozens of languages! – and then he became a Trappist monk.

SAKI, British writer, 'Reginald at the Carlton', 1904

Richard III's mother:
Thou cam'st on earth to make the
    earth my hell
Thy schooldays frightful,
A grievous burthen was thy birth
    to me;
Tetchy and wayward was thy infancy.

WILLIAM SHAKESPEARE, *Richard III*, 1591

Beat your son every day; you may not know why, but he will.

ANON

Patriotism

Can anything be stupider than that a man has the right to kill me because he lives on the other side of a river and his ruler has a quarrel with mine, though I have not quarrelled with him?

BLAISE PASCAL

I hate the idea of causes, and if I had to choose between betraying my country and betraying my friend, I hope I should have the guts to betray my country.

E. M. FORSTER, 1879–1970

'My country, right or wrong' is a thing no patriot would ever think of saying except in a desperate case. It is like saying 'My mother, drunk or sober.'

G. K. CHESTERTON

Patriots always talk of dying for their country and never of killing for their country.

BERTRAND RUSSELL

Heroism on command, senseless violence, and all the loathsome nonsense that goes by the name of patriotism – how passionately I hate them!

ALBERT EINSTEIN

If I knew something that would serve my country but would harm mankind, I would never reveal it; for I am a citizen of humanity first and by necessity, and a citizen of France second, and only by accident.

MONTESQUIEU, French philosopher, 1689–1755

It is lamentable, that to be a good patriot one must become the enemy of the rest of mankind.

VOLTAIRE, *Philosophical Dictionary*

Patriotism is the last refuge of the sculptor.

WILLIAM PLOMER, South African-born English writer, 1903–73

Politics

You have all the characteristics of a popular politician: a horrible voice, bad breeding, and a vulgar manner.

ARISTOPHANES, Greek dramatist, 450–388 BC

I have a habit of comparing the phraseology of communiqués, one with another across the years, and noting a certain similarity of words, a certain similarity of optimism in the reports which followed the summit meetings and a certain similarity in the lack of practical results during the ensuing years.

MARGARET THATCHER, b. 1925

You see how this House of Commons has begun to verify all the ill prophecies that were made of it – low, vulgar, meddling with everything, assuming universal competency, and flattering every base passion – and sneering at everything noble, refined and truly national. The direct tyranny will come on by and by, after it shall have gratified the multitude with the spoil and ruin of the old institutions of the land.

SAMUEL TAYLOR COLERIDGE

There is no art which one government sooner learns of another than that of draining money from the pockets of other people.

ADAM SMITH, Scottish economist, 1723–90

My Lord Bath, you and I are now as two insignificant men as any in England.

SIR ROBERT WALPOLE, 1676–1745, letter on promotion to the House of Lords

That grand impostor, that loathsome hypocrite, that detestable traitor, that prodigy of nature, that opprobrium of mankind, that landscape of iniquity, that sink of sin, that compendium of baseness who now calls himself our Protector.

The ANABAPTISTS, in an address to King Charles II, on Oliver Cromwell

He [Gladstone] speaks to me as if I was a public meeting.

QUEEN VICTORIA

I don't go to the House of Lords any more. I did go once but a bishop stole my umbrella.

LORD BERNERS, British composer, 1883–1950

When a nation's young men are conservative, its funeral bell is already rung.

HENRY WARD BEECHER, *Proverbs from Plymouth Pulpit*, 1887

This island is almost made of coal and surrounded by fish. Only an organizing genius could produce a shortage of coal and fish in Great Britain at the same time.

ANEURIN BEVAN, 1945

When they circumcised Herbert Samuel, they threw away the wrong bit.

DAVID LLOYD GEORGE, 1863–1945, of a fellow Liberal

A poll by Quinnipiac University in 2006 asked US voters who was the worst president since 1945:

George W. Bush (34%)
Richard Nixon (17%)
Bill Clinton (16%)
Jimmy Carter (13%)
Lyndon Johnson (4%)

One of the penalties for refusing to participate in politics is that you end up being governed by your inferiors.

PLATO, 428/427–348/347 BC

Washington DC: Too small to be a state but too large to be an asylum for the mentally deranged.

ANNE BURFORD, US environmentalist, 1942–2004

This woman is headstrong, obstinate and dangerously self-opinionated.

ICI PERSONNEL OFFICER, explaining why a young Margaret Thatcher didn't get the job

This is a rotten argument, but it should be enough for their lordships on a hot summer afternoon.

Footnote to a ministerial brief, mistakenly read out in the House of Lords

Men enter local politics solely as a result of being unhappily married.

C. NORTHCOTE PARKINSON, *Parkinson's Law*, 1957

When I gave my longest speech in the Lords, the longest letter I received was from a lady who wanted to know where I had bought my blouse.

BARONESS JAY, b. 1939

Religion

Man is the religious animal. He is the only religious animal. He is the only animal that has the True Religion – several of them. He is the only animal that loves his neighbour as himself and cuts his throat, if his theology isn't straight. He has made a graveyard of the globe in trying his honest best to smooth his brother's path to happiness and heaven.

MARK TWAIN

BISHOP: Who is it that sees and hears all we do, and before whom even I am but as a crushed worm?

PAGE: The missus, my Lord.

Punch cartoon, 1880

I like your Christ. I do not like your Christians. Your Christians are so unlike your Christ. The materialism of affluent Christian countries appears to contradict the claim of Jesus Christ that says it's not possible to worship both Mammon and God at the same time.

MAHATMA GANDHI

For most people the Church has become little more than a useful landmark by which to offer directions.

Attributed to an ARCHBISHOP OF YORK

Just in terms of allocation of time resources, religion is not very efficient. There's a lot more I could be doing on a Sunday morning.

BILL GATES, b. 1955

The more I study religions the more I am convinced that man never worshipped anything but himself.

SIR RICHARD FRANCIS BURTON, English explorer and writer, 1821–90

Religions are not imaginative, not poetic, not soulful. On the contrary, they are parochial, small-minded, niggardly with the human imagination, precisely where science is generous.

RICHARD DAWKINS, b. 1941

What lasts longer: a Pope or a wine gum?

Graffito, 1978, after John Paul I died 33 days into his papacy

We have just enough religion to make us hate, but not enough to make us love one another.

JONATHAN SWIFT, *Thoughts on Various Subjects*, 1711

To Banbury came I, O profane one,
Where I saw a Puritan
Hanging of his cat on Monday
For killing of a mouse on Sunday

RICHARD BRATHWAITE, *Barnabee's Journal*, 1638

Religion has much blood on its hands, thanks to the various Crusades of the Middle Ages (around 100,000 killed); the burning alive of witches (tens of thousands); the Spanish Inquisition, 1478–1834 (around 30,000); and it is, of course, impossible to estimate just how many have died in wars fought in the names of various gods – or have yet to die.

Religion is comparable to a childhood neurosis.

SIGMUND FREUD

When Jehovah's Witnesses knock on our doors, clutching copies of The Watchtower, they do so in the hope that we will give them the chance to explain that Armageddon is imminent, the wicked will be destroyed, the survivors, as well as some resurrected people, will form a new society ruled by a heavenly government, etc., etc. The bad news is that those of us lucky enough to survive Christ's showdown with Satan will then be involved in an unseemly scramble with our new friends to bag one of the 144,000 places reserved for those being raised to heaven. Lengthening the odds of booking a berth to eternity still further, Witnesses believe that God started selecting the 144,000 shortly after Christ's death and that there are now only roughly 9,000 spots available.

To become a popular religion, it is only necessary for a superstition to enslave a philosophy.

WILLIAM RALPH INGE, *Idea of Progress*, 1920

I see it as an elderly lady, who mutters away to herself in a corner, ignored most of the time.

GEORGE CAREY, Archbishop of Canterbury, of the Church of England in 1991

Reviews and Critics

She couldn't get a laugh if she pulled a kipper out of her cunt.

NOËL COWARD, of an actress

This is not a novel to be tossed aside lightly. It should be thrown with great force.

DOROTHY PARKER, on Mussolini's *The Cardinal's Mistress*

It seems a great pity that Jane Austen was allowed to die a natural death.

MARK TWAIN

To say Agatha Christie's characters are cardboard cut-outs is an insult to cardboard.

RUTH RENDELL, British novelist, b. 1930

I enjoyed talking to [Virginia Woolf] but I thought nothing of her writing. I considered her a beautiful little knitter.

Attributed to EDITH SITWELL, English poet, 1887–1964

The more I read Socrates, the less I wonder that they poisoned him.

THOMAS MACAULAY, 1800–59

The Beatles are not merely awful. They are so unbelievably horrible, so appallingly unmusical, so dogmatically insensitive to the magic of the art, that they qualify as crowned heads of anti-music.

WILLIAM F. BUCKLEY, US journalist, 1925–2008

… most poisonous of all the poisonous haters of England; despiser, distorter of the plain truths whereby men live; topseyturvey perverter of all human relationships; menace to ordered social thought and ordered social life; irresponsible braggart, blaring self-trumpeter; idol of opaque intellectuals and thwarted females; calculus contrariwise; flippertygibbet pope of chaos; portent and epitome of this generation's moral and spiritual disorder.

HENRY ARTHUR JONES, playwright, 1851–1929, of George Bernard Shaw

Can't act. Can't sing. Slightly bald. Can dance a little.

Talent scout, of FRED ASTAIRE

School Reports

Sir Isaac Newton (1643–1727)

Idle and inattentive.

Free Grammar School, Grantham

Napoleon Bonaparte (1769–1821)

Commanding character, imperious and opinionated.

Examiner at the École Militaire, Paris

Charlotte Brontë (1816–55)

Writes indifferently ... Knows nothing of grammar, geography, history or accomplishments.

Cowan Bridge School, near Leeds

Sir Winston Churchill (1874–1965)

Is a constant trouble to everybody and is always in some scrape or other. He cannot be trusted to behave himself anywhere.

St George's School, Ascot

Benito Mussolini (1883–1945)

... passionate and unruly. He opposes every order and discipline of the college. Nothing fulfils him: in a group of people he feels sad and lonely. He wants to be alone.

L'Istituto Salesiano, Faenza

Robert Graves (1895–1985)

Well, goodbye, Graves and remember that your best friend is the waste-paper basket.

Headmaster's valedictory report, Charterhouse

Sir Peter Ustinov (1921–2004)

He shows great originality, which must be curbed at all costs.

Westminster School

Eric Morecambe (1926–84)

This boy will never get anywhere in life.

Headmaster's report, Lancaster Road Junior School

Richard Briers (b. 1934)

It would seem that Briers thinks he is running the school and not me. If this attitude persists one of us will have to leave.

Headmaster's report, Rokeby School, Wimbledon

Beryl Bainbridge (b. 1934)

Her knowledge is so poor as to make one wonder if she is simple-minded.

Geography report, Merchant Taylors School, Crosby

Alan Coren (1938–2007)

Coren's grasp of elementary dynamics is truly astonishing. Had he lived in an earlier eon, I have little doubt but that the wheel would now be square and the principle of the lever just one more of man's impossible dreams.

Physics report, East Barnet Grammar School

Jilly Cooper (b. 1938)

Jilly has set herself an extremely low standard which she has failed to maintain.

Godolphin School, Salisbury

Harry Enfield (b. 1961)

Sometimes I think he is just a spectator who has strayed.

Rugby report, Arundale School

Diana, Princess of Wales (1961–97)

She must try to be less emotional in her dealings with others.

West Heath School

Science

Science is but an exchange of ignorance for that which is another kind of ignorance.

LORD BYRON

A science is any discipline in which the fool of this generation can go beyond the point reached by the genius of the last generation.

MAX GLUCKMAN, British anthropologist, *Politics, Law and Ritual,* 1965

Science is the record of dead religions.

OSCAR WILDE, *Phrases and Philosophies for the Use of the Young,* 1894

There has never been an age so full of humbug. Humbug everywhere, even in science. For years now the scientists have been promising us every morning a new miracle, a new element, a new metal, guaranteeing to warm us with copper discs immersed in water, to feed us with nothing, to kill us at no expense whatever and on a grand scale, to keep us alive indefinitely, to make

iron out of heaven knows what ... In the meantime the cost of living rises, doubles, trebles; there is a shortage of raw materials; even death makes no progress – as we saw at Sebastopol, where men cut each other to ribbons – and the cheapest goods are still the worst goods in the world.

The BROTHERS GONCOURT, French writers, *Journals,* 7 January 1833

The only thing that science has done for man in the last hundred years is to create for him fresh moral problems.

LORD FISHER, Archbishop of Canterbury, *Observer,* 1950

The road to Hell is paved with good inventions.

F. L. LUCAS, English critic, 1894–1967

For a list of all the ways technology has failed to improve the quality of life, please press three.

ALICE KAHN, US writer, b. 1943

All the stamped metals, and artificial stones, and imitation woods and bronzes, over the invention of which we hear daily exultation – all the short, and cheap, and easy ways of doing that whose difficulty is its honour – are just so many new obstacles in our already encumbered road. They will not make us happier or wiser – they will extend neither the pride of judgement nor the privilege of enjoyment. They will only make us shallower in our understanding, colder in our hearts, and feebler in our wits. And most justly. For we are not sent into this world to do any thing into which we cannot put our hearts.

JOHN RUSKIN, *The Seven Lamps of Architecture*, 1849

About the telephone:
This 'telephone' has too many shortcomings to be seriously considered as a means of communication. This device is inherently of no value to us.

Western Union Internal Memo

About the gramophone:
Sirs, I have tested your machine. It adds a new terror to life and makes death a long-felt want.

HERBERT BEERBOHM TREE, English actor-manager, 1853–1917

About the railways:
I fear that the development of railways will destroy the need for waterproof coats.

Attributed to CHARLES MACKINTOSH, mac inventor, 1766–1843

About printing:
The greatest misfortune that ever befell man was the invention of printing. Printing has destroyed education …

BENJAMIN DISRAELI, 1804–81

About computers:
There is no reason anyone would want a computer in their home.

KEN OLSON, president of Digital Equipment Corp., 1977

I think there is a world market for maybe five computers.

THOMAS J. WATSON, president of IBM, 1874–1956

To err is human, but to really foul things up requires a computer.

Farmer's Almanac, 1978

———

It is claimed by the International Peace Institute, Stockholm, that almost half the world's scientists – some half a million people – are working on weapons research and production.

———

I am sorry to say that there is too much point to the wisecrack that life is extinct on other planets because their scientists were more advanced than ours.

JOHN F. KENNEDY, speech, 1959

Scientific men, who imagine that their science affords an answer to the problems of existence, are perhaps the most to be pitied of mankind; and contemned.

ROBERT LOUIS STEVENSON

――――

Truth at Any Price

Is *there any reason to hope that scientists might step back from the brink, realizing that some of their inventions are just not worth the risk? History tells us that this is unlikely. Scientists may have concluded that there was no chance of the first atomic test, Trinity, setting fire to the atmosphere, but it was still a dangerous experiment, with as-yet-unfolding consequences. In* The Day After Trinity *the physicist Freeman Dyson said this:*

'I have felt it myself. The glitter of nuclear weapons. It is irresistible if you come to them as a scientist. To feel it's there in your hands, to release this energy that fuels the stars, to let it do your bidding. To perform these miracles, to lift a million tons of rock into the sky. It is something that gives people an illusion of illimitable power,

and it is, in some ways, responsible for all our troubles – this, what you might call technical arrogance, that overcomes people when they see what they can do with their minds.'

If only I had known. I should have become a watchmaker.

ALBERT EINSTEIN, of his making the atom bomb possible, 1945

On the explosion of the first atomic bomb, the Trinity test, near Alamogordo, New Mexico, 16 July 1945:
I remembered the line from the Hindu scripture, the Bhagavad Gita … 'I am become Death, the Destroyer of Worlds'.

J. ROBERT OPPENHEIMER, US physicist, 1904–67

Thus were they defiled with their own works, and went a-whoring with their own inventions.

The Bible, Psalm 106:39

――――

It's not just the old 'NBC' (nuclear, biological and chemical) technologies of the last century that still haunt us (the question of what to do with nuclear waste; the probability of a nuclear bomb and associated fallout; the mass and unwitting experiment being wrought on the planet by the astonishing number of manmade chemicals – some 80,000 –

released into our environment in the last 50 years; the appalling spectre of runaway global warming caused by our careless use of fossil fuel). No: believe it or not, there are worse, unfamiliar things than these to worry about. It's not only possible that physicists might accidentally create a 'Doomsday device' – an experimental mishap that could destroy the Earth and solar system; recent advances in 'GNR' technologies – that is, genetics, nanotechnology and robotics – also threaten us in ways that make our old nightmares look like sweet dreams. At the beginning of the Millennium, in Wired magazine, Bill Joy, the former chief scientist of Sun Microsystems, warned that these technologies 'pose a different threat than the technologies that have come before'. Joy continues: 'I think it is no exaggeration to say we are on the cusp of the further perfection of extreme evil, an evil whose possibility spreads well beyond that which weapons of mass destruction bequeathed to the nation-states, on to a surprising and terrible empowerment of extreme individuals.' Then, of course, there's the question of how dangerous we are to ourselves. The philosopher John Leslie looked at how much danger we are in from all of our technologies – nuclear, chemical, biological, nanotechnological, genetic and robotic – and concluded that the risk of human life extinguishing itself is at least 30 per cent.

I almost think it is the ultimate destiny of science to exterminate the human race.

THOMAS LOVE PEACOCK, English novelist, 1785–1866

Absolutely smashing

The Large Hadron Collider (LHC), the world's largest particle accelerator, which has been built near Geneva in collaboration with over two thousand physicists from around the world, is due to be at full operating capacity by mid-2009. Scientists are hoping that the smashing of protons head-on at phenomenal speeds (thus simulating the Big Bang) will result in the appearance of the elusive Higgs boson or 'God particle'; if such a thing were actually proved to exist it would, among other things, help scientists in their search for a Grand Unified Theory. But not everybody is so delighted by the project. In March 2008, a lawsuit was filed in Honolulu to delay the opening of the LHC on the grounds that it might accidentally create a 'strangelet', a fragment that would convert our planet into strange matter; or that the particle accelerator might give birth to an ever-expanding black hole that could swallow the planet, starting with Geneva. According to scientists, such a doomsday mishap is exceptionally unlikely, but not impossible.

Sex

No man knows what true happiness is until he has a complete set of false teeth and has lost all interest in the opposite sex.

Attributed to LORD ROSEBERY, British politician, 1882–1974

I've tried several varieties of sex. The conventional position makes me claustrophobic and the others give me a stiff neck or lockjaw.

TALLULAH BANKHEAD

I rose very disconsolate, having rested very ill by the poisonous infection raging in my veins and anxiety and vexation boiling in my breast. I could scarcely credit my own senses. What! thought I. Can this beautiful, this sensible, and this agreeable woman be so sadly defiled? Can corruption lodge beneath so fair a form? Can she who professed delicacy of sentiment and sincere regard for me, use me so very basely and so very cruelly? No, it is impossible. I have just got a gleet by irritating the parts too much with excessive venery. And yet these damned twinges, that scalding heat, and that deep-tinged loathsome matter are the strongest proofs of an infection. But she certainly must think that I would soon discover her falsehood. But perhaps she was ignorant of her being ill. A pretty conjecture indeed! No, she could not be ignorant. Yes, yes, she intended to make the most of me … And am I then taken in? Am I, who have had safe and elegant intrigues with fine women, become the dupe of a strumpet?

JAMES BOSWELL, *Diary*, 20 January 1763

In Delicato Flagranto Morto

People who have died during sex include Félix Faure, president of France, in 1899, while being fellated; Nelson Rockefeller, US vice-president (allegedly); Attila the Hun, on his wedding night, thanks to a burst artery; Errol Flynn, the hell-raising film star (rumoured); and several medieval popes. Given that relatives tend to conceal the truth in order to leave the corpse's reputation and dignity intact, the true extent of sex-related deaths will probably never be known (although it's estimated that around 700 men and women die each year in the US from auto-asphyxiation).

Humans have been trying to avoid having too many children for thousands of years. Here is a list of tried and tested techniques, some more satisfactory than others:

- Abortion
- Anal intercourse – *the preferred method of ancient Greek courtesans*
- Anaphrodisiacs – *potions and methods of quenching desire include Pliny's suggestions of rubbing a woman's loins with the blood of the ticks on a wild black bull, eating snail excrement, and using a liniment of mouse dung; and the medieval German trick where a woman could destroy a man's lust for her by putting some of her faeces in his shoe – an approach that's still highly effective today*
- Chastity – *legs crossed is a better approach than fingers crossed, but the vows taken by the religious were not always kept, to put it mildly; in fact, they seem often to have been an incitement to licentious behaviour. Orgies were not unknown in the Vatican; some popes made their*

catamites into cardinals or vice versa; and one pope ran a brothel. The not-so Innocent VIII (1484–92) even had the following poem written in his honour:

He begot eight sons, with as many
   daughters;
And Rome might with good reason
   call him father.
But, O! Innocent VIII,
   wherever you lie buried,
Filthiness, gluttony, covetousness and
   sloth will lie with thee!

- Coitus interruptus – *don't try this at home!*
- Contraception – *from the crocodile-dung plugs favoured by the Egyptians, the elephant-dung spermicides used in the Islamic world, various plant-based potions throughout all times and cultures, condoms made from goats' intestines or fish skins, to the sexual revolution and the Pill now used by some 100 million women*
- Infanticide – *Polynesian tribes put two thirds of their children to death; other cultures simply exposed them to the elements to die*
- Vatican roulette – *working out when the woman is in her 'safe period'*
- Zoophilia – *not uncommon in pastoral societies, but not welcome in every culture. In 1012, a German bishop detailed 194 different sexual sins and their penalties, among which*

*sex with a horse, cow or donkey
would earn you forty days on bread
and water once a year for seven years*

Reports of the death of slavery are premature and sex trafficking is on the increase. The number of people forced to work as prostitutes (mostly women and children from South America, the former USSR and west and south-east Asia) is estimated at about 2 million worldwide, with half-a-million women trafficked annually, and 5,000 children working as sex slaves in the UK alone.

I abhor the slimie kisse,
Which to me most loathsome is.
Those lips please me which are plac't
Close, but not too strictly lac't;
Yielding I would have them yet
Not a wimbling tongue admit …

ROBERT HERRICK, 1591–1674, 'Kisses Loathsome'

Nothing in our culture, not even home computers, is more overrated than the epidermal felicity of two featherless bipeds in desperate congress.

QUENTIN CRISP, 1908–99, *An Evening with Quentin Crisp*

Regime de Vivre

I rise at eleven, I dine about two,
I get drunk about seven, and the next
    thing I do,
I send for my whore, when for fear of
    the clap,
I spend in her hand, and I spew in
    her lap;
Then we quarrel and scold, till I fall
    fast asleep,
When the bitch growing bold, to my
    pocket does creep.
Then slyly she leaves me, and to
    revenge the affront,
At once she bereaves me of money
    and cunt.
If by chance then I wake, hot-headed
    and drunk,
What a coil do I make for the loss of
    my punk!
I storm, and I roar, and I fall in a rage,
And missing my whore, I bugger
    my page.
Then crop-sick all morning I rail at
    my men,
And in bed I lie yawning till
    eleven again.

LORD ROCHESTER, Restoration wit

The pleasure is momentary, the position ridiculous, and the expense damnable.

LORD CHESTERFIELD, 1694–1773, *Letters to His Son*

Seduction is often difficult to distinguish from rape. In seduction, the rapist bothers to buy a bottle of wine.

ANDREA DWORKIN, US feminist writer, 1976

Cybersex abuse
Dr Alvin Cooper, of the San Jose Marital and Sexuality Center, calls the internet 'the crack cocaine of sexual compulsivity'. In 2007, he and his colleagues studied 9,000 internet users and found that 15 per cent were 'addicted' to sexual sites, spending an average of 11 hours a week online for sexual purposes, with three quarters of them keeping their compulsion secret.

I could be content that we might procreate like trees, without conjunction, or that there were any way to perpetuate the world without this trivial and vulgar way of coition: it is the foolishest act a wise man commits in all his life; nor is there anything that will more deject his cool'd imagination, when he shall consider what an odd and unworthy piece of folly he hath committed.

SIR THOMAS BROWNE, English philosopher, 1605–82

Connoisseurs of coition aver
That the best British girls never stir.
This condition in Persia
Is known as inertia:
It depends what response you prefer.

ANON

Who is the Greek chap Clitoris they're talking about?

Attributed to various members of the House of Lords

I am happy now that Charles calls on my bedchamber less frequently than of old. As it is, I now endure but two calls a week and when I hear his steps outside my door I lie down on my bed, close my eyes, open my legs and think of England.

ALICE, LADY HILLINGDON, *Journal*, 1912

Historically, society's response to gay sex has usually – with a very few exceptions – ranged from casual intolerance to horrific persecution. Homosexuals were tortured to death by the Aztecs, burned alive by the Incas, castrated in the Byzantine Empire, put to death as felons for the 'abominable Crime of Buggery' in Victorian England, and made the objects of a policy of total extermination by the

Nazis. Today, although in 2001 the first same-sex marriages were legalized in the Netherlands, and in 2003 a Supreme Court decision overturned sodomy laws throughout the US, homosexual acts between consenting adults are still illegal in about a third of countries throughout the world, with several countries, such as Pakistan, Saudi Arabia, Sudan and Iran, imposing the death penalty.

Who Said Romance was Dead?

A few days since, I brought a male of Mantis Carolina to a friend who had been keeping a solitary female as a pet. Placing them in the same jar, the male, in alarm, endeavoured to escape. In a few minutes the female succeeded in grasping him. She first bit off his left front tarsus, and consumed the tibia and femur. Next she gnawed out his left eye. At this the male seemed to realize his proximity to one of the opposite sex, and began to make vain endeavours to mate. The female next ate up his right front leg, and then entirely decapitated him, devouring his head and gnawing into his thorax. Not until she had eaten all of his thorax except about three millimetres, did she stop to rest. All this while the male had continued his vain attempts to obtain entrance at the valvules, and he now succeeded, as she voluntarily spread the parts open, and union took place. She remained quiet for four hours, and the remnant of the male gave occasional signs of life by a movement of one of his remaining tarsi for three hours. The next morning she had entirely rid herself of her spouse, and nothing but his wings remained.

L. O. HOWARD, *Science Magazine*, 1886

[The universal] disobedience of this member which thrusts itself forward so inopportunely when we do not want it to, and which so inopportunely lets us down when we most need it.

MICHEL DE MONTAIGNE

20 reasons to stay in on a Saturday night:

• Chancroid • chlamydia • cytomegalovirus (CTV) • donovanosis • genital herpes • genital warts • gonorrhea (the clap) • Hepatitis B • HIV/AIDS • human papillomavirus (HPV) • jock itch • Kaposi's sarcoma-associated herpesvirus (KSHV) • molluscum (MC) • pelvic inflammatory disease • pubic lice • scabies • syphilis (the pox) • trichomoniasis • urethritis • yeast infection

I'd rather have a cup of tea.

BOY GEORGE, pop star, b. 1961

Sleep

Yet a little sleep, a little slumber, a little folding of the hands to sleep, So shall thy poverty come as one that travelleth, and thy want as an armed man.

The Bible, Proverbs 6:10–11

Sleep tight! Don't let the bedbugs bite!

If you're particularly itchy at night you may well have an infestation of bedbugs. Look for the tell-tale little stains on your sheets. These can range in colour from reddish to brown depending on whether the bedbugs are excreting while feeding on your blood. Bedbugs cluster round buttons in mattresses, folds in sheets and objects near the bed, or the actual bed frame. There are a number of bedbug insecticides to deal with the problem.

I sleep like a baby too – every two hours I wake up screaming.

COLIN POWELL, on hearing that President George W. Bush slept like a baby, *New Yorker*, 2003

Insomnia affects 5 per cent of the population at any time, and 10 per cent will experience it at some point in their lives.

A 2003 study performed at the University of Pennsylvania School of Medicine proved that cognitive performance declines with less than eight hours of sleep a night. A University of California, San Diego psychiatry study found, though, that the people who live the longest sleep for just six to seven hours each night.

Sleep deprivation is extremely harmful to the body. Experiments in rodents show that animals exposed to continued wakefulness die after a few weeks. In humans, sleep deprivation can bring on disruption of concentration, loss of libido and memory, lower immunity, depression and anxiety. There are no firm statistics on the subject, but it is thought that sleepy drivers cause thousands of accidents a year.

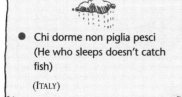

- Chi dorme non piglia pesci
  (He who sleeps doesn't catch fish)

  (ITALY)

The sleep industry in the USA alone is reckoned to be worth about US$20 billion. Much of this is spent on sleeping pills. According to the UK Sleep Council, which represents the bed-and-mattress industry, two thirds of people say they get less sleep now than they did a few years ago.

There are up to 80 distinct sleeping disorders. These are made up of four main types: 1) dyssomnias, 2) parasomnias, 3) medical or psychiatric sleep disorders and 4) sleep problems related to other issues such as pregnancy.

If life and existence were an enjoyable state, then everyone would reluctantly approach the unconscious state of sleep and would gladly rise from it again. But the very opposite is the case, for everyone very willingly goes to sleep and unwillingly gets up again.

ARTHUR SCHOPENHAUER

Researchers at Oxford University have discovered that the traditional cure for sleeplessness, counting sheep, believed to date from the 19th century, does not work because it is simply too boring to keep the mind off problems.

Sleep is cousin-german unto death:
Sleep and death differ, no more, than a carcass
And a skeleton

THOMAS TRAHERNE, 1636–74,
A Serious and a Curious Night-Meditation

Famous Insomniacs

Catherine the Great
Marlene Dietrich
Alexandre Dumas
W. C. Fields
Judy Garland
Franz Kafka
Groucho Marx
Marcel Proust
Mark Twain

Do you suffer from Spousal Arousal Syndrome? Not as exciting as it sounds, this condition is when snorers repeatedly wake their partners at night.

Smoking

Ashes to Ashes

- Smoking and other forms of tobacco use are the second biggest cause of death in the world, claiming 5 million lives a year – roughly one in 10 adults.

- There are an estimated 1.3 billion smokers worldwide and half of them are expected to die prematurely of a tobacco-related disease.

- About 12 times more British people have died from smoking than from hostilities in the Second World War.

- Every cigarette consumed by long-term smokers cuts at least five minutes of life on average – roughly the time taken to smoke it.

- Second-hand smoke contains thousands of identified chemicals, at least 250 of which are known to be carcinogenic or otherwise toxic.

- At least a quarter of all deaths from heart diseases and about three-quarters of the world's chronic bronchitis cases are related to smoking.

Hence it is that the lungs of the tobacconist are rotted, the liver spotted, the brain smoked like the backside of the pig woman's booth, here, and the whole body within, black as her pan you saw e'en now without.

BEN JONSON, *Bartholomew Fair*, 1614

A custom loathsome to the eye, hateful to the nose, harmful to the brain, dangerous to the lungs, and in the black, stinking fume thereof, nearest resembling the horrible Stygian smoke of the pit that is bottomless.

JAMES I of England, VI of Scotland, 1566–1625

Synonyms for cigarettes

Coffin nails
Cancer sticks
Gaspers
Wheezers
Lung dusters

A cigarette is a pipe with a fire at one end and a fool at the other.

ANON

Sport

Go jogging? What, and get hit by a meteor?

Robert Benchley, US humorist, 1889–1945

Serious sport has nothing to do with fair play. It is bound up with hatred, jealousy, boastfulness, disregard of all rules and sadistic pleasure in witnessing violence. In other words: it is war minus the shooting.

George Orwell, 1903–50

Whenever I get the urge to exercise, I lie down until the feeling passes away.

Robert M. Hutchins, US academic, 1929

Citius, Altius, Fortius – Swifter, Higher, Stronger – is the Olympic motto. With this in mind, each successive venue for the Olympics tries to surpass the last in grandeur and prestige. China's 2008 Beijing Olympics cost more than any Games in the past – four times more than the amount spent by the Greeks in 2004. The Greeks, Koreans and Spanish are all still paying for their Olympics, and Britain, which is set to host them in 2012, is already about three times over its original budget of £2.375 billion.

Sir, The sooner it is realised that golf is merely a pleasant recreation and inducement to indolent people to take exercise the better. Golf has none of the essentials of a great game. It destroys rather than builds up character, and tends to selfishness and ill-temper. It calls for none of the essential qualities such as pluck, endurance, physical fitness and agility, unselfishness and esprit de corps, or quickness of eye and judgement. Games which develop these are of assistance for the more serious pursuits of life.

… The present tendency is undoubtedly towards the more effeminate and less exacting pastimes, but the day that sees the youth of England given up to lawn tennis and golf in preference to the more manly pursuits (cricket, football, polo &c.) will be a sad omen for the future of the race.

BERNARD BOSANQUET, cricketer, letter to *The Times*, 4 June 1914

You ought to be suspicious when you line up against girls with moustaches.

MAREE HOLLAND, Australian sprinter, Seoul Olympics, 1988

I will not permit 30 men to travel 400 miles to agitate a bag of wind.

ANDREW D. WHITE, president of Cornell University, forbidding the university's first intercollegiate football game with the University of Michigan, 1873

Eight minds with but a single thought – if that!

MAX BEERBOHM, 1872–1956, of a rowing eight

There will be more football in a moment but first we've got the highlights of the Scottish League Cup final.

GARY NEWBON, football commentator

Football, wherein is nothing but beastly fury, and extreme violence, whereof proceedeth hurt, and consequently rancour and malice do remain with them that be wounded.

THOMAS ELYOT, *Book of the Governor*, 1531

I do not see why I should break my neck because a dog chooses to run after a nasty smell.

ARTHUR BALFOUR, 1848–1930 on why he didn't hunt

Golf always makes me so damned angry.

KING GEORGE V

I have no intention of watching undersized Englishmen perched on horses with matchstick legs race along courses planned to amuse Nell Gwynne.

GILBERT HARDING, journalist and broadcaster, 1907-60

I believe that every human has a finite number of heartbeats. I don't intend to waste any of mine running around doing exercises.

NEIL ARMSTRONG, astronaut, b. 1930

Travel

I have recently been all round the world and have formed a very poor opinion of it.

SIR THOMAS BEECHAM, British conductor, 1879–1961

How can you wonder your travels do you no good, when you carry yourself around with you?

SOCRATES, 469–399 BC

Space travel is bunk!

SIR HAROLD SPENCER JONES, Astronomer Royal of Britain, two weeks before Sputnik was launched, 1957

It can hardly be a coincidence that no language on Earth has ever produced the expression 'as pretty as an airport'.

DOUGLAS ADAMS, *The Long Dark Tea-time of the Soul*, opening words, 1988

Car-nage

When Irish scientist Mary Ward was run over by a steam-powered car in 1869, she was only the first in a very

● Been there, done that, got the T-shirt

long line of victims; today's global death toll on the roads is astonishingly high, with ten million people estimated to have been run over since 2000 – one every six seconds.

Going Nowhere, Not Very Fast

If the 210,000 miles of road in mainland Britain were joined up and made into one continuous road, it would nearly reach the moon. But we wouldn't get very far; it's reckoned that, in the British Isles during rush hour, there are more people sitting in cars than live in the whole of central London.

Railroad, n. The chief of many mechanical devices enabling us to get away from where we are to where we are no better off. For this purpose the railroad is held in highest favour by the optimist, for it permits him to make the transit with great expedition.

AMBROSE BIERCE, *The Devil's Dictionary*, 1911

Sir, Saturday morning, although recurring at regular and well-foreseen intervals, always seems to take this railway by surprise.

W. S. GILBERT, 1836–1911, letter to the stationmaster at Baker Street, London

———

Punch magazine advised readers never to travel by train without 'a small bottle of water, a tumbler, a complete set of surgical instruments, a packet of lint, and directions for making a will'.

———

The only way of catching a train I ever discovered is to miss the train before.

G. K. CHESTERTON

In the Middle Ages people were tourists because of their religion, whereas now they are tourists because tourism is their religion.

ROBERT RUNCIE, Archbishop of Canterbury, 1988

Bird Flu south for the winter

Ever since Columbus and crew returned to Europe from their travels, introducing the bacteria that went on to become venereal syphilis, countries have enthusiastically exchanged life-threatening diseases. Nowadays, though, via aeroplane travel, the potential speed and scope of a pandemic are truly awesome. In 2007, the World Health Organization warned that new infectious diseases are emerging at an 'unprecedented rate', with 39 new pathogens (including SARS, HIV/AIDS *and Ebola) identified since 1969, and that, with airlines carrying two billion passengers a year, these hideous afflictions are likely to go on holiday too. The outbreak of* SARS, *in 2003, was a warning shot across our bows, spreading easily from China to Hong Kong, Singapore and Canada via the skies. Our increased – and increasing – mobility is a pathogen's dream.*

———

On a train, why do I always end up sitting next to the woman who's eating the individual fruit pie by sucking the filling out through the hole in the middle?

VICTORIA WOOD, British comedian, b. 1953

What good is speed if the brain has oozed out on the way?

KARL KRAUS, Austrian writer, 1874–1936

Arrival-Angst is closely connected with guilt, with the dread of something terrible having happened in our absence. Death of parents. Entry of Bailiffs. Flight of loved one. Sensations worse at arriving in the evening than in the morning, and much worse at Victoria and Waterloo, than at Paddington.

CYRIL CONNOLLY, *The Unquiet Grave*, 1944

Airplane travel is nature's way of making you look like your passport photo.

AL GORE, Nobel Peace Prize winner, b. 1948

Why don't they make the whole plane out of that black box stuff?

STEVEN WRIGHT, US comedian, b. 1955

Attempts to 'offset' carbon emissions when you fly are more akin to buying a papal indulgence in the Middle Ages than getting to grips with the problem. By 2020, UK airports are predicted to be handling around 400 million passengers, a threefold increase on today's levels. As Tony Blair once said, 'You can't expect people not to fly.' Go to www.planestupid.com for a reality check.

Having set off from home to give a lecture, the famously absent-minded G. K. Chesterton sent the following telegram to his wife:

AM IN MARKET HARBOROUGH STOP WHERE OUGHT I TO BE STOP

Truth

The truth is the safest lie.

Graffito

I never give them hell. I just tell them the truth and they think it is hell.

HARRY S. TRUMAN, interview in *Look*, 1956

I see there's truth in no man, nor
    obedience
But for his own ends.

FRANCIS and JOHN BEAUMONT,
A King and No King, 1612

Truth, Sir, is a cow, that will yield such people no more milk, and so they are gone to milk the bull.

SAMUEL JOHNSON, *Of Sceptics*, 1763

The best way to keep one's word is not to give it.

NAPOLEON BONAPARTE

● There is no truth

If you want truth to go round the world you must hire an express train to pull it; but if you want a lie to go round the world, it will fly: it is as light as a feather, and a breath will carry it. It is well said in the old proverb, 'a lie will go round the world while truth is pulling its boots on'.

CHARLES HADDON SPURGEON, *Gems from Spurgeon*, 1859

Facts are stupid things.

RONALD REAGAN, 1911–2004

● Light reveals shadows and
    truth mystery
    (LATIN)

The broadsheet Pravda *('The Truth') was the official mouthpiece of the Soviet Union's Communist Party until it ceased publication in 1991. In the West it became synonymous with state propaganda and misinformation.*

Telling the truth loses you friends; not telling it gains you enemies.

JUAN RUIZ, *Libro de Buen Amor*, c. 1330

The first casualty when war comes is truth.

HIRAM WARREN JOHNSON, speech to US Senate, 1917

● All truth is subjective

In a world where it is so easy to neglect, deny, pervert and suppress the truth, the scientist may find his discipline severe. For him, truth is so seldom the sudden light that shows new order and beauty; more often, truth is the uncharted rock that sinks his ship in the dark.

SIR JOHN WARCUP CORNFORTH, Nobel Prize speech, 1975

The public does not always know how to desire the truth.

DENIS DIDEROT, 1713–84

Truths uncovered by intelligence become sterile.

ANATOLE FRANCE, *La Vie littéraire*, 1892

● A lie told often enough becomes the truth
● A half-truth is a whole lie

I know not what I may appear to the world, but to myself I seem to have been only like a boy playing on the sea shore, and diverting myself in now and then finding a smoother pebble or a prettier shell than ordinary, whilst the great ocean of truth lay all undiscovered before me.

SIR ISAAC NEWTON

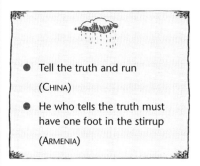

● Tell the truth and run (CHINA)
● He who tells the truth must have one foot in the stirrup (ARMENIA)

United States

Three quarters of the American population literally believe in religious miracles. The numbers who believe in the devil, in resurrection, in God doing this and that – it's astonishing. These numbers aren't duplicated anywhere else in the industrial world. You'd have to maybe go to mosques in Iran or do a poll among old ladies in Sicily to get numbers like this. Yet this is the American population.

NOAM CHOMSKY, US academic, b. 1928

America is the only nation in history which miraculously has gone directly from barbarism to degeneration without the usual interval of civilisation.

GEORGES CLEMENCEAU

I hereby accuse the North American empire of being the biggest menace to our planet.

HUGO CHAVEZ, president of Venezuela, b. 1954

America's one of the finest countries anyone ever stole.

ANON

We, with God's help, call on every Muslim who believes in God and wishes to be rewarded to comply with God's order to kill the Americans and plunder their money wherever and whenever they find it. We also call on Muslim ulema, leaders, youths, and soldiers to launch the raid on Satan's U.S. troops and the devil's supporters allying with them, and to displace those who are behind them so that they may learn a lesson.

OSAMA BIN LADEN, February 1998

It is a pity that instead of the Pilgrim Fathers landing on Plymouth Rock, Plymouth Rock had not landed on the Pilgrim Fathers.

CHAUNCEY DEPEW, US senator, 1881

You have to be sure that the Americans will commit all the stupidities they can think of, plus some that are beyond imagination.

CHARLES DE GAULLE, *Time* magazine, December 1967

Sitting at the table doesn't make you a diner, unless you eat some of what's on that plate. Being here in America doesn't make you an American. Being born here in America doesn't make you an American.

MALCOLM X, human rights activist, 1925–65

The breathless haste with which they [the Americans] work – the distinctive vice of the new world – is already beginning ferociously to infect old Europe and is spreading a spiritual emptiness over the continent.

FRIEDRICH NIETZSCHE, 1844–1900

In almost every case [where the United States has fought wars] our overwhelming commitment to freedom, democracy and human rights has required us to support those regimes that would deny freedom, democracy and human rights to their own people.

GORE VIDAL

With what morality can the [US] leaders talk of human rights in a country where there are millionaires and beggars, where blacks face discrimination, women are prostituted, and great masses of Chicanos, Puerto Ricans and Latin Americans are deprecated, exploited and humiliated?

FIDEL CASTRO, 26 July 1978

Americans are the great Satan, the wounded snake.

AYATOLLAH KHOMEINI, Iranian spiritual and political leader, 1902–89

———

With these now infamous words, under a floating banner proclaiming 'Mission Accomplished', President George W. Bush stood on the deck of a US battleship in May 2003 and declared the Iraq war over: 'Admiral Kelly, Captain Card, officers and sailors of the USS Abraham Lincoln, my fellow Americans: Major combat operations in Iraq have ended. In the Battle of Iraq, the United States and our allies have prevailed. And now our coalition is engaged in securing and reconstructing that country.' Hundreds of thousands of Iraqis and hundreds of US and allied soldiers are now dead, and about $12.5 billion is being spent per month on this ongoing war alone. Mission Accomplished ... or Mission Impossible?

War

I know not with what weapons World War III will be fought, but World War IV will be fought with sticks and stones.

ALBERT EINSTEIN, letter to Harry S. Truman

I hope to God that I have fought my last battle. It is a bad thing to be always fighting. While in the thick of it I am too much occupied to feel anything; but it is wretched just after. It is quite impossible to think of glory. Both mind and feelings are exhausted. I am wretched even at the moment of victory, and I always say that, next to a battle lost, the greatest misery is a battle gained. Not only do you lose those dear friends with whom you have been living, but you are forced to leave the wounded behind you … At such moments every feeling is deadened. I am now just beginning to regain my natural spirits, but I never wish for any more fighting.

DUKE OF WELLINGTON to Lady Shelley, July 1815, three weeks after Waterloo

This is the biggest fool thing we have ever done. The bomb will never go off, and I speak as an expert in explosives.

ADMIRAL WILLIAM LEAHY, US Chief of Staff to President Truman, on the atomic bomb, 1945

What passing-bells for these who die
   as cattle?
Only the monstrous anger of
   the guns.
Only the stuttering rifles' rapid rattle
Can patter out their hasty orisons.

WILFRED OWEN, 'Anthem for Doomed Youth'

I have many times asked myself whether there can be more potent advocates of peace upon earth through the years to come than this massed multitude of silent witnesses to the desolation of war.

KING GEORGE V, visiting war graves in Flanders, 1922

Airplanes are interesting toys but of no military value.

MARSHAL FERDINAND FOCH, French general, before the First World War

How horrible, fantastic, incredible, it is that we should be digging trenches and trying on gas-masks here because of a quarrel in a far-away country between people of whom we know nothing!

NEVILLE CHAMBERLAIN, British prime minister, 1938

———

It's been calculated that there have only been about 230 years of real peace in the 'civilized' world in 3,500 years.

———

We do not, generally speaking, like the thoughts of peace. I expect I shall remain abroad for three or four years, which, individually, I would sooner spend in war than in peace. There is something indescribably exciting in the former.

GENERAL CHARLES 'CHINESE' GORDON, 1856. Gordon's head was displayed on a pike after he was decapitated by Mahdi Mohammed Ahmed's soldiers at the siege of Khartoum.

They now ring the bells, but they will soon wring their hands.

SIR ROBERT WALPOLE, on Britain's declaration of war with Spain, 1739

In 2008, robotics expert Professor Noel Sharkey, of Sheffield University, warned that an international robot arms race is now beginning, and it may not be long before terrorists start to replace suicide bombers with robots.

———

What difference does it make to the dead, the orphans and the homeless, whether the mad destruction is wrought under the name of totalitarianism or the holy name of liberty or democracy?

MAHATMA GANDHI, Non-Violence in Peace and War

Older men declare war. But it is youth that must fight and die. And it is youth who must inherit the tribulation, the sorrow and the triumphs that are the aftermath of war.

HERBERT HOOVER, US president, 1874–1964

I am young, I am twenty years old; yet I know nothing of life but despair, death, fear, and fatuous superficiality cast over an abyss of sorrow. I see how peoples are set against one another, and in silence, unknowingly, foolishly, obediently, innocently slay one another.

ERICH MARIA REMARQUE, All Quiet on the Western Front, 1929

Wealth

A rich man is nothing but a poor man with money.

W. C. FIELDS, 1880-1946

Lay not up for yourselves treasures upon earth, where moth and rust doth corrupt, and where thieves break through and steal.

The Bible, St Matthew 6:19

There's no money in poetry, but then there's no poetry in money either.

ROBERT GRAVES

- The rich man knows not who is his friend
- Riches serve a wise man but command a fool
- He is rich enough that wants nothing
- Health is better than wealth
- Behind every great fortune there is a crime

The expression 'paying through the nose' comes from a Viking practice of cutting people's noses in two if they failed to pay their taxes.

It's the same the whole world over,
It's the poor wot gets the blame,
It's the rich wot gets the pleasure,
Ain't it all a bleedin' shame?

Chorus of 'She was poor but she was honest', a song popular among British soldiers during the First World War

Ten Poorest Countries by GNP per capita

Burundi $90
Ethiopia $110
Democratic Republic of Congo $110
Liberia $110
Malawi $160
Guinea-Bissau $160
Eritrea $190
Niger $210
Sierra Leone $210
Rwanda $210

(World Bank, 2006)

The Pessimist's Handbook

What difference does it make how much you have? What you do not have amounts to much more.

SENECA

In 1908 a former member of the Argyllshire school board wrote to newspapers of the day suggesting poor children should walk to school barefoot. He argued that by doing so they would harden their feet and be prevented from catching cold.

Plutomania: a craving for money; the delusion that one is already wealthy; obsession with money

---

It is an unfortunate human failing that a full pocketbook often groans more loudly than an empty stomach.

FRANKLIN D. ROOSEVELT, 1882–1945

Famous bankrupts

P. T. Barnum (showman)
Cervantes (writer)
Daniel Defoe (writer)
Ulysses S. Grant (US general)
Buster Keaton (actor)
Rembrandt (artist)
Mark Twain (writer)

In 2006 the UN Development Programme reported that the combined income of the world's 500 richest people was equal to the income of the world's poorest 420 million: a ratio described as one small village in South America harbouring as much wealth as the rest of the continent. The gap between Britain's richest and poorest is currently the widest it's been for more than 40 years. In the sixties the salaries of CEOs were 30 times greater than that of the average worker. Today, they are between 150 and 200 times greater.

In the worst stock-market crash in history, which took place in 1930–2, investors lost 86 per cent of their money, and this followed hard on the heels of the 1929 crash when investors lost 48 per cent. The markets didn't recover their full value until 1954.

Annual income twenty pounds, annual expenditure nineteen nineteen six, result happiness. Annual income twenty pounds, annual expenditure twenty pounds ought and six, result misery.

CHARLES DICKENS, Mr Micawber in *David Copperfield*, 1848–50

Repeated research into the effects of wealth on happiness show that when it lifts people out of poverty into comfort it makes them enormously happy, but from there on up, there is no increase in happiness and often a downturn.

More than two trillion (or two million million) dollars are traded each day on foreign exchange markets, which is roughly 100 times more than the trading volume of all the stock markets of the world together. Only 2 per cent of these trades relate to the real economy (i.e. movements of real goods and services in the world); the rest is purely speculative, phantom money.

[The coming economic times] are arguably the worst they've been in 60 years, and I think it's going to be more profound and long-lasting than people thought.

ALISTAIR DARLING, UK chancellor, Guardian, 30 August 2008

In 1923, at the highest point of German hyperinflation, the exchange rate was one trillion marks to one dollar; a wheelbarrow of money couldn't buy a newspaper and the prices on menus changed by the minute. When a student at Freiburg University ordered a cup of coffee for 5,000 marks at a café, and then a second, he was surprised to be given a bill for 14,000 marks. 'To save money,' the waiter told him, 'you should order them both at the same time.'

He who dies rich, dies disgraced.

ANDREW CARNEGIE, Scottish industrialist and philanthropist, 1835–1919

Despite being – and possibly because they are – three times richer than they were in the 1950s, people in Britain are far less happy. The proportion of people saying they are 'very happy' has fallen from 52 per cent in 1957 to less than 40 per cent today. GfK NOP's opinion poll mirrors data from America, where happiness levels and life satisfaction have also been in gradual decline – and are still falling.

Weather

An English summer – three fine days and a thunderstorm.

ANON

What dreadful hot weather we have! It keeps me in a continual state of inelegance.

JANE AUSTEN, 1796

The rain it raineth every day
Upon the just and unjust fella,
But more upon the just because
The unjust hath the just's umbrella.

ANON

Who wants to be foretold the weather? It is bad enough when it comes, without our having the misery of knowing about it beforehand.

JEROME K. JEROME, 1859–1927

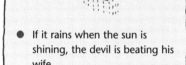

● If it rains when the sun is shining, the devil is beating his wife

The comic almanacs give us dreadful pictures of January and February; but, in truth, the months which should be made to look gloomy in England are March and April. Let no man boast himself that he has got through the perils of winter till at least the seventh of May.

ANTHONY TROLLOPE, 1815–82, *Doctor Thorne*

Very high and very low temperatures extinguish all human sympathy and relations. It is impossible to feel any affection beyond 78 and below 20 Fahrenheit; human nature is too solid or too liquid beyond these limits.

SYDNEY SMITH

Summer has set in with its usual severity.

SAMUEL TAYLOR COLERIDGE, letter to Vincent Novello, 1826

Weather bad. Attacked by inflammation of the testicles and groaned all day.

GEORGE GISSING, diary, 5 October 1895

I cannot command winds and weather.

LORD NELSON

The English often kill themselves – it is a malady caused by the humid climate.

NAPOLEON

I no longer wonder why these people talk so much of the weather; they live in the most inconstant of all climates, against which it is so difficult to take any effectual precaution, that they have given the matter up in despair, and take no precautions at all. Their great poet, Milton, describes the souls of the condemned as being hurried from fiery into frozen regions: perhaps he took the idea from his own feelings on such a day as this, when, like me, he was scorched on one side and frost-bitten on the other;

and, not knowing which of the two torments was the worst, assigned them to the wicked both in turn.

ROBERT SOUTHEY, writing as Don Manuel Alvarez Espriella, *Letters from England*, 1803

How misty is England! I have spent four years in a gray gloom.

NATHANIEL HAWTHORNE, US novelist, 1804–64

I'm leaving because the weather is too good. I hate London when it's not raining.

GROUCHO MARX

5 biggest changes to the weather scientists expect climate change to bring

Dry regions get drier, wet regions wetter.

More violent and longer hurricanes and storms.

Shorter winters, less snow.

More heatwaves and droughts.

More floods, rising sea levels.

Women

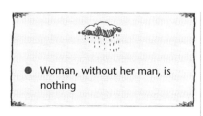

● Woman, without her man, is nothing

Be to her virtues very kind;
Be to her faults a little blind;
Let all her ways be unconfined;
And clap your padlock – on her mind.

MATTHEW PRIOR, 'An English Padlock', 1705

The Queen is most anxious to enlist every one who can speak or write to join in checking this mad, wicked folly of 'Woman's Rights', with all its attendant horrors, on which her poor feeble sex is bent, forgetting every sense of womanly feeling and propriety.

QUEEN VICTORIA, letter to Theodore Martin, 29 May 1870

Unto the woman He said: 'I will greatly multiply thy pain and thy travail; in pain thou shalt bring forth children; and thy desire shall be to thy husband, and he shall rule over thee.'

The Bible, Genesis 3:16

No woman in my time will be Prime Minister or Foreign Secretary.

MARGARET THATCHER, 1974

You'll Be the Death of Me
Every year, 600,000 women die from complications during pregnancy and childbirth, with a woman in Somalia 700 times more likely to die than a woman in the UK.

A woman, especially if she have the misfortune of knowing anything, should conceal it as well as she can.

JANE AUSTEN, 1775–1817

Written while in medical school:

The Professor of Gynaecology began his course of lectures as follows: 'Gentlemen, woman is an animal that micturates once a day, defecates once a week, menstruates once a month, parturates once a year and copulates whenever she has the opportunity.'

I thought it a prettily-balanced sentence.

W. SOMERSET MAUGHAM, *A Writer's Notebook*

When a man gives his opinion he's a man. When a woman gives her opinion she's a bitch.

BETTE DAVIS, 1908-89

A man is seldom ashamed of feeling that he cannot love a woman so well when he sees a certain greatness in her: nature having intended greatness for men.

GEORGE ELIOT, *Middlemarch*, 1871–2

Women used to have time to make mince pies and had to fake orgasms. Now we can manage the orgasms, but we have to fake the mince pies.

ALLISON PEARSON, b. 1960, *I Don't Know How She Does It*

Nice Work if You Can Get It

Globally, it's reckoned that women do two thirds of the work – mostly unwaged; but even when they are paid for what they do, they are still undervalued. In the UK, in spite of the 1970s Sex Discrimination and Equal Pay Acts, women are still earning about £7,000 less per annum than men. And although it's illegal to pay a woman less than a man for the same kind of work, this disparity may now even be increasing, with an average man earning £569 a week and an average woman £436, according to the Office for National Statistics.

How to Keep a Woman in Her Place

Foot binding may have been outlawed in China – not before an estimated billion women had been crippled by it – but in some parts of the world female genital mutilation has not yet been outlawed. There are at least four types of FGM, which may be inflicted, usually without anaesthetic, on infants, girls or mature women depending on the culture. In almost all cases the clitoris is cut off; in 15 per cent of procedures, infibulation (the cutting off of all the external genitalia, and the stitching up of the vaginal opening) is practised. Immediate complications include shock, haemorrhage, infection and death; long-term problems include *incontinence, sexual dysfunction, difficulties in childbirth and depression. The World Health Organization estimates that well over 100 million women have undergone FGM, mostly in Africa, Asia and the Middle East, but also in other places where the practice has been imported. The reasons given for performing it include: because it's more hygienic, more healthy and more aesthetic; because religion demands it; because it maintains chastity in the female before marriage and fidelity afterwards (by making sex painful); and, last and not least, because it increases male sexual pleasure. Every year, a further 2 million girls will be genitally mutilated – that's around 6,000 a day.*

● Hell hath no fury like a woman scorned

If all men are born free,
How is it all women are born slaves?

MARY ASTELL, *Some Reflections upon Marriage*, 1706

Some advice from Lord Chesterfield to his son:

Women, then, are only children of a larger growth: they have an entertaining tattle, and sometimes wit; but for solid, reasoning good-sense, I never knew in my life one that had it, or who reasoned or acted consequentially for four and twenty hours together.

And further:

A man of sense only trifles with them, plays with them, humours and flatters them, as he does with a sprightly and forward child; but he neither consults them about, nor trusts them with, serious matters.

Only the male intellect, clouded by sexual impulse, could call the undersized, narrow-shouldered, broad-hipped, and short-legged sex the fair sex.

ARTHUR SCHOPENHAUER, 'On Women', 1851

A Few Facts about Rape

- *It did not become illegal for a man to rape his wife in the US until 1993, when it became a crime in all 50 states.*
- *Scotland, 2001: A senior judge in the Scottish High Court ruled that 'to have sexual intercourse with a woman without her consent in itself is not rape. There seems to be a*

common perception that lack of consent is enough for a charge of rape.'

- Thanks to 'rape' drugs such as Rohypnol, GHB, ketamine, 'Fry' and Burundanga, date rape statistics are rocketing.
- Since before the rape of the Sabine women, sexual violence has been used as a deliberate tool of war. For example: during the Second World War, Japanese soldiers forced hundreds of thousands of women into sexual slavery; in the 1990s, during the ethnic cleansing campaign in Bosnia, thousands of Muslim women were raped; during Rwanda's 1994 genocide, at least a quarter of a million women were raped. Subsequently, many of these women were deemed shameful, and rejected by their husbands and family.
- In the UK, one in twenty women has experienced rape, but fewer than one in five bothered to report it, partly, no doubt, because fewer than 6 per cent of reported rapes end in a conviction.

According to the Russian scientist Elie Metchnikoff, the natives of Tierra del Fuego used to slaughter and eat their old women, rather than their dogs, in times of famine. The reason was simple: whereas the dogs were good at catching seals, the old women weren't so great.

Can the fact that our Lord chose men as his twelve Apostles be lightly dismissed?

One of the BISHOPS OF WINCHESTER

Don't Worry Your Pretty Little Head

No parliament in the world has as many female MPs as male, and in the UK fewer than one in five MPs is a woman. Surely it's no coincidence that, around the world, fewer women than men bother to go to the polls? In any case, in Saudi Arabia, women are still not emancipated; in other nations, where women have the vote in theory, they are often disenfranchised through intimidation and violence; in Bhutan, where each household has only one vote, you may be sure that it's not the wife who gets to use it.

Proverbially, women:

- are the snares of Satan
- have long hair and short brains

Furthermore,

- Never trust a woman, even if she has borne you seven children
- A woman, a dog, and a walnut tree, the more you beat them the better they be
- There is no devil so bad as a she-devil

And biblically:

- As a jewel of gold in a swine's snout, so is a fair woman which is without discretion
- All wickedness is but little to the wickedness of a woman

Words of Wisdom

Advice is seldom welcome; and those who want it the most always like it the least.

LORD CHESTERFIELD, *Letters to His Son*

Believe everything you hear about the world; nothing is too impossibly bad.

HONORÉ DE BALZAC

There's no need to worry – Whatever you do, life is hell.

WENDY COPE, b. 1945, 'Advice to Young Women'

If one cannot catch the bird of paradise, better take a wet hen.

NIKITA KHRUSHCHEV, *Time* magazine, 1958

All of men's problems stem from one single thing, which is their inability to stay quietly in a room at home.

BLAISE PASCAL, *Pensées*

If you can't be a good example, then you'll just have to be a horrible warning.

CATHERINE AIRD, English writer, b. 1930

Be Not Too Hard

Be not too hard for life is short
And nothing is given to man;
Be not too hard when he is sold and
    bought
For he must manage as best he can;
Be not too hard when he gladly dies
Defending things he does not own;
Be not too hard when he tells lies
And if his heart is sometimes like a
    stone
Be not too hard – for soon he dies,
Often no wiser than he began;
Be not too hard for life is short
And nothing is given to man.

CHRISTOPHER LOGUE, b. 1926

Live with yourself: get to know how poorly furnished you are.

PERSIUS, AD 34–62, *Satires*

If you are foolish enough to be contented, don't show it, but grumble with the rest.

JEROME K. JEROME

A man must swallow a toad every morning if he wishes to be sure of finding nothing still more disgusting before the end of the day.

NICOLAS CHAMFORT

Cheer up! The worst is yet to come!

PHILANDER CHASE JOHNSON, US journalist, in *Everybody's Magazine*, 1920

How many of our daydreams would darken into nightmares if there seemed any danger of their coming true!

LOGAN PEARSALL SMITH, *Afterthoughts*, 1931

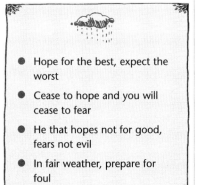

- Hope for the best, expect the worst
- Cease to hope and you will cease to fear
- He that hopes not for good, fears not evil
- In fair weather, prepare for foul

Never do to-day what you can put off till to-morrow.

Punch

If we see light at the end of the tunnel, It's the light of the oncoming train.

ROBERT LOWELL, 1917–77, 'Day by Day'

Biblical pointers:

When thou hast enough, remember the time of hunger.

Ecclesiastes 18:25

Say not thou, What is the cause that the former days were better than these? For thou dost not enquire wisely concerning this.

Ecclesiastes 7:10

Take therefore no thought for the morrow: for the morrow shall take thought for the things of itself. Sufficient unto the day is the evil thereof.

Matthew 6:34

Love thy neighbour, but don't take down the fence.

BENJAMIN FRANKLIN

My only solution for the problem of habitual accidents (and, so far, nobody has asked me for my solution) is to stay in bed all day. Even then, there is always the chance that you will fall out.

ROBERT BENCHLEY, 'Safety Second', 1949

Do not bite at the bait of pleasure till you know there is no hook beneath it.

THOMAS JEFFERSON

Men should do with their hopes as they do with tame fowl: cut their wings that they may not fly over the wall.

VISCOUNT HALIFAX, English political writer and statesman, 1633–95

If a thing is worth doing, it is worth doing badly.

G. K. CHESTERTON

Advice to Officers of the British Army, 1782
To appear more warlike, you should ride with your sword drawn; but take care you do not cut your horse's ear off.

CAPTAIN FRANCIS GROSE, antiquary, 1731–91

The best defence against the atom bomb is not to be there when it goes off.

British Army Journal, 1949

- Don't count your chickens before they are hatched
- First catch your hare

… because I called but you refused to listen, because I stretched out my hand but no one paid attention, because you neglected all my advice, and did not comply with my rebuke, so I myself will laugh when disaster strikes you.

The Bible, Proverbs 1:24–6

On a Gravestone at St Osyth, Essex
Where e'er ye be,
Always let your wind go free,
For keeping it in
Was the death of me.

Pessimism … is, in brief, playing the sure game. You cannot lose at it; you may gain. It is the only view of life in which you can never be disappointed.

THOMAS HARDY, 1840–1928

Call no man happy this side of the grave; he is at best but fortunate.

SOLON, c. 640–c. 558 BC

Work

It is wonderful, when a calculation is made, how little the mind is actually employed in the discharge of any profession.

SAMUEL JOHNSON

Ergophobia is the abnormal and recurring phobia of work. For many people it is a severe ailment that torments weekends and turns Monday morning into a nightmare. The word was first invented by Dr W. D. Spanton in the British Medical Journal in 1905. He recognized, as many others do, that one can feel properly sick and traumatized at the idea of work and the workplace.

On yer bike!

NORMAN TEBBIT, 1981, to the unemployed

A desk is a dangerous place from which to view the world.

Sign on the desk of American Express president Louis Gerstner

The law firm Peninsula conducted a survey of 1,200 employees and found that four out of five people lost their temper at work, most of the time through frustration at another colleague's behaviour. This is a common trend across offices worldwide. The survey recommended regular breaks and a good lunch to calm people down.

According to a study in the Medical Journal of Australia, top managers and directors are less likely to have cancer than employees lower down in the work hierarchy.

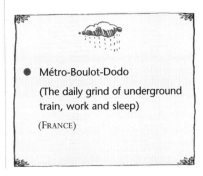

- Métro-Boulot-Dodo

(The daily grind of underground train, work and sleep)

(FRANCE)

Work expands so as to fill the time available for its completion.

C. NORTHCOTE PARKINSON, *Parkinson's Law*, 1957

———

Office politics are a minefield. Everyone is looking out for themselves and you can be sure that you'll be blamed if something goes wrong. There are, please note, certain office no-go areas so as not to alienate your work colleagues. These include: 1) plastering your desk and walls with pictures of your smiling friends and family, 2) eating pungent food loudly at your desk, 3) talking stridently on the phone, 4) arriving late, leaving before everyone else, 5) changing your behaviour when the boss is around, 6) talking endlessly and stealing the limelight at meetings.

———

A man willing to work, and unable to find work, is perhaps the saddest sight that fortune's inequality exhibits under the sun.

THOMAS CARLYLE, *Chartism*, 1839

Work is a necessary evil to be avoided.

PUBLIUS TERENTIUS AFER (TERENCE), 195 or 185–159 BC, *Phormio*

———

If you persistently eat in front of your computer or in your office, an Arizona University study has discovered, you may have up to 400 times more bacteria on your desk than on your toilet seat.

———

Working in an 'open space' environment is very stressful, a Cornell University study has found. Even low-level noise in open-plan offices results in stress.

———

In a hierarchy every employee tends to rise to his level of incompetence; the cream rises until it sours.

PETER LAURENCE and RAYMOND HULL, *The Peter Principle*, 1968

Term, holidays, term, holidays, till we leave school, and then work, work, work, till we die.

C. S. LEWIS, *Surprised by Joy*, 1955

———

They'll work you into the ground
The number of work-related accidents and illnesses continues to rise, with up to 2.2 million deaths a year. According to the International Labour Organization, 268 million non-fatal accidents are also reported annually.

Youth and Childhood

One cannot love lumps of flesh, and little infants are nothing more.

SAMUEL JOHNSON

The question that is so clearly in many potential parents' minds: 'Why should we stunt our ambitions and impoverish our lives in order to be insulted and looked down upon in our old age?'

JOSEPH ALOIS SCHUMPETER, *Capitalism, Socialism, and Democracy*, 1942

He that doth get a wench with child and marries her afterwards it is as if a man should shit in his hat and then clap it on his head.

SAMUEL PEPYS, 1633–1703

Children are haughty, disdainful, angry, envious, curious, interested, lazy, fickle, shy, self-indulgent, liars, deceivers … they do not wish to suffer evil, but like to do evil.

JEAN DE LA BRUYÈRE

- 10.5 million children still die every year worldwide.

- 29,000 children under the age of five die every day, nearly 4,000 simply because they lack safe water and sanitation.

- 12 million children worldwide have been orphaned by AIDS.

- 146 million children regularly go hungry.

- 640 million lack adequate shelter.

- 250 million work as cheap labour, 2 million as prostitutes.

- Conflict has claimed the lives of 2 million children in 1998–2008, and left 6 million wounded and disabled.

- 300,000 children worldwide are forced to carry a gun.

- 72 million children are still not going to school.

UNESCO

Youth is something very new: twenty years ago no one mentioned it.

COCO CHANEL

Street children are a global and escalating phenomenon, particularly in large cities of the developing world. These children who work and live on the street, often abandoned by their families and society, risk disease and rejection and are generally forced to beg or hawk to survive. An estimated 90 per cent of street children use solvents and glues to get intoxicated and alleviate their suffering and hunger. Life expectancy for these children is low. UNICEF estimates the number of street children to be over 100 million worldwide.

I don't know what Scrope Davies meant by telling you I liked Children, I abominate the sight of them so much that I have always had the greatest respect for the character of Herod.

LORD BYRON, letter to Augusta Leigh, *Letters and Journals*, Vol. 2, 1810–12

Youth, large, lusty, loving – youth full
    of grace, force, fascination,
Do you know that Old Age may come
    after you with equal grace, force,
    fascination?

WALT WHITMAN, 'Youth, Day, Old Age and Night', 1881

US bumper sticker

● Be nice to your kids. They'll choose your nursing home.

The youth of the present day are quite monstrous. They have absolutely no respect for dyed hair.

OSCAR WILDE, *Lady Windermere's Fan*, 1892

● Children should be seen and not heard

The Society for Threatened Peoples published a human rights report in 2006 containing the news that the breast milk of Inuit women in Greenland is so contaminated with dioxins, DDT and other persistent organic pollutants that mothers are advised not to breastfeed their babies. So far, women in other countries are still being told that breast is best, but do watch this space.

Children today are tyrants. They contradict their parents, gobble their food and tyrannize their teachers.

SOCRATES

Goodbye

May the curse of Mary Malone and her nine blind illegitimate children chase you so far over the hills of Damnation that the Lord himself can't find you with a telescope.

(IRELAND)

the circumference. round other each chase no and yes while

THE
OPTIMIST'S
HANDBOOK

a companion to hope

NIALL EDWORTHY
& PETRA CRAMSIE

Illustrations by Emily Faccini

Doubleday

LONDON · TORONTO · SYDNEY · AUCKLAND · JOHANNESBURG

www.rbooks.co.uk

TRANSWORLD PUBLISHERS
61–63 Uxbridge Road, London W5 5SA
A Random House Group Company
www.rbooks.co.uk

First published in Great Britain
in 2008 by Doubleday
an imprint of Transworld Publishers

A CIP catalogue record for this book
is available from the British Library.

ISBN 9780385614115

Addresses for Random House Group Ltd companies outside the UK
can be found at: www.randomhouse.co.uk
The Random House Group Ltd Reg. No. 954009

The Random House Group Limited supports The Forest Stewardship
Council (FSC), the leading international forest-certification organization. All
our titles that are printed on Greenpeace-approved FSC-certified paper carry
the FSC logo.

Mixed Sources
Product group from well-managed
forests and other controlled sources
www.fsc.org   Cert no. TT-COC-2139
© 1996 Forest Stewardship Council
FSC

Our paper procurement policy can be found at
www.rbooks.co.uk/environment

Typeset in La Gioconda
Printed and bound in Great Britain by CPI Mackays, Chatham, ME5 8TD

2 4 6 8 10 9 7 5 3 1

*To all children, especially Hope, Alfie, Francesco,
Eliza, Joe, Delfina, Marianna and Danny*

acknowledgements

The authors and publishers are grateful to the following for permission to reproduce copyright material: Winston Churchill quotations are reproduced with permission of Curtis Brown Ltd, London, on behalf of the Estate of Winston Churchill. Copyright Winston Churchill; extract from *The Power and the Glory* by Graham Greene, published by Random House; extract from 'My Believing Bones' by Sydney Carter (1915-2004) © 1971 Stainer & Bell Ltd, 23 Gruneisen Road, London N3 1DZ, England. Reprinted by permission from *The Two-Way Clock*; 72 words from THE KORAN translated by N. J. Dawood (Penguin Classics 1956, Fifth revised edition 1990). Copyright © N. J. Dawood, 1956, 1959, 1966, 1968, 1974, 1990, 1993, 1997, 1999, 2003; Barbara Cartland quotations are reprinted with kind permission of Cartland Promotions and Rupert Crew Ltd; Desmond Tutu quotation is © Desmond Tutu, all rights reserved; 'The Peace of Wild Things' is copyright © 1999 by Wendell Berry from *The Selected Poems of Wendell Berry*. Reprinted by permission of the publisher; quotations from *Afterthoughts* by Logan Pearsall Smith quoted by kind permission of the London Library; excerpt from *Swanson on Swanson* reproduced by permission of Gloria Swanson Inc., c/o Migdal, Pollack & Rosencrantz LLP, 41 East 57th Street, New York; Tom Sharpe quotation is © Tom Sharpe and reproduced by permission of Sheil Land Associates Ltd; excerpt from *Long Walk to Freedom* by Nelson Mandela, published by Little, Brown; excerpt from *The Grapes of Wrath* by John Steinbeck (Penguin Books, 2001). Copyright 1939 by John Steinbeck; 'The Bright Field' originally published in *R. S. Thomas – Laboratories of the Spirit*, London, Macmillan, 1975 © Kunjana Thomas 2001; lines from *Dr Spock's Baby and Child Care* by Dr Spock, published by the Bodley Head. Reprinted by permission of The Random House Group Ltd; extract from *The Comforters* by Muriel Spark, Penguin 1957; extract from *Eleanor Roosevelt* by Blanche Wiesen Cook published by Bloomsbury; list of Top Twenty Greatest Engineering Achievements of the Twentieth Century reprinted with permission from *A Century of Innovation: Twenty Engineering Achievements that Transformed Our Lives* © 2003 by the National Academy of Sciences, Courtesy of the National Academies Press, Washington DC; lines from *The French Lieutenant's Woman* are copyright © John Fowles 1969; 'Ourstory' is taken from *Stitching the Dark: New & Selected Poems* by Carole Satyamurti (Bloodaxe Books, 2004); lines from Sigmund Freud's Letter to Marie Bonaparte reproduced by arrangement with Paterson Marsh Ltd, London; lines from *Collected Poetry of Aldous Huxley*. Copyright © 1970 by Aldous Huxley. Reprinted by permission of Georges Borchardt, Inc., for the Estate of Aldous Huxley; 'School Reports': mostly sourced from *Could Do Better* (Pocket Books, 2002) and *Could Do (Even) Better* (Pocket Books, 2004) by Catherine Hurley; lines from 'The Nature of Architecture' by Patrick Nuttgens, in *Companion to Contemporary Architectural Thought* by Ben Farmer and Hentie Louws (eds), 1993, reprinted by permission of Taylor and Francis Books UK; lines from 'My Own View' by Isaac Asimov in *The Encyclopedia of Science Fiction*, Holdstock, ed. 1978, p. 5, published by Octopus Books, reprinted by permission of the Estate of Isaac Asimov, c/o Ralph M. Vicinanza Ltd; lines from *The New Testament in Scots*, translated by William L. Lorimer, first published in Great Britain by Canongate Books Ltd, 14 High Street, Edinburgh, EH1 1TE.

categories

PREFACE

'For myself I am an optimist – it does not seem to be much use being anything else.'

WINSTON CHURCHILL

CAN YOU BELIEVE that, for every academic paper written on the subject of happiness, there are over a hundred written about depression? What is *wrong* with people? Does the sun not rise for these doom-mongers each morning? Do birds not sing and flowers not bloom for the pessimist? Stung into action by this outrage, we have produced *The Optimist's Handbook,* an exhaustively researched and beautifully crafted work, to prove that these sour-faced miners of misery have been hacking away in the wrong pit all these years. As someone's cheerful grandmother probably once said: 'Pessimist! Leave thy slagheap of misery behind, and come celebrate life's wealth of riches!'

If only they knew where to dig, they would quickly discover that, right beneath their dirty, sodden boots, lies a bottomless mine positively bursting with sparkling seams of nuggets and gems that celebrate Life. That's *celebrate,* not *denigrate.* With infinite care, untold pleasure, and the encouragement of our superb editor, we have weighed and polished our precious finds for your enjoyment, trying them this way and that, moving some about, honing others into shape, always discarding the imperfect. As you will see, only the most glittering jewels remain, and each and every one of them has found its ideal setting, not only complementing its neighbours perfectly, but making its own unique contribution to the whole illuminating display.

'We are all in the gutter,
but some of us are looking at the stars.'
Oscar Wilde

A BEGINNER'S GUIDE

IT is never too late to become what you might have been.

ANON

HAD I been present at the Creation, I would have given some useful hints for the better ordering of the universe.

ALFONSO 'THE WISE' OF CASTILE, Spanish monarch, 1221–84

LIFE ain't all beer and skittles, and more's the pity;
But what's the odds, so long as you're happy?

GEORGE DU MAURIER, *Punch* cartoonist, 1834–97

I CANNOT help being happy. I've struggled against it but no good. There is, I am well aware, no virtue whatever in this. It results from a combination of heredity, health, good fortune and shallow intellect.

ARTHUR MARSHALL, British broadcaster, 1910–89

The Call

Sound, sound the clarion,
  fill the fife,
Throughout the sensual
  world proclaim,
One crowded hour of glorious life
Is worth an age without a name.

THOMAS OSBERT MORDAUNT, British officer and poet, 1730–1809

I DO not believe that a world without evil, preferable in order to ours, is possible; otherwise it would have been preferred. It is necessary to believe that the mixture of evil has produced the greatest possible good: otherwise the evil would not have been permitted.

GOTTFRIED LEIBNIZ, German philosopher and mathematician, 1646–1716

ALL is for the best in the best of all possible worlds.

VOLTAIRE, *Candide, or Optimism*, 1759

THEY say everything in the world is good for something.

JOHN DRYDEN, *The Spanish Friar*, 1681

Happy Thought

The world is so full of a
   number of things,
I'm sure we should all be as
   happy as kings.

ROBERT LOUIS STEVENSON, 1850–94

OPTIMISM is essential to achievement and it is also the foundation of courage and true progress.

NICHOLAS MURRAY BUTLER, US presidential adviser, 1862–1947

TRULY the light is sweet, and a pleasant thing it is for the eyes to behold the sun.

The Bible, Ecclesiastes 11:7

WHAT doesn't kill me only makes me stronger.

FRIEDRICH NIETZSCHE, 1844–1900

I HAVE tried too in my time to be a philosopher; but, I don't know how, cheerfulness was always breaking in.

OLIVER EDWARDS to Samuel Johnson, in Boswell's *Life of Johnson*, 1791

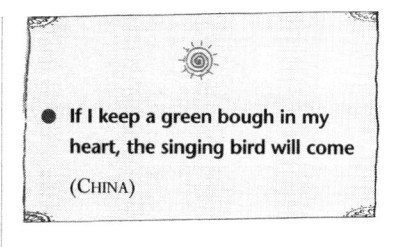

● If I keep a green bough in my heart, the singing bird will come

(CHINA)

THERE is one thing which gives radiance to everything. It is the idea of something around the corner.

G. K. CHESTERTON, 1874–1936

OPTIMISM is the cheerful frame of mind that enables a kettle to sing, though in hot water up to its nose.

ANON

WHAT'S lost upon the roundabouts we pulls up on the swings!

PATRICK REGINALD CHALMERS, Irish writer, 1872–1942, *Green Days and Blue Days*

What's the use of worrying?
It was never worthwhile.
So pack up your troubles in your
   old kit-bag
And smile, smile, smile.

GEORGE ASAF, English lyricist, 1880–1951

---

from 'The Collar'

Is the year only lost to me?
Have I no bays to crown it?
No flowers, no garlands gay?
All blasted?
All wasted?
Not so, my heart; but there is fruit,
And thou hast hands

GEORGE HERBERT, English poet, 1593–1633

IT is one of the strange discoveries a man can make that life, however you lead it, contains moments of exhilaration; there are always comparisons that can be made with worse times; even in danger and misery the pendulum swings.

GRAHAM GREENE, *The Power and the Glory*, 1940

HOPE ...

... is the poor man's bread.
GEORGE HERBERT

... springs eternal in the human breast.
ALEXANDER POPE, 1688–1744

... is the last thing to abandon the unhappy.

---

but wotthehell archy wotthehell
jamais triste archy jamais triste
that is my motto.

DON MARQUIS, US writer, *archy & mehitabel*, 1927

From *Optimism* by
Helen Keller, 1880–1968

... MY optimism is grounded in two worlds, myself and what is about me. I demand that the world be good, and lo, it obeys. I proclaim the world good, and facts range themselves to prove my proclamation overwhelmingly true. To what is good I open the doors of my being, and jealously shut them against what is bad. Such is the force of this beautiful and wilful conviction, it carries itself in the face of all opposition. I am never discouraged by absence of good. I never can be argued into hopelessness. Doubt and mistrust are the mere panic of timid imagination, which the steadfast heart will conquer, and the large mind transcend.

HOW wonderful to wake up in the morning and feel that one is lovely One!

DIANA MOSLEY, 1910–93, during her incarceration in Holloway Prison

I AM of a constitution so general, that it consorts and sympathiseth with all things. I have no antipathy, or rather idiosyncrasy, in diet, humour, air, anything.

SIR THOMAS BROWNE, 1605–82

Invictus

Out of the night that covers me,
Black as the Pit from pole to pole,
I thank whatever gods may be
For my unconquerable soul.

In the fell clutch of circumstance
I have not winced nor cried aloud.
Under the bludgeonings of chance
My head is bloody, but unbowed.

Beyond this place of wrath
    and tears
Looms but the Horror of the shade,
And yet the menace of the years
Finds, and shall find me, unafraid.

It matters not how strait the gate,
How charged with punishments
    the scroll,
I am the master of my fate:
I am the captain of my soul.

W. E. HENLEY, English poet, 1849–1903

There's a divinity that shapes
    our ends,
Rough-hew them how we will

WILLIAM SHAKESPEARE, 1564–1616,
Hamlet

SIR, I have never complained of the world; nor do I think that I have reason to complain. It is rather to be wondered at that I have so much.

SAMUEL JOHNSON, 1709–84

I CAME into the world at the right time, and I shall leave the world at the right time. I am content with whatever happens between the womb and the tomb; neither joy nor sorrow can touch me. I am free from all bonds.

CHUANG TZU, Taoist, 3rd century BC

MY country is the world, and my religion is to do good.

TOM PAINE, *The Rights of Man*, 1791

I AM by Nature made for my own good; not my own evil.

EPICTETUS, Stoic philosopher,
AD c. 55–135

I HAVE become my own version of an optimist. If I can't make it through one door, I'll go through another door – or I'll make a door. Something terrific will come no matter how dark the present.

RABINDRANATH TAGORE, Winner of the Nobel Prize for Literature, 1861–1941

GIVE me somewhere to stand, and I will move the earth.

ARCHIMEDES, 287–212 BC

Haiku

The thief left it behind:
the moon at my window.

RYOKAN, Japanese poet, 1758–1831

THIS week has really been a week of great delight. Never have I had such irresistible, perpetual, & continued urgings of future greatness. I have been like a man with air balloons under his armpits and ether in his soul. While I was painting, or walking, or thinking, these beaming flashes of energy followed & impressed me! O God, grant they may not be presumptuous feelings. Grant they may be the fiery anticipations of a great Soul born to realise them …

B. R. HAYDON, English writer, *Journals*, 29 April 1815

I AM always pleased to see my friends, happy to be with my wife and family, but the high-spot of every day is when I first catch a glimpse of myself in the shaving mirror.

ROBERT MORLEY, British actor, 1908–92

ERROR has never approached my spirit.

PRINCE METTERNICH, Austrian statesman, 1773–1859

WHAT a beautiful day for putting on a kilt, standing upside down in the middle of the road, and saying 'How's that for a table lamp?'

KEN DODD, British comedian, *Guardian*, 1991

- While there's life there's hope

- There is more delight in hope than in enjoyment

- In the land of hope there is never any winter

I BELIEVE in the ultimate decency of things.

ROBERT LOUIS STEVENSON, Scottish writer, 1850–94

Hence, loathed Melancholy,
Of Cerberus and Blackest
 Midnight born
In Stygian cave forlorn,
'Mongst horrid shapes and
 shrieks and sights unholy!

JOHN MILTON, 1608–74, 'L'Allegro'

ADVENTURE

IT is not the mountain we conquer but ourselves.

Sir Edmund Hillary, 1919–2008, with Sherpa Tenzing the first man to climb Everest

A FOOL … is a man who never tried an experiment in his life.

Erasmus Darwin, English physician, 1731–1802

THE first question which you will ask and which I must try to answer is this, 'What is the use of climbing Mount Everest?' and my answer must at once be, 'It is no use.' There is not the slightest prospect of any gain whatsoever. Oh, we may learn a little about the behaviour of the human body at high altitudes, and possibly medical men may turn our observation to some account for the purposes of aviation. But otherwise nothing will come of it. We shall not bring back a single bit of gold or silver, not a gem, nor any coal or iron. We shall not find a single foot of earth that can be planted with crops to raise food. It's no use. So, if you cannot understand that there is something in man which responds to the challenge of this mountain and goes out to meet it, that the struggle is the struggle of life itself upward and forever upward, then you won't see why we go. What we get from this adventure is just sheer joy. And joy is, after all, the end of life. We do not live to eat and make money. We eat and make money to be able to enjoy life. That is what life means and what life is for.

English mountaineer George Mallory, who died on the slopes of Everest in 1924. The discovery of his body in 1999 revived speculation as to whether he and his climbing partner Andrew Irvine had made it to the summit before they perished.

THE church says the earth is flat, but I know that it is round, for I have seen the shadow on the moon, and I have more faith in a shadow than in the church.

Ferdinand Magellan, Portuguese explorer, c. 1480–1521

In 2002, Brock Enright, a 25-year-old artist, launched a 'designer kidnapping' business for bored New Yorkers looking for some adventure in their lives. Dozens of customers paid Brock and his team between $1,500 and $4,000 to be violently abducted. (Costs varied according to the level of danger involved.) Each kidnap was tailored to meet the tastes and phobias of the client, but most chose to be seized at a secret location, bound, gagged, blindfolded, taken away and slapped around for hours, or even days. Customers were abducted in the street, or in their beds at night. 'It's about stepping outside of yourself. I wanted to see what I could do,' said Jason, a carpenter, after his third abduction.

DO just once what others say you can't do, and you will never pay attention to their limitations again.

CAPTAIN JAMES COOK, English explorer, 1728–79

'IT'S an incredible bargain at $100 million a seat,' says Eric Anderson, president and CEO of Space Adventures about his plans to fly two private citizens to the far side of the moon. 'I believe there's a bigger market than people might imagine.' Space Adventures, the pioneers of space tourism, have already flown five customers to the International Space Station (ISS) at a cost to each of roughly $25 million, but the lunar adventure is by far their most ambitious project to date. The US firm promises that, for $100 million, the intrepid lunar tourist will get to lead the first important manned space expedition of the 21st century; become a catalyst for humankind's expansion into space; join the ranks of the world's greatest explorers; experience the majesty and wonder of earthrise and explore and experience the far side of the moon.

I AM actually not at all a man of science, not an observer, not an experimenter, not a thinker. I am by temperament nothing but a conquistador – an adventurer, if you want it translated – with all the curiosity, daring, and tenacity characteristic of a man of this sort.

SIGMUND FREUD, letter to Wilhelm Fliess, 1 February 1900

MAN cannot discover new oceans unless he has the courage to lose sight of the shore.

ANDRÉ GIDE, French writer, 1869–1951

Africa

EX Africa semper aliquid novi.
(Something new always comes
out of Africa.)

<small>PLINY THE ELDER, AD 23–79</small>

THE future is bright. We are
dealing with positive changes ...
The economies are better,
elections are taking place in
many African states, presidents
are willing to leave offices, and
there are no coups these days.

<small>SIR QUETT KETUMILE JONI MASIRE, former
president of Botswana, b. 1925</small>

*The earliest known proof of
human existence and civilization
came from Africa. Lucy, our
common ancestor, the 3.2-million-
year-old fossil celebrity, was
uncovered in an archaeological
dig in Ethiopia. She lies in a
specially constructed safe at the
palaeoanthropology laboratories
of the National Museum of
Ethiopia in Addis Ababa.*

*When it comes to culture in all
its forms, Africa is on top.
Recent years have seen many*

*African writers rewarded.
Nigerian novelist Chinua Achebe
won the 2007 Man Booker
International Prize and
Chimamanda Ngozi Adichie,
also Nigerian, won the Orange
Prize for Fiction. The same year,
Ethiopian émigré Dinaw
Mengestu won the* **Guardian**
*First Novel Award. In France,
Congolese writer Alain
Mabanckou won the prestigious
Prix Renaudot in 2006. Africa
too, in many ways, is music's
past and future. Without Africa
there would be no blues, samba,
calypso, gospel, soul, reggae,
rap, salsa, jazz, etc. As for
football, Africa is a hotbed of
talent. From Didier Drogba to
Emmanuel Eboué, Africa's
footballers are providing the
world's clubs with energy and
skill. According to Robert
Nouzaret, coach of the Guinea
team, the 2010 World Cup is
bound to have African teams
reaching the semi-finals.*

Nelson Mandela remains one of the most revered figures of our times. This is the man who once said, 'It always seems impossible until it's done.' He also famously declared in a courtroom in 1964: 'I have dedicated my life to this struggle of the African people. I have fought against white domination, and I have fought against black domination. I have cherished the ideals of a democratic and free society in which all persons live together in harmony with equal opportunities. It is an ideal which I hope to live for, and to see realized. But my lord, if needs be, it is an ideal for which I am prepared to die.'

The Xhosa people of South Africa have a word, Ubuntu. It means that we are human in and through one another. We are all inter-twined and part of each other.

I AM not interested in picking up crumbs of compassion thrown from the table of someone who considers himself my master. I want the full menu of human rights.

ARCHBISHOP DESMOND TUTU, South African activist, b. 1931

Necessity is the mother of invention. Nowhere is this truer than in Africa, where people recycle plastic bags into mats, tins into suitcases and tyres into shoes. Poverty in Africa has bred inventiveness and resilience, rather than submission. To see or buy some of the extraordinary objects made from recycled material in Africa visit www.csao.fr and www.larbreduvoyageur.com, two gallery shops in Paris.

A HANDFUL OF OPTIMISTIC AFRICAN NATIONAL MOTTOS:

Burkina Faso: Unité, Travail, Progrès (Unity, Work, Progress)

Cameroon: Paix, Travail, Patrie (Peace, Work, Fatherland)

Côte d'Ivoire: Unité, Discipline, Travail (Unity, Discipline, Work)

Kenya: Harambee (Let's Work Together)

Mali: Un Peuple, Un But, Une Foi (One People, One Goal, One Faith)

Rwanda: Unity, Work and Patriotism

afterlife

Coming and going by the
    dance, I see
That what I am not is a part of me.
Dancing is all that I can ever trust,
The dance is all I am, the rest
    is dust.
I will believe my bones and
    live by what
Will go on dancing when
    my bones are not.

SYDNEY CARTER, 1915–2004, from 'My
Believing Bones'

… IN the next world I shan't be
doing music, with all the
striving and disappointments. I
shall be being it.

RALPH VAUGHAN WILLIAMS, English
composer, 1872–1958

MY heaven will be filled with
wonderful young men and
dukes.

DAME BARBARA CARTLAND, 1901–2000

BUT the true servants of God
shall be well provided for,
feasting on fruit, and honoured
in the gardens of delight.
Reclining face to face upon soft
couches, they shall be served
with a goblet filled at a gushing
fountain, white, and delicious to
those who drink it. It will neither
dull their senses nor befuddle
them. They shall sit with bashful,
dark-eyed virgins, as chaste as the
sheltered eggs of ostriches.

The Koran, Surah 37:39–47, translated by
N. J. Dawood

BEHOLD, I show you a mystery;
We shall not all sleep, but we
shall all be changed, In a
moment, in the twinkling of
an eye, at the last trump: for
the trumpet shall sound, and
the dead shall be raised
incorruptible, and we shall be
changed. For this corruptible
must put on incorruption, and
this mortal must put on
immortality. So when this
corruptible shall have put on
incorruption, and this mortal

shall have put on immortality, then shall be brought to pass the saying that is written, Death is swallowed up in victory. O death, where is thy sting? O grave, where is thy victory?

The Bible, 1 Corinthians 15: 51–5

O Death, where is thy
  sting-a-ling-a-ling,
O Grave, thy victoree?
The bells of Hell go
  ting-a-ling-a-ling,
For you, but not for me.

First World War army song

I'll be wrapped around your finger

Nowadays, carbon-based life-forms needn't end up as ashes or bones, we can be made into jewellery and be on hand at all times. LifeGem, of Chicago, Illinois, will take a few grains of your cremated remains and subject them to high pressure and temperature. After 18 weeks, you'll emerge sparkling. Go to www.LifeGem.com to find out more about becoming a Memorial Diamond.

HOW can it enter into the thoughts of man, that the soul, which is capable of such immense perfections, and of receiving new improvements to all eternity, shall fall away into nothing almost as soon as it is created?

JOSEPH ADDISON, English essayist, 1672–1719

For the ancient Egyptians, death was a mere break in existence, and nothing to fear if you had a clear conscience. Your friends would mummify you to help you on your way, and you would then, after journeying to the land of the dead, enter the 'Hall of Double Justice', in order to affirm to the 42 judges that you had committed no sin. After having your heart weighed against Truth in a huge pair of scales, Osiris, the God of the Dead, would give judgement. If the scales were in equilibrium he would pronounce in your favour, and from then on you would lead a life of eternal happiness in the kingdom of the dead.

A BBC MORI poll, conducted in 2003, found that 52 per cent of people in the United Kingdom believed in Heaven, but only 32 per cent believed in Hell.

A thousand tymes have I herd
   men telle
That ther ys joy in hevene
   and peyne in helle,
And I acorde wel that it ys so;
But, natheless, yet wot I wel also
That ther nis noon dwelling in
   this contree,
That eyther hath in hevene or
   helle ybe,
Ne may of hit noon other
   weyes witen,
But as he hath herd seyd, or
   founde it written;
For by assay ther may not man
   it preve.

GEOFFREY CHAUCER, c. 1343–1400, 'The
Legend of Good Women'

WILFRID Blunt's idea of Heaven
was to be laid to sleep in a
garden with running water near
for 100,000 years, then to be
woke [sic] by a bird singing and
to call out to the person one
loved best 'Are you there?' 'Yes,
are you?' then turn round and
go to sleep for another 100,000
years.

GEORGE LYTTELTON, 1883–1962,
Commonplace Book

[HENRY Luttrell's] idea of
Heaven is, eating *pâté-de-foie-
gras* to the sound of trumpets.

SYDNEY SMITH, English wit, 1771–1845

*In 1950, when the great sage
Ramana Maharshi was on his
deathbed, he heard faintly from
without the wails and sobbing
of those who were preparing to
face life without him. A look of
bewilderment passed over his
face, and he murmured, 'But
where do they imagine that I
could possibly go?'*

THERE never was a time when
I, you, and all these warriors
here did not exist, and there
never will be a time when any
of us shall cease to be.

   As the self travels in this body
from childhood to youth to old
age, so the self moves into
another body at death. The wise
are not confused by this change.

The Bhagavad Gita, 2:12–13

Dante's **Paradiso** *lists nine spheres
of Heaven, named after the
planets, each more wonderful than
the last, to reward those souls who
have done well on earth. Among
them, the fourth sphere, the Sun, is
reserved for the souls of the wise,
and the sixth, Jupiter, for the just.
In the ninth and best sphere, the
'Primum Mobile', live the nine
orders of angels (Seraphim,
Cherubim, Thrones; Dominions,
Virtues, Powers; Principalities,*

Archangels, Angels) who surround God. Beyond this lies 'the Empyrean', the source of true light, where angels fly between a gigantic rose made up of the souls of believers, and the hive – God Himself.

Old Shepherd's Prayer

Up to the bed by the window,
    where I be lyin',
Comes bells and bleat of the flock
    wi' they two children's clack.
Over, from under the eaves there's
    the starlings flyin',
And down in yard, fit to burst
    his chain, yapping out at Sue I
    do hear young Mac.

Turning around like a
    falled-over sack
I can see team ploughin' in
    Whithy-bush field and meal carts
    startin' up road to Church-Town;
Saturday arternoon the men
    goin' back
And the women from market,
    trapin' home over the down.

Heavenly Master, I wud like to
    wake to they same green places
Where I be know'd for breakin'
    dogs and follerin' sheep.
And if I may not walk in th' old
    ways and look on th' old faces
I wud sooner sleep.

CHARLOTTE MEW, 1869–1927

All is not lost! Even wandering spirits can eventually find peace in the Afterlife. The Chinese celebrate a Ghost Month, the seventh in the calendar, when the gates of hell are thrust open, liberating hungry ghosts who search the Earth for food or to take revenge on those who have upset them by entering their bodies and causing illness. To entertain these spirits and ward off their evil, people perform street operas, burn 'hell money' and cook feasts. The ghosts are then guided with lanterns in the direction of Heaven.

If you think it would be a shame to die when your turn comes, go to www.alcor.org to find out more about how you, or just your brain, can be preserved after your death. Cryonically suspended in liquid nitrogen at minus 196°, awaiting medical advances, you may one day be able to take up life again where you left off.

WE may be surprised at the people we find in heaven. God has a soft spot for sinners. His standards are quite low.

ARCHBISHOP DESMOND TUTU

ANIMALS

McTAGGART, the celebrated philosopher, always wore a string round one of his waistcoat buttons. Gilbert Murray asked him why and he answered, 'I keep it handy in case I should meet a kitten.'

GEORGE LYTTELTON, *Commonplace Book*

ANIMALS are such agreeable friends – they ask no questions, they pass no criticisms.

GEORGE ELIOT, 1819–80, *Mr Gilfil's Love-Story*

Animal Rights, Part One

Recently, there have been moves towards including certain creatures in a 'community of equals' with humans. The Seattle-based Great Ape Project is calling for the UN to adopt a Declaration on Great Apes, in which chimps, bonobos, gorillas and orang-utans have the right to life, the protection of individual liberty, and the prohibition of torture.

The Peace of Wild Things

When despair for the world
   grows in me
and I wake in the night at the
   least sound
in fear of what my life and
   my children's lives may be,
I go and lie down where the
   wood drake
rests in his beauty on the water, and
   the great heron feeds.
I come into the peace of wild things
who do not tax their lives with
   forethought
of grief. I come into the presence of
   still water.
And I feel above me the
   day-blind stars
waiting with their light. For a time
I rest in the grace of the world,
   and am free.

WENDELL BERRY, American writer, b. 1934

For as little as £2.50 a month, you can 'adopt' an endangered animal such as an orang-utan, tiger or panda, and help WWF safeguard their future: www.wwf.org.uk.

Chimps are from Mars, Bonobos are from Venus

Whereas the well-known Common Chimpanzee is marauding, murdering and brutally dominant, the lesser-known Bonobo is cooperative, friendly and peace-loving. So why don't we see more Bonobos in zoos? Perhaps part of the answer is that these gentle apes spend an extraordinary amount of time having sex with every member of the group and in every conceivable (and inconceivable) position, which might not suit your average Sunday School outing. In the wild, whereas chimps tend to kill each other during territorial disputes, Bonobos usually make love not war, with females rushing to begin an orgy with the enemy, which usually ends with all the adults grooming each other while their children play. We share almost 100 per cent of our DNA with both kinds of chimp, so is it too much to hope that, one day, we'll allow our inner Bonobo out of the bedroom and on to the battlefield?

ALL the really good ideas I ever had came to me while I was milking a cow.

GRANT WOOD, American painter, 1891–1942

HOW I hate the man who talks about the 'brute creation', with an ugly emphasis on *brute*. Only Christians are capable of it. As for me, I am proud of my close kinship with other animals. I take a jealous pride in my Simian ancestry. I like to think that I was once a magnificent hairy fellow living in the trees and that my frame has come down through geological times *via* sea jelly and worms and Amphioxus, Fish, Dinosaurs, and Apes. Who would exchange these for the pallid couple in the Garden of Eden?

W. N. P. BARBELLION, British naturalist, 1889–1919

Busy, curious, thirsty fly,
Gently drink, and drink as I;
Freely welcome to my cup.
WILLIAM OLDYS, English antiquary, 1696–1761

THE great pleasure of a dog is that you may make a fool of yourself with him and not only will he not scold you, but he will make a fool of himself too.
SAMUEL BUTLER, British writer, 1835–1902

Inscription on the Monument of a Newfoundland Dog belonging to Lord Byron

Near this spot are deposited the
Remains of one
who possessed Beauty without
Vanity,
Strength without Insolence,
Courage without Ferocity,
and all the virtues of Man without
his Vices.
This praise, which would be
unmeaning Flattery,
if inscribed over human Ashes,
is but a just tribute to the Memory
of BOATSWAIN, A DOG.

JOHN CAM HOBHOUSE, British politician,
1786–1869

IN return for a place by the fireside, a friendly bone and an occasional pat over the past 15,000 years, dogs guard us, help us catch or bring home our prey, pull our sleds, rescue us on mountains, find us in rubble after disasters, help us to detect landmines, drugs, criminals and cancer, help us to see or hear, comfort us in our illness and, last but not least, accompany us in our loneliness. Every year, stories abound of the myriad ways in which dogs enhance our lives, and now the UK's largest dog welfare charity, Dogs Trust, has launched an annual award ceremony with five categories. Send your nominations to *www.dogstrust.org.uk*.

In Praise of the Horse

Where in this wide world can man
find nobility without pride,
Friendship without envy, or beauty
without vanity?
Here where grace is laced with
muscle and strength by gentleness
confined.
He serves without servility; he has
fought without enmity.
There is nothing so powerful,
nothing less violent;
There is nothing so quick, nothing
more patient.
England's past has been borne on his
back.
All our history is his industry.
We are his heirs;
He is our inheritance.
Ladies and Gentlemen – the Horse!

RONALD DUNCAN, British playwright,
1914–82

- **Don't look a gift horse in the mouth**

- **What's good for the goose is good for the gander**

- **Every dog has his day**

Animal Rights, Part Two

The founder of utilitarian philosophy, Jeremy Bentham, stated that, when considering whether or not a being should have rights, 'The question is not, "Can they reason?", nor "Can they talk?" but "Can they suffer?" As People for the Ethical Treatment of Animals founder Ingrid Newkirk says, 'When it comes to pain, love, joy, loneliness, and fear, a rat is a pig is a dog is a boy. Each one values his or her life and fights the knife.' Throw away your fur coat and go to www.peta.org for more information.

I FIND penguins at present the only comfort in life. One feels everything in the world so sympathetically ridiculous, one can't be angry when one looks at a penguin.

JOHN RUSKIN, 1819–1900

Chain reaction

On 26 April 1986, in Ukraine, the worst accident in history occurred, when Reactor No. 4 at the Chernobyl nuclear power plant exploded. A 30-km exclusion zone was set up – and it is here that a most remarkable reversal has taken place. In the twenty years since the explosion, the deserted and heavily irradiated towns, villages and surrounding countryside have become one of Europe's richest wildlife habitats, with a staggering diversity of species. Indeed, Michael Bondarkov, the director of the International Radioecology Laboratory just outside the zone, says that nearly 50 globally endangered species of animals and plants are thriving. Some 180 species of bird are breeding there; freshwater fish are doing well; large mammals such as moose, wild boar, deer, wolves and lynx are firmly established. It is hoped that a permanent, protected nature reserve will be set up – and that human beings, who left in a hurry, will never return.

WHEN the insects take over the world, we hope they will remember with gratitude how we took them along on all our picnics.

BILL VAUGHAN, US columnist, 1915–77

architecture

The Burj Dubai tower, currently under construction in the Gulf, is set to be the world's tallest building with a projected height of 2,275 feet. Its spire will be seen up to 60 miles away. The lifts will travel at 40 miles per hour.

IN the final analysis, all architecture reveals the application of human ingenuity to the satisfaction of human needs. And among these needs are not only shelter, warmth and accommodation, but also the needs, felt at every moment in every part of the world in endlessly different ways, for something more profound, evocative and universal, for beauty, for permanence, for immortality.

PATRICK NUTTGENS, British architect, 1930–2004

GOOD architecture is like a piece of beautifully composed music crystallized in space that elevates our spirits beyond the limitation of time.

TAO HO, Chinese architect, b. 1936

THE great thing about being an architect is you can walk into your dreams.

HAROLD E. WAGONER, architect

The charity Maggie's Centres has turned architecture into a weapon against cancer. It creates tranquil and inspirational buildings which cancer sufferers and their families can visit for advice. Frank Gehry, Kisho Kurosawa and Zaha Hadid are just some of the major names who have designed unique buildings.

UNESCO – the United Nations Educational, Scientific and Cultural Organization – seeks to protect the world's most precious buildings with its World Heritage List. This list contains some of humanity's most iconic buildings and architectural achievements which have been singled out for preservation for future generations. There are 851 sites on this list. See http://whc.unesco.org.

ART

TO be an artist is to believe in life.

HENRY MOORE, English artist and sculptor, 1898–1986

ART – the one achievement of Man which has made the long trip up from all fours seem well advised.

JAMES THURBER, *Forum and Century*, June 1939

———

London tops the world for most-visited museums. Tate Modern attracts around 5.2 million visitors a year, the British Museum 4.8 million and the National Gallery 4.1 million.

———

AT the age of six I wanted to be a cook. At seven I wanted to be Napoleon. And my ambition has been growing steadily ever since.

SALVADOR DALI, 1904–89

DON'T look for obscure formulas or mystery in my work. It is pure joy that I offer you.

CONSTANTIN BRANCUSI, abstract sculptor, 1876–1957

DO not fail, as you go on, to draw something every day, for no matter how little it is it will be well worth while, and it will do you a world of good.

CENNINO CENNINI, c. 1370–c. 1440, *The Craftsman's Handbook*

THERE is no must in art because art is free.

WASSILY KANDINSKY, abstract artist, 1866–1944

THE purpose of art is washing the dust of daily life off our souls.

PABLO PICASSO, 1881–1973

GREAT art picks up where nature ends.

MARC CHAGALL, 1887–1985

———

Art therapy is a method of using the creative process to improve mental, physical and emotional welfare. Widely used in hospitals as well as schools, it is of particular value in helping traumatized children process horrors they cannot put into words, as workers from Human Rights Watch recently showed when they gave children in Darfur crayons and paper.

BALDNESS

THE most delightful advantage of being bald – one can *hear* snowflakes.

R. G. DANIELS, British magistrate, 1916–93

I DON'T consider myself bald. I'm simply taller than my hair.

TOM SHARPE, English author, b. 1928

Baldness may well be a blessing, but in October 2006 a UK biotechnology firm announced they could 'cure' it by removing hair follicles from the back of the neck, multiplying them and then implanting the cells into the scalp. This method of hair multiplication proved successful in 70 per cent of male patients, and the treatment will be available to the public by 2009. Another technique has been pioneered in Italy. Pierluigi Santi, of Genoa, has successfully used stem cells to 'multiply' hair roots, and his method will soon be available to paying customers.

HE wore baldness like an expensive hat, as if it were out of the question for him to have hair like other men.

GLORIA SWANSON, Hollywood star, 1897–1983, on first meeting Cecil B. de Mille

THERE is more felicity on the far side of baldness than young men can possibly imagine.

LOGAN PEARSALL SMITH, *Afterthoughts*, 1931

There is no consensus as to why male pattern baldness exists, but the most likely theory suggests that it has evolved in males through sexual selection as a signal of enhanced status, social maturity, and ability to maintain a mate in the lifestyle to which she is accustomed. So if you're growing old and shiny-pated, just remember the words of Dolly Parton: 'I love bald men. Just because you've lost your fuzz don't mean you ain't a peach.'

Beauty

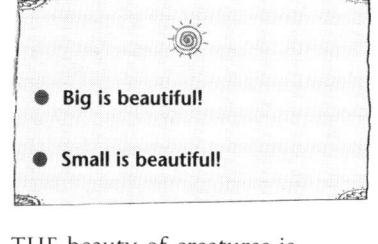

- Big is beautiful!

- Small is beautiful!

THE beauty of creatures is nothing other than the image of the divine beauty in which things participate.

ST THOMAS AQUINAS, *Commentarium in Dionysii de Divinibus Nominibus*, 1260

Years back the world might have voted Greta Garbo, Ava Gardner, Marlene Dietrich, Grace Kelly or Brigitte Bardot the most beautiful woman, but who would win today? In a recent poll Angelina Jolie got the most votes. Her love, Brad Pitt, has often been voted the world's most handsome man. Together, they form the world's most beautiful couple, now termed 'Brangelina'.

IF eyes were made for seeing, then Beauty is its own excuse for being.

RALPH WALDO EMERSON, 1803–82

THERE is nothing ugly; I never saw an ugly thing in my life: for let the form of an object be what it may, light, shade, and perspective will always make it beautiful.

JOHN CONSTABLE, British painter, 1776–1837

What makes for a beautiful appearance or so-called 'wow' factor in a face? Research published in the journal **Proceedings of the Royal Society, Biological Sciences,** *finds that it is, in fact, a perfectly balanced face, one in which the symmetry is clear and striking to the eye. Many well-known actors and actresses, for instance, have symmetrical faces. People with lopsided features or irregular jaws and noses are not (no surprise there!) considered attractive by the majority of people.*

'BEAUTIFUL! Beautiful!'

EDWIN BUZZ ALDRIN's first words as he stepped on to the moon in 1969

It would appear we human beings really are beauty-conscious! Good looks are worth their weight in gold. Studies out of the University of Texas and Michigan State University show that the more attractive you are the more likely you are to earn better money. Basically, unattractive employees earn 5 to 10 per cent less than others. Those considered 'good-looking', in turn, earn more than those deemed 'average' in looks.

The beauty of the world is almost the sole way by which we can allow God to penetrate us ... the beauty of the world is the commonest, easiest and most natural way of approach.

SIMONE WEIL, 1909–43, *Attente de Dieu*

Researchers at Columbia University's Business School used data from an online dating site to show that people with comparable attractiveness tend to pair up. Unattractive men, however, are more likely to try to ask unattainable beauties out on a date!

BEAUTY is the first test: there is no permanent place in the world for ugly mathematics.

GODFREY HAROLD HARDY,
A Mathematician's Apology, 1941

- Those who look for beauty, find it

- There is beauty in everything

IF Nature had not befriended us with beauty, and other good graces, to help us insinuate our selves into men's affections, we should have been more enslaved than any other of Nature's creatures she hath made.

MARGARET CAVENDISH, Duchess of Newcastle, *Sociable Letters*, 1664

A thing of beauty is a joy for ever:
Its loveliness increases, it will never
Pass into nothingness, but still will
     keep
A bower quiet for us, and a sleep
Full of dreams, and health, and
     quiet breathing.

JOHN KEATS, 'Endymion', 1818

EVERY time you smile at someone, it is an action of love, a gift to that person, a beautiful thing.

MOTHER THERESA, 1910–97

BOOKS and READING

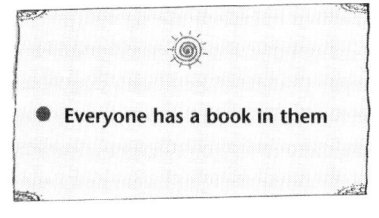

● **Everyone has a book in them**

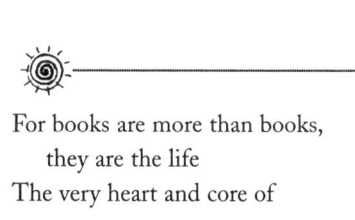

For books are more than books,
    they are the life
The very heart and core of
    ages past,
The reason why men lived and
    worked and died,
The essence and quintessence
    of their lives.

AMY LOWELL, 'The Boston Atheneum', 1912

I NEVER read any novels except
my own. When I feel worried,
agitated or upset, I read one
and find the last pages soothe
me and leave me happy. I quite
understand why I am popular
in hospitals.

DAME BARBARA CARTLAND

A Novel Way to Proceed

*A sixth of the world's trees are
cut down to make paper, so it's
heartening to hear that part of
the new M6 toll road has been
built on copies of pulped novels –
including Mills & Boon love
stories – to prevent it cracking.
Copies of the books were shredded
into a paste and added to a
mixture of asphalt and Tarmac
in a refreshing combination of
romance and environmental
thinking.*

A TRULY good book is
something as wildly natural
and primitive, mysterious and
marvellous, ambrosial and
fertile, as a fungus or a lichen.

HENRY DAVID THOREAU, journal entry,
16 November 1850

BOOKS are cold and sure
friends.

VICTOR HUGO, *Les Misérables*, 1862

The first digital library in the world was set up in 1971 by Michael Hart to make available free electronic copies of out-of-copyright books, or those where the copyright had been donated. The number of digitalized books reached 11,000 by 2004. Some 350 new titles are added each month. Michael Hart's dream is to have 1 million titles available by 2015.

PEOPLE say that life is the thing, but I prefer reading.

LOGAN PEARSALL SMITH, *Afterthoughts*, 1931

READING is to the mind what exercise is to the body.

SIR RICHARD STEELE, *Tatler*, 18 March 1710

Studies have shown that American children who learn to read by the third grade are less likely to end up in prison, drop out of school, or take drugs. Adults who read literature on a regular basis are nearly three times as likely to attend a performing arts event, almost four times as likely to visit an art museum, more than two-and-a-half times as likely to do volunteer or charity work, and one-and-a-half times as likely to participate in sporting activities.

IF the dullest person in the world would only put down sincerely what he or she thought about his or her life, about work and love, religion and emotion, it would be a fascinating document.

A. C. BENSON, *From a College Window*, 1906

When Aaron Lansky realized, in 1980, that thousands of Yiddish books which had survived the horrors of the Nazi years were being chucked out, all over the USA, by people who were unable to read Yiddish as their grandparents had done, he resolved to do something about it. After all, the literature of an entire civilization was at stake. Lansky put out an appeal for unwanted Yiddish books, and has ended up with 1.5 million books which are now housed in the National Yiddish Book Center.

[READING] consoles me in my retreat; it relieves me of the weight of distressing idleness and, at any time, can rid me of boring company. It blunts the stabs of pain whenever pain is not too overpowering and extreme. To distract me from morose thoughts, I simply need to have recourse to books.

MICHEL DE MONTAIGNE, 1533–92

MEN of power have not time to read, yet men who do not read are not fit for power.

MICHAEL FOOT, British politician, b.1913

BOOKS cannot be killed by fire. People die, but books never die. No man and no force can abolish memory ... in this war, we know, books are weapons. And it is a part of your dedication always to make them weapons for man's freedom.

FRANKLIN ROOSEVELT, US president, message to the booksellers of America, 6 May 1942

IT is not true that we have only one life to live; if we can read, we can live as many more lives and as many kinds of lives as we wish.

Attributed to S. I. HAYAKAWA, American academic, 1908–92

A survey carried out for World Book Day in 2006 showed that 41 per cent of people have a definite preference for books with happy endings.

CELEBRATED OPTIMISTIC LITERARY CHARACTERS:

TOM JONES (in the novel by Henry Fielding)

POLLYANNA (in the novel by Eleanor H. Porter, first published in 1913 and now a children's classic. The book introduced the term 'pollyanna' into common parlance, to depict a person who is readily optimistic and who has a big-hearted attitude towards others. In contradiction to the essence of the book, it also came to mean a naive optimist who expects people to behave decently, despite all evidence.)

HEIDI (in the novel by Johanna Spyri)

PROFESSOR PANGLOSS (in *Candide* by Voltaire)

DON QUIXOTE (in the novel by Miguel de Cervantes)

BEATRICE (in *Much Ado About Nothing* by William Shakespeare): '... my mother cried, but then there was a star danced, and under that was I born'

MR MICAWBER (in *David Copperfield* by Charles Dickens): 'I have known him come home to supper with a flood of tears and a declaration that nothing was now left but a jail; and go to bed making a calculation of the expense of putting bow-windows to the house, "in case anything turned up," which was his favourite expression.'

SCARLETT O'HARA (in *Gone with the Wind* by Margaret Mitchell): 'After all, tomorrow is another day.'

BOREDOM

BOREDOM is the highest mental state.

Attributed to ALBERT EINSTEIN, German-born US physicist, 1879–1955

WHAT'S wrong with being a boring kind of guy?

GEORGE W. BUSH, US president, b.1946

Why not celebrate being bored? Click onto www.bored.com or www.Iambored.org.uk. If even that doesn't make you happily bored, go to www.pointlesssites.com.

EXTREME boredom serves to distract us from boredom.

DUC DE LA ROCHEFOUCAULD, 1613–80

IT is better that aged diplomats be bored than for young men to die.

WARREN AUSTIN, US diplomat, 1877–1962

Everybody is somebody's bore.

Attributed to EDITH SITWELL, British poet, 1887–1964

Don't despair at the sound of that familiar moan from kids, 'I'm booooored …' According to some child psychologists, children need to experience boredom to relax, rest and initiate social interaction of their own accord. Without a good dose of boredom they'll always seek outside stimulation and spend life with the bitter taste of dissatisfaction in their mouths. Within Buddhism and Hinduism, boredom is a path to awakening greater self-awareness. It offers you the chance to empty yourself of superficial needs and feelings.

THE secret to being a bore is to tell everything.

VOLTAIRE, 1694–1778

BRITISH EMPIRE

THERE has never been anything so great in the world's history as the British empire, so great an instrument for the good of humanity.

LORD CURZON, Viceroy of India, 1859–1925

WITHOUT the empire we would be victims of world politics, pushed and bullied. Being part of the empire is both our sword and our shield.

WILLIAM HUGHES, prime minister of Australia, 1862–1952

C is for Colonies
Rightly we boast
That of all the great nations
Great Britain has the most

MRS ERNEST AMES, An ABC for Baby Patriots, 1890s

I THOUGHT [poet] Benjamin Zephaniah showed ignorance of history when he refused an honour because it was associated with the British Empire, denouncing imperial rule as cruel and oppressive: if he had read certain accounts of missionaries trying to stop little girls of nine being sold into a dubious marriage or widows being saved from the funeral pyre by the intervention of the Imperial Crown, surely he would not take such an ill-informed view. The British Empire was often a force for good.

MARY KENNY, The Times, 8 November 2004

WE the English seem, as it were, to have conquered and peopled half the world in a fit of absence of mind.

SIR JOHN SEELEY, 'The Expansion of England', 1883

NOW I know it's unfashionable to refer to colonialism in anything other than negative terms. And certainly, no part of the world is unscarred by the excesses of empires. But in the Canadian context, the actions of

the British Empire were largely benign and occasionally brilliant.

STEPHEN HARPER, Canadian prime minister, b. 1959

… THE extension of British rule throughout the world, the perfecting of a system of emigration from the United Kingdom, and of colonisation by British subjects of all lands where the means of livelihood are attainable by energy, labour and enterprise, and especially the occupation by British settlers of the entire Continent of Africa, the Holy Land, the Valley of the Euphrates, the Islands of Cyprus and Candia, the whole of South America, the Islands of the Pacific not heretofore possessed by Great Britain, the whole of the Malay Archipelago, the seaboard of China and Japan, the ultimate recovery of the United States of America as an integral part of the British Empire, the inauguration of a system of Colonial representation in the Imperial Parliament which may tend to weld together the disjointed members of the Empire and, finally, the foundation of so great a Power as to render wars impossible, and promote the best interests of humanity.

CECIL RHODES, excerpt from his first will, 1875, written at age 22

WHATEVER the Empire's early crimes, and there were many, the British succeeded, before the Empire's demise, in atoning for most of them and transforming the institution into what it became: a Commonwealth for the common wealth … Should the British be proud of the Empire they left behind? Of course they should … There is a sort of love for the old British Empire that remains warm among most of those who belonged to it, and that is its greatest monument. The test of the greatness of the British Empire is that its former subjects treat its surviving servants as friends, and not only them but the British as a people also. Of what other Empire is that true?

Historian JOHN KEEGAN, foreword to the *Daily Telegraph*'s *The British Empire*, 1997

───────────────

The banners of England, unfurled
     across the sea,
Floating out upon the wind,
     were beckoning to me;
Storm-rent and battle torn,
     smoke stained and grey,
The banners of England – and
     how could I stay?

From 'For England' by CORPORAL JAMES DRUMMOND BURNS, Australian soldier killed at Gallipoli in 1915, aged 20

change

Only idiots don't change

(FRANCE)

NOTHING is so perfectly amusing as a total change of ideas.

LAURENCE STERNE, *Tristram Shandy*, 1766–7

LOSS is nothing else but change, and change is Nature's delight.

MARCUS AURELIUS, AD 121–80

If any book is ever going to change you it's 365 Ways to Change the World. Author Michael Norton tells us how each and every one of us can change the world and make a difference. No time like the present, get changing! For links to this book, ideas and other change organizations, visit www.365act.com.

THE true revolutionary is guided by feelings of great love.

ERNESTO CHE GUEVARA, 1928–67

THE quintessential revolution is that of the spirit, born of an intellectual conviction of the need for change in those mental attitudes and values which shape the course of a nation's development … It is not enough to merely call for freedom, democracy and human rights. There has to be a united determination to persevere in the struggle, to make sacrifices in the name of enduring truths, to resist the corrupting influences of desire, ill-will, ignorance, and fear.

AUNG SAN SUU KI, Burmese dissident leader, Nobel Peace Prize speech, 1991

No pain – no gain

NEVER doubt that a small band of committed people can change the world. Indeed, it is the only thing that ever has.

Attributed to MARGARET MEAD, American cultural anthropologist, 1901–78

ONE of the things I learnt when I was negotiating was that until I changed myself I could not change others.

NELSON MANDELA, *Sunday Times*, 2000

LORD grant me the serenity to accept the things I cannot change, the courage to change the things I can, and the wisdom to know the difference.

All ALCOHOLICS ANONYMOUS meetings begin with this prayer

YOU must be the change you wish to see in the world.

MAHATMA GANDHI, 1869–1948

TO-DAY is not yesterday: we ourselves change; how can our Works and Thoughts, if they are always to be the fittest, continue always the same? Change, indeed, is painful; yet ever needful; and if Memory have its force and worth, so also has Hope.

THOMAS CARLYLE, 1795–1881, *Essays*, 'Characteristics'

IT is change, continuing change, inevitable change, that is the dominant factor of our society.

ISAAC ASIMOV, *My Own View*, 1978

YOU can't step twice into the same river.

HERACLITUS, C. 513 BC

- It's never too late to change

- Change or die!

- It's an ill wind that blows nobody any good

THE thing that lies at the foundation of positive change, the way I see it, is service to a fellow human being.

LECH WALESA, b. 1943

THE urgent question of our time is whether we can make change our friend and not our enemy.

BILL CLINTON, inaugural speech, 1993

A state without the means of some change is without the means of its conservation.

EDMUND BURKE, *Reflections on the Revolution in France*, 1790

The old order changeth, yielding
    place to new,
And God fulfils himself in
    many ways,
Lest one good custom should
    corrupt the world.

ALFRED, LORD TENNYSON, *Idylls of the King*, 1869

civilization

BY the test of our faith the highest standard of civilization is the readiness to sacrifice for others.

DAVID LLOYD GEORGE, speech in Queen's Hall, 1914

Civilization (from the Latin meaning city) is nothing more or less than testimony to our superb ability to cooperate. The urban revolution began about five thousand years ago, in several different places all over the world, as farming technology – the plough, irrigation and fertilizers – freed mankind from the overwhelming day-to-day tyranny of finding food, and men began to build cities, job-share, specialize: in short, evolve into citizens. The world's first empires, such as that of the Akkadians, in Mesopotamia's 'Fertile Crescent', and those of Meso-America, were the cradle of astronomy, mathematics, writing and craftwork; in Africa, people learnt to fuse tin and copper to make ornaments and weapons of bronze. Today, cities and all their associated freedoms still appear to be our destiny: in 2008, there were, for the first time in history, more city-dwellers worldwide than country-dwellers and, by 2030, 5 billion of us will be living urban lives.

JESUS wept and Voltaire smiled. Of that divine teardrop and the sweetness of that human smile present civilization is made.

VICTOR HUGO, speech on Voltaire's centenary, 1878

THAT'S one small step for (a) man. One giant leap for mankind.

NEIL ARMSTRONG, landing on the moon, 21 July 1969

SOCIETY is indeed a contract … it becomes a partnership not only between those who are living, but between those who are living, those who are dead, and those who are to be born.

EDMUND BURKE, *Reflections on the Revolution in France*, 1790

CLOCK

The Clock of the Long Now

Time was when nothing much was invented, and nothing much changed. Huge excitement when the windmill was introduced into England in the 12th century — not much was new before or for a long while after. Nowadays, of course, the pace of change is such that no sooner has one learnt to operate a particular kind of something than it is superseded by a new prototype. With such an exciting present, it's difficult to give much thought to the future.

Step forward the Long Now Foundation, whose task is, according to founder Stewart Brand, 'to foster long-term responsibility'. One project is the 10,000 Year Clock, which is being designed and built by Danny Hillis: a timepiece so huge that people will be able to walk through it, like a monument, and so slow that, as Hillis first described it, 'It ticks once a year, bongs once a century, and the cuckoo comes out every millennium.' The Clock will serve as a reminder that, however fast our lives seem now, there are still aeons of eternity before us — and it will also show those in the future that we care about them, that we were thinking about them, way back when. There's a small prototype of the Clock at London's Science Museum, and the foundation's website is www.longnow.org.

countryside

WHEN I go out into the countryside and see the sun and the green and everything flowering, I say to myself 'Yes indeed, all that belongs to me!'

HENRI 'LE DOUANIER' ROUSSEAU, French artist, 1844–1910

The total farming area covered by Environmentally Sensitive Areas and Countryside Stewardship Schemes in the UK increased from 650,000 hectares in 1999 to 1,170,000 in 2003.

And this our life, exempt from
    public haunt,
Finds tongues in trees, books in
    the running brooks,
Sermons in stones, and good
    in everything.

WILLIAM SHAKESPEARE, *As You Like It*

TRULY it may be said that the outside of a mountain is good for the inside of a man.

GEORGE WHERRY, *Alpine Notes and the Climbing Foot*, 1896

In a 2005 survey by the agency Natural England, 72 per cent of people living in the countryside said that they were very satisfied with the areas in which they live, compared to 45 per cent of people in urban areas. Indeed, living in the country is better for your mental health than being a city-dweller, according to a 2006 British Journal of Psychiatry *study.*

From 'The Wanderers'
Forget six counties overhung with
    smoke,
Forget the snorting steam and
    piston stroke
Forget the spreading of the hideous
    town;
Think rather of the pack-horse on
    the down,
And dream of London, small and
    white and clean,
The clear Thames bordered by its
    gardens green.

WILLIAM MORRIS, British designer, socialist reformer, poet, 1834–96

The Manor Farm

The rock-like mud unfroze a little
and rills
Ran and sparkled down each side
of the road
Under the catkins wagging in the
hedge.
But earth would have her sleep out,
spite of the sun;
Nor did I value that thin gliding
beam
More than a pretty February thing
Till I came down to the old
Manor Farm,
And church and yew-tree opposite,
in age
Its equals and in size. The church
and yew
And farmhouse slept in a Sunday
silentness.
The air raised not a straw. The
steep farm roof,
With tiles duskily glowing,
entertained
The mid-day sun; and up and down
the roof
White pigeons nestled. There was
no sound but one.
Three cart-horses were looking over
a gate
Drowsily through their forelocks,
swishing their tails
Against a fly, a solitary fly.

The Winter's cheek flushed as if he
had drained
Spring, Summer, and Autumn at a
draught

And smiled quietly. But 'twas not
Winter –
Rather a season of bliss
unchangeable
Awakened from farm and church
where it had lain
Safe under tile and thatch for
ages since
This England, Old already, was
called Merry.

EDWARD THOMAS, English poet,
1878–1917

*The 300,000 miles of hedgerows
and another 65,000 miles of
drystone walls that remain in
England and Wales are now
protected under the Hedgerow
Regulations 1997, meaning that
no countryside hedge may be
removed without the permission
of the local authority. In 2006,
Natural England was happy to
report: 'The quality and size of
many hedgerows have improved
and the widespread removal of
this distinctive feature of the
English landscape has all but
ceased.'*

*The three-year survival rate of
business enterprises registered in
2002 in rural areas was 76 per
cent, which was 6 per cent higher
than in urban areas.*

THE tree which moves some to tears of joy is in the eyes of others only a green thing that stands in the way. Some see nature all ridicule and deformity … and some scarce see nature at all. But to the eyes of the man of imagination, nature is imagination itself.

WILLIAM BLAKE, 1757–1827

Otters were once a common sight in the English countryside but by the late 1970s they had become virtually extinct owing to pollution levels in rivers. Numbers were thought to have fallen below a hundred. Thanks to a combination of protective legislation and improvements in water quality, wildlife experts estimate that the population is now 4,000.

A 2006 report by the Botanical Society of the British Isles and the charity Plantlife showed that while 16 per cent of plant species are in decline, another 18 per cent are doing better than they were in a similar survey 18 years earlier. A number of plants were benefiting from the warmer environment, including species of orchids and ferns.

'I only went out for a walk, and finally concluded to stay out til sundown, for going out, I found, was really going in' (John Muir). Those who frequently travel by Shanks's pony live longer and enjoy better health than non-walkers. Why not have a look at the Ramblers' Association (www.ramblers.org.uk) and join 139,000 other people religiously wearing out their shoe leather?

LET children walk with Nature, let them see the beautiful blendings and communions of death and life, their joyous inseparable unity, as taught in woods and meadows, plains and mountains and streams of our blessed star, and they will learn that death is stingless indeed, and as beautiful as life.

JOHN MUIR, pioneering conservationist, 1838–1914

NEVER, no never, did Nature say one thing and Wisdom say another.

EDMUND BURKE, philosopher, 1729–97

DEATH

I WENT out to Charing Cross, to see Major-General Harrison hanged, drawn, and quartered; which was done there, he looking as cheerful as any man could do in that condition.

SAMUEL PEPYS, *Diary*, 13 October 1660

DEATH has something to be
    said for it:
There's no need to get out of
    bed for it.

KINGSLEY AMIS, 1922–95

PERHAPS the best cure for the fear of death is to reflect that life has a beginning as well as an end. There was a time when we were not: this gives us no concern – why then should it trouble us that a time will come when we shall cease to be? ... To die is only to be as we were before we were born; yet no one feels any remorse, or regret, or repugnance, in contemplating this last idea.

WILLIAM HAZLITT, English essayist, 1778–1830, *Table Talk*, 'On the Fear of Death'

TO die would be an awfully big adventure.

J. M. BARRIE, 1860–1937, *Peter Pan*

WITH the dead there is no rivalry. In the dead there is no change. Plato is never sullen. Cervantes is never petulant. Demosthenes never comes unseasonably. Dante never stays too long.

LORD MACAULAY, 1800–59, 'Lord Bacon'

Look out for the dead and they will look out for you! Seven years after death, in a ceremony called the **famadihana**, *or turning of the bones, Madagascan people dig their loved ones up and parade their bones around, telling them all the local gossip. The bones are then carefully cleaned and wrapped in a new shroud for reburial. The old shroud is often presented to a newly-wed couple in the family for them to make love on, so that the ancestor's power will live on in any children who result.*

WE can be certain that more than a hundred thousand persons die in the world every day. So that a man who has lived for thirty years has escaped this tremendous destruction about one thousand, four hundred times.

NICOLAS CHAMFORT, French writer, 1741–94

You may not want to die, but consider the alternative. In Greek mythology, the goddess of the Dawn, Eos, fell in love with Tithonus, a handsome mortal. Eos begged Zeus to grant her lover the gift of eternal life; Zeus did so, but neglected to give him eternal youth. Increasingly demented, Tithonus lived for ever, becoming a tiny, debilitated, twittering wreck, driving Eos crazy with his babbling, and finally turning into a grasshopper. In our times, we're getting ever nearer the possibility of life-extension treatments that could enable us to live eternally (presumably with a full set of marbles), as 'transhumans'. But what would life be without death – would it be any kind of life at all? The influential Leon Kass, a bioethicist at the University of Chicago, is among those who hold that death is what gives our lives shape, for without the definition and certainty it brings, many of

the things that give our lives meaning – art, love, beauty – would be lost; while the political economist Francis Fukuyama believes that to abandon death would be, essentially, to abandon our humanity; he has called Transhumanism 'the World's Most Dangerous Idea'.

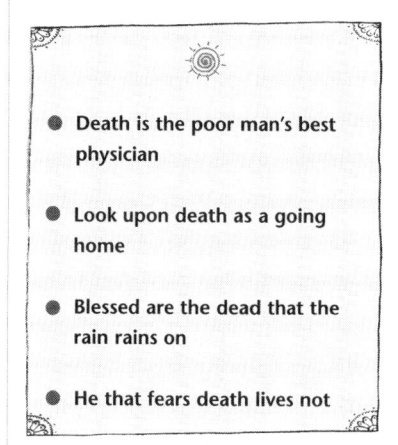

- **Death is the poor man's best physician**

- **Look upon death as a going home**

- **Blessed are the dead that the rain rains on**

- **He that fears death lives not**

BELOW my window in Ross, when I'm working in Ross, for example, there at this season, the blossom is out in full now, there in the west early. It's a plum tree, it looks like apple blossom but it's white, and looking at it, instead of saying 'Oh that's nice blossom' … last week looking at it through the window when I'm writing, I see it is the whitest, frothiest, blossomest blossom that there ever could be, and I can see it. Things are both more trivial than they ever were, and more important than

they ever were, and the difference between the trivial and the important doesn't seem to matter. But the nowness of everything is absolutely wondrous, and if people could see that, you know. There's no way of telling you; you have to experience it, but the glory of it, if you like, the comfort of it, the reassurance … not that I'm interested in reassuring people – bugger that. The fact is, if you see the present tense, boy do you see it! And boy can you celebrate it.

DENNIS POTTER, British playwright, on his imminent death from cancer, 1994

I'VE a great fancy to see my own funeral afore I die.

MARIA EDGEWORTH, 1767–1849, *Castle Rackrent*

DEATH belongs to life as birth does. The walk is in the raising of the foot as in the laying of it down.

RABINDRANATH TAGORE, 1861–1941

It ain't over till it's over. The following organs and tissues can be donated and grafted from a dead body to ensure a new or improved life in another human being: lungs, pancreas, liver, kidneys, intestines, heart; veins, heart valves, skin, tendons, *bone and corneas. Visit www.uktransplant.org.uk or the national organization of your country, and live on!*

ETERNAL law has arranged nothing better than this, that it has given us one way into life, but many ways out.

SENECA, Stoic philosopher, c. 4 BC– AD 59

Traditional British burials use MDF or hardwood coffins, and the embalming process uses formaldehyde that leaches into the soil; every cremation produces on average 50kg of CO_2, and a worrying amount of mercury vapour. Why not go green when you go? Visit www.naturaldeath.org.uk for all sorts of eco-friendly ideas.

An Irish Blessing

● May you die in bed at 95, shot by a jealous spouse.

To a fellow pallbearer at the funeral of escapologist Harry Houdini:
I BET you a hundred bucks he ain't in here.

Dreams

IT is better to dream your life than to live it, and even though you live it, you will still dream it.

MARCEL PROUST, *Les Plaisirs et les Jours*, 1896

Come to me in my dreams, and
   then
By day I shall be well again!
For then the night will more than
   pay
The hopeless longing of the day.

MATTHEW ARNOLD, 'Longing', *Empedocles on Etna and Other Poems*, 1852

AND he said, 'Hear my words: If there is a prophet among you, I the Lord make myself known to him in a vision; I speak with him in a dream.'

The Bible, Numbers 12:6

DREAMS pass into the reality of action. From the action stems the dream again; and this interdependence produces the highest form of living.

Attributed to ANAÏS NIN, 1903–77

SINCE Life is but a Dream, Why toil to no avail?

LI PO, Chinese poet, 701–62

I HAVE a dream. I have a dream that my four little children will one day live in a nation where they will not be judged by the colour of their skin but by the content of their character.

MARTIN LUTHER KING, Washington rally, 15 June 1963

WE grow great by dreams. All big men are dreamers.

WOODROW T. WILSON, US president, 1856–1924

A MAN'S dreams are an index to his greatness.

ZADOC RABINOWITZ, 1823–1900

EVERYTHING you can imagine is real.

PABLO PICASSO

● **Live your dreams**

● **Never lose sight of your dreams**

Utopias have come to mean imaginary and good places, dreamed paradises. The term was coined by Sir Thomas More from the Greek word for no-place. There have been many utopias throughout history (each and every one of us probably creates one in our mind), but some have shaped human destiny. Plato's **Republic**, c. 360 BC, is the earliest known European utopia and had a far-reaching influence on political thought. Tennyson's 'Lotos-Eaters' created a land where those who tasted the 'honey-sweet fruit of the lotos' became overwhelmed by a dreamy forgetfulness. James Hilton, in 1933, described the land of Shangri-La in his novel **Lost Horizon**. It was so mythical, mysterious and beautiful that it is now synonymous with the notion of an earthly paradise, a land of the constantly happy.

CASTLES in the air – they are so easy to take refuge in. And so easy to build, too.

HENRIK IBSEN, *The Master Builder*, 1892

Psychologists estimate that we daydream for about a third to a half of our waking hours. Each single daydream may last only a few seconds or a couple of minutes. Children and adults alike are often chided for daydreaming yet it fulfils an essential function in our lives. It allows us, for example, to imagine and manage stressful situations and conflict, control our behaviour, foresee relationship tensions, relax and recharge our minds, etc. It can also be a moment of particular revelation. Chemist Friedrich August Kekulé, 1829–96, puzzled by how the carbon atoms of benzene fitted together, suddenly came to a clear realization while daydreaming on a Clapham omnibus. Next time you see a friend staring into space don't wave your hand in front of his or her eyes.

No, there is nothing half so sweet
   in life
As love's young dream.

THOMAS MOORE, *Irish Melodies*, 'Love's Young Dream', 1807

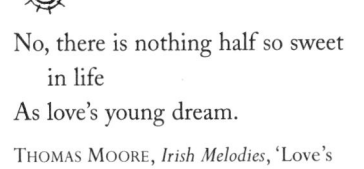

I DO not know whether I was then a man dreaming I was a butterfly, or whether I am now a butterfly dreaming I was a man.

CHUANG TZU, 389–286 BC

DRINK AND DRINKING

BEER is proof that God loves us and wants us to be happy.

BENJAMIN FRANKLIN, writer, scientist, diplomat, 1706–90

OUR country has deliberately undertaken a great social and economic experiment, noble in motive and far-reaching in purpose.

HERBERT HOOVER, US president, on Prohibition, 1919

Anthony Burgess's modern classic A Clockwork Orange *might never have been completed if it wasn't for the numbing effects of booze. 'I had to write* A Clockwork Orange *in a state of near drunkenness in order to deal with the material that upset me so much,' Burgess recalled.*

GIVE beer to those who are perishing, wine to those who are in anguish; let them drink and forget their poverty and remember their misery no more.

The Bible, Proverbs 31: 6–7

If it wasn't for an unruly mob of drunkards, high on rum punch, Americans might still be pledging allegiance to the Union Jack rather than the Stars and Stripes. The American Revolution, leading to independence from the UK four years later, began with the Boston Tea Party in 1773, when 50 colonials, cross about being taxed but not represented in Westminster, converged on the Boston home of printer Benjamin Edes in the late afternoon with a view to staging some kind of protest. Edes provided the patriots with a huge bowl of powerful punch, which his son Peter continually refilled, and as the hours passed by the men grew steadily more inebriated. Their courage suitably fortified, the colonials decided to change into makeshift Indian costumes (fooling no one) and then staggered down to Griffins Wharf where they proceeded to throw 45 tons of tea into the harbour, thereby sparking a constitutional

crisis that led to the birth of a country that would soon become the most powerful in the world.

- Ale will make a cat speak
- There are more old drunkards than old doctors
- It is a good wind that blows a man to the wine

THANK God for something warm at last.

BENJAMIN DISRAELI, British prime minister, 1804–81, on being handed a glass of champagne with his pudding

NO poems can please for long or live that are written by water-drinkers.

HORACE, Roman poet, 65–8 BC

WHAT ideas are more inseparable than beer and Britannia.

SYDNEY SMITH

The US Constitution was born out of the Philadelphia Convention over the summer of 1787 when 55 Founding Fathers of the new republic met to discuss issues arising out of independence from Great Britain. Two days before drafting their agreements,

the delegates retired for lunch to a neighbouring tavern, where they drank 54 bottles of Madeira, 60 bottles of claret, 8 whisky, 22 port, 8 strong cider and 7 bowls of punch so large that, it was said, ducks could swim around in them. And then returned to the conference table to add some final touches to the fledgling American constitution.

WELL-KNOWN WRITERS WHO DRANK HEAVILY

Kingsley Amis

Lord Byron

Truman Capote

Raymond Carver

Winston Churchill

John Donne

William Faulkner

F. Scott Fitzgerald

Ernest Hemingway

Samuel Johnson

Jack London

Malcolm Lowry

Herman Melville

Eugene O'Neill

Dorothy Parker

Dylan Thomas

Evelyn Waugh

Oscar Wilde

Drugs

THOU hast the keys of paradise, oh just, subtle and mighty opium!

THOMAS DE QUINCEY, *Confessions of an English Opium Eater*, 1822

It's the Real Thing

Concocted by John Stith Pemberton, a former lieutenant in the Confederate army, Coca-Cola began life in 1886 as 'valuable brain-tonic and cure for all nervous afflictions'. The new beverage, sold at chemists across Atlanta, was known as Pemberton's French Wine Coca, and according to the blurb, offered 'the virtues of coca without the vices of alcohol'. Each recommended serving contained a significant quantity of cocaine until the drug was removed from the production process in 1903.

ONLY when committing adultery.

US senator WYCHE FOWLER when asked if he smoked marijuana in the sixties

In 1863 Italian chemist Angelo Mariani patented a wine called Vin Mariani which contained 12 per cent alcohol and 6.5 mg of cocaine in every ounce. His Holiness Pope Leo XIII, who carried around a hipflask of the wine, was so impressed he awarded Mariani a coveted 'gold medal'. Other well-known figures who innocently enjoyed the effects of cocaine included the writers Henrik Ibsen, Émile Zola, Jules Verne, Alexandre Dumas and Sir Arthur Conan Doyle. Robert Louis Stephenson was said to have written The Strange Case of Dr Jekyll and Mr Hyde *during a week-long cocaine binge. Royal dabblers included Queen Victoria, King Alphonse XIII of Spain and the Shah of Persia, while US presidents William McKinley and Ulysses S. Grant were also enthusiasts.*

A radically liberal drug policy introduced in Zurich at the end of the 1990s has led to an 82 per cent decline in new users of heroin, according to a report published in the Lancet *in early 2008. Drug addicts in the Swiss city are offered 'substitution' treatment, including injectable heroin, oral methadone, needle exchange and 'shooting galleries' where they can get their fix. The controversial new approach is succeeding, the report says, by removing the perceived glamour of taking heroin and presenting it as a serious illness. 'Finally, heroin seems to have become a loser drug, with its attractiveness fading for young people,' said Carlos Nordt of the Psychiatric University Hospital in Zurich. While the policy led to a dramatically steep decline in the numbers of new users, the overall number of heroin addicts in the city declined by 4 per cent a year.*

IF even a small fraction of the money we now spend on trying to enforce drug prohibition were devoted to treatment and drug rehabilitation, in an atmosphere of compassion not punishment, the reduction in drug usage and in the harm done to users could be dramatic.

MILTON FRIEDMAN, 1976 Nobel Prize Winner for Economics

I ONLY get ill when I give up drugs.

Attributed to KEITH RICHARDS, b. 1943

Cocaine was widely used in patent medicines in the latter half of the nineteenth century and the first two decades of the twentieth. One well-known medicine, Ryno's Hay Fever and Catarrh Remedy, was 99.9 per cent pure cocaine. During the First World War, Harrods sold a kit described as 'A Welcome Present for Friends at the Front' containing cocaine, morphine, syringes and needles.

Popular in the 1930s, the Brompton Cocktail, a mixture of cocaine, morphine, alcohol and sweet syrup, was prescribed to terminally ill patients in order to give them a euphoric send-off from this world. So named after the Royal Brompton Hospital in London where it was invented, it was also administered as a cough sedative to TB sufferers.

DRUGS may be the road to nowhere, but at least they're the scenic route.

ANON

EDUCATION

EDUCATION is a fundamental human right. It is the key to sustainable development and peace and stability within and among countries, and thus an indispensable means for effective participation in the societies and economies of the twenty-first century ... Achieving Education for All goals should be postponed no longer. The basic learning needs of all can and must be met as a matter of urgency.

UN-sponsored World Education Forum, Dakar, Senegal, 26–8 April 2000

ESTABLISHING lasting peace is the work of education; all politics can do is keep us out of war.

Maria Montessori, 1870–1952

THERE is nothing training cannot do. Nothing is above its reach. It can turn bad morals to good; it can destroy bad principles and recreate good ones; it can lift men to angelship.

Mark Twain, 1835–1910

EDUCATION is the great engine of personal development. It is through education that the daughter of a peasant can become a doctor, that a son of a mineworker can become the head of the mine, that a child of farm workers can become the president of a great nation. It is what we make out of what we have, not what we are given, that separates one person from another.

Nelson Mandela, b. 1918

EACH diploma is a lighted match ... Each one of you is a fuse.

Edward Koch, former mayor of New York, addressing students, 1983

GIVE instruction to a wise man, and he will be still wiser; teach a righteous man, and he will increase in learning.

The Bible, Proverbs 9:9

THE roots of education are bitter, but its fruit is sweet.

Aristotle, 384–322 bc

A MAN'S education begins when he is born; before speaking, before understanding, he is already teaching himself.

JEAN-JACQUES ROUSSEAU, *Émile, ou Traité de l'éducation*, 1762

Studies coming out of Harvard Medical School show that people with more than 12 years of education can look forward to an extra 7 years of life compared to those who had 12 or fewer years spent in education. Those who stayed in education the longest can currently expect to live to 82, while those with less time in education only to 75. What was the rush to leave school?

LET us reform our schools, and we shall find little need of reform in our prisons.

JOHN RUSKIN

WHOSO neglects learning in his youth loses the past and is dead for the future.

EURIPIDES, 480–406 BC

I HAVE never met a man so ignorant that I couldn't learn something from him.

GALILEO GALILEI, Italian astronomer, 1564–1642

I AM indebted to my father for living, but to my teacher for living well.

ALEXANDER THE GREAT, 356–323 BC

Educating girls and women reduces family size, delays marriage and increases the chances of having and maintaining healthy babies. It is reckoned, by the World Bank and intergovernmental sources, that one year of female education reduces fertility by 10 per cent, even more so at secondary level. Women with formal education are more likely to get medical advice, delay marriage, combat HIV/AIDS and have nutritional knowledge to care for their children. It also increases women's income and generates greater productivity. A girl who goes to school is also a woman who is more likely to send her own children to school.

A FOOL has a lot to teach a wise man.

FRANÇOIS RABELAIS, c. 1494–1553

I AM not afraid of storms for I am learning to sail my ship.

LOUISA MAY ALCOTT, US novelist, 1832–88

● **In teaching others we teach ourselves**

(CHINA)

environment

Thank God men cannot fly, and lay waste the sky as well as the earth.

HENRY DAVID THOREAU, US writer and naturalist, 1817–62

GLOBAL WARMING: reasons to be cheerful

- Agricultural diversification

- Increase in tourism and leisure pursuits

- Less cold-related illness

- Less winter transport disruption

- Longer growing seasons

- Reduced demand for winter heating

- Shift to healthier outdoor-orientated lifestyles

More than $100 billion in venture capital, private equity, corporate research and development and government support was invested in environmental start-up ventures in 2007.

WE come away from this project with a strong sense that something large, perhaps even revolutionary, is struggling to be born as business leaders, investors, politicians, and the general public create the architecture of sustainable economics. Indeed, it is breathtaking to see how much innovation has been unleashed by the wave of concern about climate change that has broken across the world in the past year, culminating in the awarding of the Nobel Peace Prize to the world's leading climate scientists and their most effective evangelist, Al Gore.

CHRISTOPHER FLAVIN, president of the Worldwatch Institute, 2008

The Kyoto protocol, in which countries around the world pledged to do their bit in the fight against climate change, is up for renegotiation in 2012. But, since the US, which generates a quarter of the world's greenhouse gas emissions, refuses to take Kyoto

seriously, believing it to give an unfair advantage to the developing countries, is there any point in yet more thousands of hours of incredibly complicated meetings between nations, ending up with another toothless agreement that makes no appreciable difference? Step forward C&C (Contraction & Convergence). This framework, conceived by Aubrey Meyer of the Global Commons Institute, proposes that the world decides how much more CO_2 it is safe to emit, and then shares that allowance out equally – but, crucially, not between countries, which leads to terrible squabbles, but per individual – carbon rationing, in effect. It's fair, it's simple, and it could even work.

IT is easy to be pessimistic in the face of the daunting environmental challenges that every one of us faces. But the prospect of environmental innovation makes me an optimist, at least over the longer term … No company or industry can today afford to ignore energy costs, pollution issues, and other environmental challenges. Those that do risk competitive disadvantage.

DANIEL C. ESTY, director of the Yale Center for Environmental Law and Policy, 2008

Man-made emissions of greenhouse gases are causing average temperatures to rise towards a tipping point where climate change will become dangerous, and possibly irreversible. What to do? Here's some ideas from our brightest and best:

- 'Sequester' carbon – capture emissions at source and bury them underground.
- Fit power stations with 'carbon scrubbers' to drastically cut CO_2 emissions.
- Develop an intelligent tree-management project – cut them down and bury them deep, with their carbon safely locked inside.
- Alter the 'albedo', or reflecting capability of the earth, by seeding clouds with seawater to make them whiter and so reflect more sunlight. Or, for the same purpose, release sulphate particles into the atmosphere.
- Reflect sunlight back into space with giant mirrors or a fleet of tiny aluminium balloons.
- Encourage giant blooms of algae in the seas which will absorb CO_2 from the air, either by sprinkling iron filings in the oceans or by putting pipes in place to bring nutrient-rich water from the deep to the surface, enhancing algal growth.

In 2007, Richard Branson launched the Virgin Earth Challenge prize, where he invited scientists to invent a method of sucking or 'scavenging' one billion tonnes of CO_2, directly from the sky, per year. $25 million is on offer to whoever succeeds in meeting the challenge, but the real prize would be the dramatic impact that this would have on global warming, and thus, as the Virgin boss puts it, 'the satisfaction of saving thousands of species and possibly mankind itself'.

When, in 2006, a US businessman told the Kenyan environmental activist and Nobel Peace Prize winner Wangari Maathai that his company was planning to plant a million trees, she replied, 'That's great. But what we really need is to plant one billion trees.' So far, she has inspired people to plant a total of 1.5 billion trees, and counting. 'The planting of trees is the planting of ideas,' says Maathai. 'By starting with the simple step of digging a hole and planting a tree, we plant hope for ourselves and for future generations.' Her official site is www.greenbeltmovement.org.

IN London this smoke is found to blight or destroy all vegetation … One of the improvements of this age, by which the next is likely to benefit, has been its contrivances of more perfect combustion; and for the condensation and sublimation of smoke. The general adoption of a system of consuming smoke would render the London air as pure as that of the country, and diminish many of the nuisances and inconveniences … It must in a future age be … difficult to believe that the Londoners could have resided in the dense atmosphere of coal-smoke above described.

SIR RICHARD PHILLIPS, 'A Morning's Walk from London to Kew', 1817

OVER the next 30 years, many agriculture-related environmental problems will remain serious. However, some problems may deepen more slowly than in the past and some may even be reversed.

UN Food and Agriculture Organization, 'World Agriculture: towards 2015/2030'

I HAVE no doubt that we will be successful in harnessing the sun's energy … If sunbeams were weapons of war, we would have had solar energy centuries ago.

SIR GEORGE PORTER, British scientist, *Observer*, 26 August 1973

WE only need to capture one part in 10,000 of the sunlight that falls on the Earth to meet 100 per cent of our energy needs. This will become feasible with nanoengineered solar panels and nanoengineered fuel cells.

RAY KURZWEIL, inventor and futurologist, February 2008

American scientist K. Eric Drexler has written about the possibilities of nanotechnology going badly wrong, famously describing the 'gray goo problem', a scenario where uncontrolled, self-replicating nanobots (hypothetical microscopic robots) reduce the biosphere to dust in a matter of days. Today, however, while still alive to the inherent dangers of the technology, he considers deliberate abuse, not accidental disaster, to be the bigger threat, and he is working with the Swedish branch of the World Wide Fund for Nature to inform decision-makers around the world of the extraordinary possibilities of advanced nanotechnologies. Among these are ways to reverse (not just stop) the accumulation of greenhouse gases, thereby solving, rather than delaying, global warming.

The great environmental challenge is on. According to veteran CND campaigner and Buddhist eco-philosopher Joanna Macy, if we learn to meet our needs without destroying the planet, then future generations will look back at this era of great transition and call it 'the time of the Great Turning'. For more inspiration about the epochal transition we are currently living, go to www.joannamacy.net.

WHATEVER the experts say about the howling gales, thunder and lightning we've had over the past two days, of one thing we can be certain. Someone, somewhere – and there is every chance it will be a politician or an environmentalist – will blame the weather on global warming. But they will be 100 per cent wrong. Global warming – at least the modern nightmare version – is a myth. I am sure of it and so are a growing number of scientists ... They say this is global warming: I say this is poppycock.

PROFESSOR DAVID BELLAMY, *Daily Mail*, 9 July 2004

Fame

FAMOUS men have the whole earth as their memorial.

PERICLES, c. 490–429 BC

I AM the greatest!

MUHAMMAD ALI, b. 1942

LET us not disdain glory too much; nothing is finer, except virtue. The height of happiness would be to unite both in this life.

FRANÇOIS-RENÉ DE CHATEAUBRIAND, 1768–1848

IF you would not be forgotten as soon as you are dead, either write things worth reading or do things worth writing.

BENJAMIN FRANKLIN

Celebrities are visible and essential role models in an age of moral disorientation. David Beckham's trip to Liberia in January 2008 as Unicef ambassador highlighted the desperate issue of child mortality in the country. His wife, Victoria, is a champion of the Meningitis Research Foundation. Bono and Bob Geldof famously brought Africa's suffering to the attention of the world. Bollywood stars raised enormous funds for tsunami victims. George Clooney has been key in bringing the world's attention to the plight of Darfur.

CELEBRITY: the advantage of being known by people who don't know you.

NICOLAS CHAMFORT, *Reflections on Life, Love and Liberty*, c. 1785

NOBODY can be exactly like me. Sometimes even I have trouble doing it.

Attributed to TALLULAH BANKHEAD, 1903–68

EVERYTHING a human being wants can be divided into four components: love, adventure, power and fame.

JOHANN WOLFGANG VON GOETHE, 1749–1832

YOU'RE not a star until they can spell your name in Karachi.

Attributed to HUMPHREY BOGART, 1899–1957

Fame pays and pays well. No doubt about it! Angelina Jolie, apparently, picks up between $15 million and $20 million per film. Nicole Kidman can expect to earn up to $15 million.

Have little care that life is brief,
And less that art is long.
Success is in the silences,
Though fame is in the song.

BLISS CARMAN, *Ballads and Lyrics*,1861–1929

THE desire for fame tempts even noble minds.

ST AUGUSTINE, 354–430, *The City of God*

FAME is no plant that grows on mortal soil.

JOHN MILTON, 'Lycidas', 1637

THE main advantage of being famous is that when you bore people at dinner parties they think it is their fault.

Attributed to HENRY KISSINGER, b. 1923

Jackie Bibby of Texas achieved fame on World Record Day in 2006 by holding 10 snakes in his mouth for 12.5 seconds.

AFTER I'm dead I'd rather have people ask why I have no monument than why I have one.

CATO THE ELDER, 234–149 BC

THE charm of fame is so great that we like every object to which it is attached, even death.

BLAISE PASCAL, 1623–66

ANDY Warhol said that, in the future, everyone will be famous for 15 minutes. That's probably a bit ambitious, but a contemporary American artist, Raul Vincent Enriquez, has come up with a cunning plan called I in the Sky, to give everyone one minute of fame by setting up a 250-metre-square screen in Times Square in New York. Portraits, taken from photo booths, are then flashed up on to the screen for the public to see and admire.

I HAVE pursued fame always in the hope of winning her love.

MADAME DE STAËL, *Corinne ou de l'Italie*, 1807

FAMOUS LAST WORDS

WHY not, why not, why not. Yeah.

TIMOTHY LEARY, US writer, 1920–96

IT'S all been rather lovely.

JOHN LE MESURIER, British actor, 1912–83

On seeing all her children at her bedside during her last illness:
AM I dying, or is this my birthday?

NANCY ASTOR, first female MP, 1879–1964

GOD will pardon me. It's his profession.

HEINRICH HEINE, German poet, 1797–1856

DON'T pull down the blinds! I feel fine. I want the sunlight to greet me.

RUDOLPH VALENTINO, Hollywood heart-throb, 1895–1926

I SHALL hear in Heaven.

LUDWIG VAN BEETHOVEN, 1770–1827

On a paper dated 23 November 1654, stitched into the lining of his coat and found after his death:
FIRE. God of Abraham, God of Isaac, God of Jacob, not of the philosophers and scholars. Certainty. Certainty. Feeling. Joy. Peace.

BLAISE PASCAL, French mathematician, 1623–62

IT'S very beautiful over there.

THOMAS EDISON, US inventor, 1847–1931

In response to a dirty joke from his doctor:
THAT'S a very good one. Tomorrow I will be telling it on the Golden Floor.

A. E. HOUSMAN, English poet, 1859–1936

THAT was a great game of golf, fellers.

BING CROSBY, 1903–77

I'VE had a hell of a lot of fun, and I've enjoyed every minute of it.

ERROL FLYNN, 1909–59

To his coach, Knute Rockne:

ONE day, when the going is tough and the big game is hanging in the balance, ask the team to win one for the Gipper. I don't know where I'll be, Rock, but I'll know about it and I'll be happy.

GEORGE GIPP, legendary US football player, 1895–1920

I'VE just had eighteen straight scotches. I do believe that is a record.

DYLAN THOMAS, 1914–53

DRINK to me!

PABLO PICASSO

Surveying the enemy lines at the Battle of Spotsylvania:

THEY couldn't hit an elephant at this dist–

GENERAL JOHN SEDGEWICK, 1813–64

Before drowning aboard the Lusitania, *1915:*

WHY fear death? It is the most beautiful adventure in life.

CHARLES FROHMAN, US theatrical producer, 1860–1915

I AM about to take my last voyage, a great leap in the dark.

THOMAS HOBBES, English philosopher, 1588–1679

FATHER, into thy hands I commend my spirit.

JESUS CHRIST

Before blowing her executioners a kiss:

DEATH is nothing, nor life either, for that matter. To die, to sleep, to pass into nothingness, what does it matter? Everything is an illusion.

MATA HARI, courtesan and spy, 1876–1917

Before his execution by the Nazis:

IN a few minutes I am going out to shape all the singing tomorrows.

GABRIEL PÉRI, French Communist, 1902–41

To his executioner:

SO the heart be right, it is no matter which way the head lies.

SIR WALTER RALEIGH, Renaissance man, 1552–1618

When asked, in front of the firing squad, for his last request:

WHY yes, a bullet-proof vest!

JAMES W. RODGERS, US criminal, d. 1960

Fashion

WE live not according to reason, but fashion.

SENECA

MAN'S earthly interests are all hooked and buttoned together, and held up, by Clothes.

THOMAS CARLYLE

I BELIEVE that style is the only real luxury that is really desirable.

Attributed to GIORGIO ARMANI, b. 1934

Recent excavations at a site in Plocnik, Serbia, dating back 7,500 years, show that young women of the Serbian Neolithic era wore short tops and miniskirts not dissimilar to those of today. Fashion was evidently an essential ingredient of being human even in prehistoric times.

A MAN with a good coat upon his back meets with a better reception than he who has a bad one.

SAMUEL JOHNSON, 1709–84

ALL the rudiments of life are to be found ironing trousers.

CHRIS EUBANK, boxing champion, *Independent*, 2003

In 2008 the burghers of Amsterdam began handing over the use of the city's infamous sex-shop windows to fashion designers, replacing real women with plastic models dressed in the latest trendy styles. It is hoped that fashion will beat the red light district's reputation for debauchery, drugs and crime.

THIS bikini made me a success.

URSULA ANDRESS, actress, b. 1936

FASHION is not something that exists in dresses only. Fashion is in the sky, in the street, fashion has to do with ideas, the way we live, what is happening.

COCO CHANEL, 1883–1971

* Fine cloth is never out of fashion.
* Good clothes open all doors.
* The present fashion is always handsome.

THOMAS FULLER, *Gnomologia*, 1732

CLOTHES make the man. Naked people have little or no influence over society.

MARK TWAIN

A WOMAN'S dress should be like a barbed-wire fence: serving its purpose without obstructing the view.

SOPHIA LOREN

The fashion industry generates sales worth around 300 billion euros worldwide each year.

THEY say – people who ought to be ashamed of themselves do – that a consciousness of being well dressed imparts a blissfulness to the human heart that religion is powerless to bestow. I am afraid these cynical persons are sometimes correct.

JEROME K. JEROME, *Idle Thoughts of an Idle Fellow*, 1886

THE only rule is don't be boring and dress cute wherever you go. Life is too short to blend in.

Attributed to PARIS HILTON, b. 1981

I DON'T design clothes, I design dreams.

Attributed to RALPH LAUREN

THERE is no woman who does not dream of being dressed in Paris.

Catalogue of the 1925 Paris Exhibition

I DON'T get out of bed for less than $10,000 a day.

LINDA EVANGELISTA, model, b. 1965

Baudelaire once said, 'The dandy must aspire to be sublime without interruption; he must live and sleep before a mirror.' Beau Brummell pretty much followed that rule. Famous for his faultless and tailored dress sense in the early 19th century, Brummell remains perhaps the most celebrated dandy of all time. He is said to have been responsible for giving us the modern suit.

FISHING

SIR Henry Wotton ... was also a most dear lover, and a frequent practiser of the art of angling; of which he would say it was an employment for his idle time, which was not then idly spent ... a rest to his mind, a cheerer of his spirits, a diverter of sadness, a calmer of unquiet thoughts, a moderator of passions, a procurer of contentedness; and that it begat habits of peace and patience in those that professed and practised it.

IZAAK WALTON, *The Compleat Angler*, 1653

It's true that many fish are in danger of extinction. But, according to the Marine Conservation Society, there are also lots of edible and delicious ones that are sustainably fished, using environmentally friendly methods. Go to www.fishonline.org for a comprehensive list of species. If everybody did this, we could ensure that there would always be plenty more fish in the sea.

Let your hook always be cast.
In the stream where you least
    expect it,
There will be a fish.

OVID, 43 BC–AD 17

Fishing for Fun – and to Wash your Soul

HERBERT HOOVER, US president, 1874–1964, book title

Man's life is but vain, for 'tis subject
    to pain
And sorrow and short as a bubble;
'Tis a hodge-podge of business and
    money and care
And care and money and trouble.

But we'll take no care when the
    weather proves fair,
Nor will we now vex though it rain;
We'll banish all sorrow, and sing til
    tomorrow,
And angle and angle again.

ANON, c. 1620

- Give a man a fish and you feed him for a day. Teach a man to fish, and you feed him for a lifetime

  (CHINA)

- Throw back the first fish you catch, and you'll catch many more

- The gods do not deduct from man's allotted span the hours spent in fishing

  (BABYLONIA)

In 2006, it was reported that, twenty years after acid rain annihilated fish stocks in the River Wye in Wales, salmon have returned to its upper reaches. Adding lime to the water has helped neutralize the chemicals and encouraged the fish to spawn again, according to the Wye and Usk Foundation, which is leading the project to reintroduce the salmon. You can support the Foundation's work by buying a passport to fish in those rivers — with some 3.3 million anglers in the UK, it's fishermen and women who will ensure that a healthy environment is more than just an abstract ideal.

Now, happy fisherman; now twitch the line!
How thy rod bends! behold, the prize is thine!

JOHN GAY, English poet, 1685–1732, 'Rural Sports'

The traveller fancies he has seen the country. So he has, the outside of it at least; but the angler only sees the inside. The angler only is brought close, face to face with the flower and bird and insect life of the rich river banks, the only part of the landscape where the hand of man has never interfered.

CHARLES KINGSLEY, 1819–75

CH. 8 – Instructions for baiting a hook with a live frog
In so doing, use him as though you loved him.

IZAAK WALTON, *The Compleat Angler*, 1653

FOOD

WE are not hungry ... Why foist this food upon us? We don't want to be choked. We have enough ... We have tons of potatoes, but the people aren't potato eaters. They have rice, but don't like it.

ROBERT MUGABE, Zimbabwe president, b. 1924

Organic farming can produce up to three times as much food as conventional farming in developing countries, according to a study published by leading US researchers in 2007. Estimates based on 293 published studies on yields from organic farming show that organic methods could produce enough food to sustain the current human population, and potentially an even larger population, without expanding the agricultural land base.

To eat well in England all you have to do is take breakfast three times a day.

W. SOMERSET MAUGHAM, English writer, 1874–1965

WHEN we no longer have good cooking in the world, we will have no literature, nor high and sharp intelligence, nor friendly gathering, nor social harmony.

ANTONIN CARÊME, chef and author, 1784–1833

The 13-year study by Cambridge academics of death rates in 20,000 people found that being physically active, eating reasonable quantities of fruit and veg, not smoking and keeping your alcohol consumption below 15 units a week can add 14 years to your life – regardless of how fat and unhealthy you are otherwise.
Study published in January 2008

NOTHING will benefit human health and increase the chances for survival of life on Earth as much as the evolution to a vegetarian diet.

ALBERT EINSTEIN

POOR Britons, there is some good in them after all -- they produced an oyster.

SALLUST, Roman historian, on the discovery of oyster beds in East Anglia

HERE we have a very versatile technology [genetically modified food crops], which has the power and the capacity to contribute to a more effective, a more benign, a more sustainable agriculture. 80 percent of the poor people that we have on this planet today are farmers or people that work on farms. So, therefore, if you can introduce biotech crops ... that will increase the income of these people, then you are making a direct contribution to the alleviation of poverty.

DR CLIVE JAMES, agricultural scientist quoted on the website of Monsanto, the world's leading producer of genetically engineered seed

BISHOP: I'm afraid you've got a bad egg, Mr Jones!

CURATE: Oh no, my lord, I assure you! Parts of it are excellent!

Punch cartoon, 1895

Edible, adj. Good to eat, and wholesome to digest, as a worm to a toad, a toad to a snake, a snake to a pig, a pig to a man, and a man to a worm.

AMBROSE BIERCE, *The Devil's Dictionary*, 1911

SIR, The hymn 'Onward Christian Soldiers', sung to the right tune and in a not-too-brisk tempo, makes a very good egg timer. If you put your egg into boiling water and sing all five verses and chorus, the egg will be just right when you come to Amen.

Letter to the *Daily Telegraph*, 1983

I WANT there to be no peasant in my kingdom so poor that he is unable to have a chicken in his pot every Sunday.

HENRY IV, King of France, at his coronation in 1589

THE discovery of a new dish does more for human happiness than the discovery of a new star.

ANTHELME BRILLAT-SAVARIN, French politician and gastronome, 1855–1926, *The Physiology of Taste*

A MAN may be a pessimistic determinist before lunch and an optimistic believer in the will's freedom after it.

ALDOUS HUXLEY, English novelist, 1894–1963

MADAM, I have been looking for a person who disliked gravy all my life; let us swear eternal friendship.

SYDNEY SMITH 1771–1845

France and the French

FRANCE ... naturally fortified against foreign attack, being almost surrounded by seas, by high mountains, or by very deep rivers. She produces an abundance of the things needed for man ... She has an unusual perfection as a state ... and her inhabitants are almost infinite in number, robust and generous, born for war, frank and disciplined.

LOUIS XIV, the Sun King

YET, who can help loving the land that has taught us six hundred and eighty-five ways to dress eggs?

THOMAS MOORE, *The Fudge Family in Paris*, 1818

VICTORIAN England was vaguely convinced that nineteenth century France had too good a time; that Frenchmen laughed too much and cooked too well ... More serious still, Victorian England suspected that the French put more into, and got more out of, sex than the English. Victorian England had not the vaguest idea of how this was done, but it was sure that the advantage was not fair, and quite sure that it was not nice.

SIR ROBERT VANSITTART, diplomat, 1881–1957

IN France everything is a matter for jest. People make quips about the scaffold, about Napoleon's defeat on the banks of the Beresina, and about the barricades of our revolutions. So, at the assizes of the Last Judgment, there will always be a Frenchman to crack a joke.

HONORÉ DE BALZAC, French writer, 1899–1950

A FRENCHMAN who, with a fund of virtue, learning and good sense, has the manners and good-breeding of his country, is the perfection of human nature.

EARL OF CHESTERFIELD, 1747

FRIENDSHIP

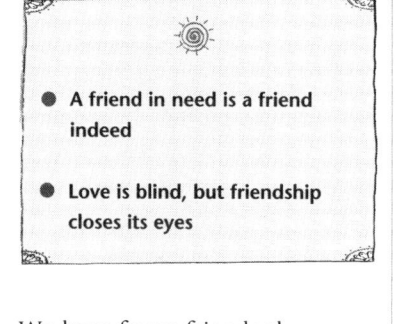

- A friend in need is a friend indeed

- Love is blind, but friendship closes its eyes

We have fewer friends than we imagine, but more than we know.

HUGO VON HOFMANNSTHAL, Austrian poet, 1874–1929

If I am pressed to say why I loved him, I feel it can only be explained by replying, Because it was he: because it was me!

MICHEL DE MONTAIGNE, of his friend Étienne de la Boétie

Old friends are best. King James used to call for his old shoes; they were easiest for his feet.

JOHN SELDEN, English antiquarian, 1584–1654

A friend may well be reckoned the masterpiece of Nature.

RALPH WALDO EMERSON

Greater love hath no man than this, that a man lay down his life for his friends.

The Bible, John 15:13

Am I not destroying my enemies when I make friends of them?

ABRAHAM LINCOLN, US president, 1809–1865

A friendship that can be ended didn't ever start.

MELLIN DE SAINT-GELAIS, French poet, c.1491–1558

Don't walk in front of me, I may not follow.
Don't walk behind me, I may not lead.
Walk beside me and be my friend.

ALBERT CAMUS, 1913–60

THE FUTURE

2012 … is when everything begins again

The ancient Mayans, who were great astronomers, had at least twenty different calendars, all of which were devilishly precise. That civilization is long gone, but their Long Count calendar, which has now been going for over 5,000 years, continues, coming to an end on 21 December 2012. The Mayans held that this date was sacred and propitious, and it is still widely believed that this auspicious moment will herald a new dawn for mankind.

The Diamond Age

Humans break their prehistory into the Ages of Stone, Bronze and Iron; and the author Neal Stephenson has proposed that we call our imminent future 'the Diamond Age', because self-replicating machines, or 'assemblers', will use **carbon** *as their basic material for manufacturing anything we require – even diamonds! This nanotechnology, as alluring as alchemy, quasi-magical but actually possible, throws up a range of practically endless possibilities, and it could literally transform our world. It's likely that the forthcoming techno-revolution will have as dramatic an impact on humanity as the agricultural and industrial revolutions once did: there seems to be no doubt that we are entering an era of unbelievable abundance –* **superabundance.**

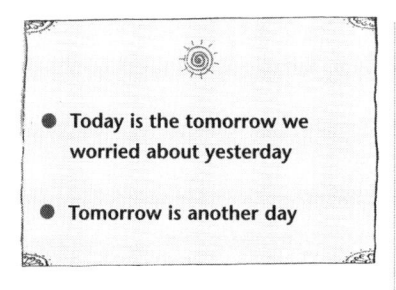

- Today is the tomorrow we worried about yesterday

- Tomorrow is another day

I SEE the nations growing wiser and realizing that the alluring woman of their destinies is nothing but an illusion after all. There will be a time when the world will have no use for armies, hypocritical religions, and degenerate art.

LEO TOLSTOY, 1828–1910

A Miss is as Good as Thousands of Miles

On 7 January 2002, a stadium-sized asteroid named 2001 YB5, big enough to wipe out an entire country, hurtled towards a rendezvous with Earth – but, luckily, we had moved on a mere four hours earlier, and it missed us by just twice the distance of the Moon – a whisker in celestial terms. In the last seventy years or so, at least 22 asteroids are known to have come even closer than this one; in fact, for every object that does hit us, such as the 1908 Siberian asteroid whose impact was 600 times that of Hiroshima, tens of thousands miss, and 100 tonnes' worth are

burned up in our atmosphere daily. Still more fortuitously, so far no object has ever hit a densely populated area. Meanwhile, Apophis, a 20-million-tonne asteroid homing in on us with a 1 in 45,000 chance that it could hit on 13 April 2036, is concentrating minds wonderfully. With the UN now taking the problem seriously, we look set to develop the means not only to locate and track such threats to our survival, but also, using solutions such as a massive spacecraft as a 'gravitational tractor', to divert them.

THE wolf also shall dwell with the lamb, and the leopard shall lie down with the kid; and the calf and the young lion and the fatling together; and a little child shall lead them.

The Bible, Isaiah 9:6

Moore and Moore

In 1965, Gordon Moore, the co-founder of Intel, observed that computing power doubles every 18 months. In other words, it increases exponentially – and this is likely to have remarkable results in the very near future. The story of the Emperor's Chessboard illustrates why the impact of 'Moore's Law' is likely to be so

It's not all stars and tea-leaves. Here are a few other tried and tested techniques for divining the future:

Augury (studying the flights or cries of birds)

Capnomancy (observing patterns in smoke)

Chiromancy (fortune-telling by the hand)

Geloscopy (watching the way somebody, usually a medium, laughs)

Gyromancy (divination by walking in a circle and falling down dizzy)

Haruspication (inspecting the entrails of animals)

Myomancy (observing the movement of mice)

Necromancy (questioning the spirits of the dead about the future)

Oneiromancy (divination by dreams)

Scatoscopy (examining excrement)

Sortilege (casting of lots)

Spodomancy (studying ashes)

dramatic. According to legend, a Chinese emperor once asked a sage to name his reward (possibly for the invention of chess). In an apparently humble request, the sage asked for rice – one grain on the first square of the chessboard, two on the second, four on the third, eight on the fourth, etc. The emperor was happy about this, up until 32 squares, when the sage had accumulated 4 billion grains, or one large field's worth. (This is about where computer power stands now, with around 32 doublings of performance since computers were invented in the Second World War.)

It is as we move into the second half of the chessboard that the leaps from square to square start to become truly awesome; ultimately, the 63 doublings from one grain of rice total 18 million trillion, enough to cover the Earth twice over. Applied to the rate of technological change, it means that we may be accelerating so quickly that we will soon reach a point, 'the Singularity' (the word for the centre of black holes, where the known laws of physics cease to apply), when, because of the evolution of a superintelligence (thanks to the rapid doubling of computer power), the world will be redefined in ways about which it is fruitless even to speculate. However, the Singularity Institute

for Artificial Intelligence in Silicon Valley (www.singinst.org) believes that, by planning for the Singularity, a positive outcome can be secured. It is working towards ensuring that any superhuman intelligence that emerges is steered in the right direction, so that not only will it be benign towards humanity, but it will transform our lives and choices, giving us, for example, the chance to expand our own intelligence, wisdom, love, happiness, creativity, health and lifespan, should we so desire.

Ring out, wild bells, to the wild sky,
The flying cloud, the frosty light:
The year is dying in the night;
Ring out, wild bells, and let him die.

Ring out the old, ring in the new,
Ring, happy bells, across the snow:
The year is going, let him go;
Ring out the false, ring in the
    true …

Ring out old shapes of foul disease;
Ring out the narrowing lust of gold;
Ring out the thousand wars of old,
Ring in the thousand years of peace.
ALFRED, LORD TENNYSON, 'In Memoriam
A. H. H.', 1849

HUMANITY has the stars in its future, and that future is too important to be lost under the burden of juvenile folly and ignorant superstition.
ISAAC ASIMOV

The Lifeboat Foundation (www.lifeboat.com) is looking to the future of humanity. If things go awry on this planet, there is always the possibility of self-sustaining space colonies. Ark I, which is currently being designed, has enough room for 1,000 people, and will at first orbit Earth at a height of 400 km. Later, it and other colonies will move further into space. One advantage of this system over Earth is that, while on this planet different kinds of people have to learn to tolerate each other (with varying degrees of success), space settlements offer the possibility of harmonious groups living together, with 'millions of miles of hard vacuum' separating those who have ideological differences. What a welcome relief from endless conflict!

THE important things of life will not perish. The greatest things will endure – faith, hope, love, and the moral nature of man.
CLAUDE M. FUESS, US historian, 1885–1963

genius

WHAT creates men of genius, or rather, what they create, is not new ideas, it is that idea – inside them – that what has been said has still not been said enough.

EUGÈNE DELACROIX, *Journal*, 1824

A MAN of genius makes no mistakes.

JAMES JOYCE, *Ulysses*, 1922

NEITHER a lofty degree of intelligence nor imagination nor both together go to the making of genius. Love, love, love, that is the soul of genius.

MOZART, 1756–91

WHEN you close your doors, and make darkness within, remember never to say that you are alone, for you are not alone, nay, God is within, and your genius is within. And what need have they of light to see what you are doing.

EPICTETUS

An IQ of 140 or over is considered to be genius. Were the great men of history all geniuses? We have no way of knowing how they would have fared in an intelligence test, but it is safe to imagine that Voltaire, Bach, Beethoven, Kant, Cervantes, Darwin, Mozart, Spinoza, Michelangelo, Leonardo da Vinci, Isaac Newton, Blaise Pascal, Ludwig Wittgenstein, etc., would have achieved high scores. Test your IQ online with www.iqtest.com or go straight to Mensa, the society for people with high IQ, and order your own IQ test form: www.mensa.org.uk/request_form. html.

MEDIOCRITY knows nothing higher than itself, but talent instantly recognizes genius.

SIR ARTHUR CONAN DOYLE, *The Valley of Fear*, 1915

What should I do,
But cocker up my genius, and
    live free
To all delights my fortune calls
    me to?

BEN JONSON, *Volpone*, 1609

WHEN a true genius appears in the world, you may know him by this sign, that the dunces are all in confederacy against him.

JONATHAN SWIFT, *Thoughts on Various Subjects*, 1711

Yehudi Menuhin was a musical prodigy, a genius performing to audiences around the world at the age of 13. Mozart was already composing aged 5. Rimbaud gave up on poetry aged 19, having composed some of the most beautiful we know. As a teenager, Picasso would routinely draw pictures most of us wouldn't manage in a lifetime of trying!

TALENT is like a marksman who hits a target that others cannot reach; genius is like the marksman who hits a target … others cannot even see.

ARTHUR SCHOPENHAUER, German philosopher, 1788–1860

PATIENCE is a necessary ingredient of genius.

BENJAMIN DISRAELI, *Contarini Fleming*, 1832

ANY fool can make things bigger, more complex, and more violent. It takes a touch of genius – and a lot of courage – to move in the opposite direction.

JOHN DRYDEN, 1631–1700, *Epistle X – To Congreve*

*Leonardo da Vinci (1452-1519) is widely regarded as the most talented man who's ever lived. A master of anatomy, mathematics, architecture, botany and music, he was the ultimate Renaissance man. Born illegitimate, this extraordinary polymath gave the world some of its most celebrated paintings (***The Mona Lisa, The Virgin of the Rocks***) and is credited, among many other things, with having invented the parachute, tank, helicopter and bicycle, as well as scissors and the hydraulic pump.*

GENIUS is an African who dreams up snow.

Attributed to VLADIMIR NABOKOV, Russian-American novelist, 1899–1977

HEALTH

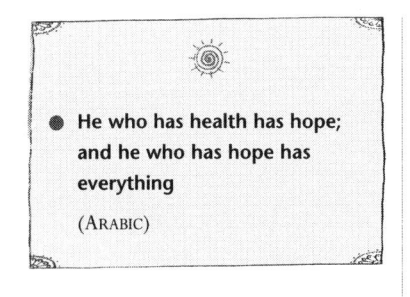

● He who has health has hope; and he who has hope has everything

(ARABIC)

I RECKON being ill as one of the greatest pleasures of life, provided one is not too ill and is not obliged to work until one is better.

SAMUEL BUTLER, *The Way of All Flesh*, 1903

THE twenty-first century offers a bright vision of better health for all. It holds the prospect not merely of longer life, but superior quality of life, with less disability and disease. As the new millennium approaches, the global population has never had a healthier outlook ... unprecedented advances in health during the twentieth century have laid the foundations for further dramatic progress in the years ahead ... there have been steady and sometimes spectacular advances in the control and prevention of other diseases, the development of vaccines and medicines, and countless other medical and scientific innovations.

World Health (Organization) Report, 1998

Émile Coué, 1857–1926, a French pharmacist, developed what he believed to be a revolutionary method, La Méthode Coué, to enable people to improve their health solely through their mind. The method works through positive thinking, focused optimism and auto-suggestion. His catchphrase was 'Every day, in every way, I am getting better and better.' This was to be said over and over several times a day, especially in the morning and evening, until it worked.

THE art of medicine consists of amusing the patient while nature cures the disease.

VOLTAIRE

saints to pray to when ill

Arthritis – St Alphonsus Liguori

Broken bones – St Drogo

Dysentery/haemorrhage – St Lucy of Syracuse

Gallstones – St Benedict

Headaches – St Teresa of Avila

Herpes – St George

Piles/venereal disease – St Fiacre

Rabies/epilepsy – St Guy of Anderlecht

Toothache – St Apollonia

Ulcers – St Charles Borromeo

ONE should pray to have a sound mind in a sound body.

JUVENAL, satirist, c. 55–c. 140

SCIATICA: he cured it by boiling his buttock.

JOHN AUBREY, English biographer, 1626–97, on Sir Jonas Moore

I REFUSE to spend my life worrying about what I eat. There is no pleasure worth forgoing just for an extra three years in the geriatric ward.

JOHN MORTIMER, English lawyer and writer, b. 1923

WE can close the books on infectious diseases.

WILLIAM H. STEWART, Surgeon General of the United States, addressing the US Congress, 1969

———

Data from the UN and WHO in 2007 showed the percentage of people with HIV has levelled off and that the number of new infections has fallen. Global HIV incidence is now estimated to have peaked in the late 1990s at over 3 million new infections per year, and is estimated in 2007 to be 2.5 million.

———

ONE finger in the throat and one in the rectum makes a good diagnostician.

SIR WILLIAM OSLER, Canadian physician, 1849–1919

CONFIDENCE and hope do more good than physic.

GALEN, Greek physician, 129–c. 200

KEEP up the spirits of your patients with the music of the viol and the psaltery, or by forging letters telling of the death of his enemies, or (if he be a cleric) by informing him that he has been made a bishop.

HENRI DE MONDEVILLE, pioneering French surgeon, 1260–1320

In the early 20th century, 65 per cent of Britons died before the age of 60. Today, the figure is just 11 per cent. The life expectancy of newborn children today is 76 years for boys and 81 years for girls. In 1901 boys were expected to live for 45 years and girls for 49 years. During the 20th century the lifespan of the average American rose from 44 years to 77.

AN improper mind is a perpetual feast.

<small>LOGAN PEARSALL SMITH, *Afterthoughts,* 'Life and Human Nature'</small>

I HAVE been accustomed for some time past, to apply leeches to the inflamed testicle, which practice has always been followed with most happy effects.

<small>WILLIAM BUCHAN, *Domestic Medicine,* 1798</small>

The brainchild of Mumbai GP Madan Kataria, who also founded World Laughter Day (the first Sunday in May every year), Laughter (Hasya) Yoga is the funniest way to de-stress and improve your health. Since the first Laughter Club was started in 1995, over 5,000 more groups in 40 countries have enjoyed the tension-releasing sessions in which the chanting of Ho-Ho-Ha-Ha in unison inevitably turns into real laughter. In 2000, Laughter Clubs and others – 10,000 people or more – gathered together in Town Hall Square in Copenhagen to laugh together in a bid to build up a global consciousness of brotherhood and friendship – and made it into The Guinness Book of World Records. *It's the best kind of yoga – and you don't have to bend over backwards to do it.*

A CLOWN is like an aspirin, only he works twice as fast.

<small>GROUCHO MARX, US comedian, 1890–1977</small>

DEVELOPMENT OF VACCINES

Polio (1962)

Measles (1963)

Mumps (1967)

Rubella (1970)

Chicken pox (1974)

Pneumonia (1977)

Meningitis (1978)

Hepatitis B (1981)

Hepatitis A (1992)

Lyme disease (1998)

Rotavirus (1998)

Human papillomavirus (2006)

Humankind

THERE are many wonderful things, and nothing is more wonderful than man.

Sophocles, c. 496–406 BC

[A creature] whose thoughts are not limited by any narrow bounds, either of place or time; who carries his researches into the most distant regions of this globe, and beyond this globe, to the planets and heavenly bodies; looks backward to consider the first origin, at least, the history of the human race; casts his eye forward to see the influence of his actions upon posterity, and the judgements which will be formed of his character a thousand years hence; a creature, who traces causes and effects to a great length and intricacy; extracts general principles from particular appearances; improves upon his discoveries; corrects his mistakes; and makes his very errors profitable.

David Hume, Scottish philosopher, 'Of the Dignity or Meanness of Human Nature', 1741

FOR man, the vast marvel is to be alive. For man, as for flower and beast and bird, the supreme triumph is to be most vividly, most perfectly alive. Whatever the unborn may know, they cannot know the beauty, the marvel of being alive in the flesh. The dead may look after the afterwards. But the magnificent here and now of life in the flesh is ours, and ours alone, and ours only for a time. We ought to dance with rapture that we should be alive and in the flesh, and part of the living, incarnate cosmos.

D. H. Lawrence, *Apocalypse*, 1930

I EXPECT to pass through this world but once; any good thing therefore that I can do, or any kindness that I can show to any fellow-creature, let me do it now; let me not defer or neglect it, for I shall not pass this way again.

Stephen Grellet, Quaker missionary, 1773–1855

Random Acts of Kindness Week is in February, and World Kindness Week every November. Check out the website www.actsofkindness.org, or go to www.join-me.co.uk and join the Karma Army. What goes around, comes around.

IT is one of the most beautiful compensations of this life that no man can sincerely try to help another without helping himself.

RALPH WALDO EMERSON

THE majority of men are subjective towards themselves and objective towards all others, terribly objective sometimes, but the real task is in fact to be objective towards oneself and subjective towards all others.

SØREN KIERKEGAARD, Danish philosopher, 1813–55

OUR virtues and our vices may be traced to the incidents which make the history of our lives, and if these incidents could be divested of every improper tendency, vice would be extirpated from the world.

WILLIAM GODWIN, English journalist, 1756–1836

Is man an ape or an angel? Now I am on the side of the angels.

BENJAMIN DISRAELI

Dr Martin Seligman, the founder of Positive Psychology, has proven through research that it is possible to be happier, regardless of one's circumstances. To that end, the Character Strengths and Virtues *handbook identifies the positive psychological traits of human beings. In a nutshell, they are:*

1 *Wisdom and Knowledge (creativity, curiosity, open-mindedness, love of learning, perspective)*
2 *Courage (bravery, persistence, integrity, vitality)*
3 *Humanity (love, kindness, social intelligence)*
4 *Justice (citizenship, fairness, leadership)*
5 *Temperance (forgiveness and mercy, humility and modesty, prudence, self-regulation)*
6 *Transcendence (appreciation of beauty and excellence, gratitude, hope, humour, spirituality)*

It's hoped that therapists, counsellors and others will use the handbook as a practical tool for change. Find out more about the University of Pennsylvania Positive Psychology Center, and participate in ongoing research into improving the human condition, at www. authentichappiness.sas.upenn.edu.

THERE is surely a piece of divinity in us, something that was before the elements, and owes no homage unto the sun.

SIR THOMAS BROWNE, English philosopher, 1605–82

If you feel that life, however wonderful, could be even better, why not join the Transhumanist movement? The aim is to use technology to improve on the basic human model, thereby eliminating such things as suffering, disease, old age and, eventually, involuntary death. In 1998, the World Transhumanist Association, dedicated to a continuous improvement in the human condition and a strongly optimistic view of future advances to ameliorate the human lot, was set up. If you believe that body modification, cybernetics, nanotechnology and bio-engineering are the way forward, and would like to consciously help humanity to evolve, go to www.transhumanism.org or to the website of the Extropy Institute, www.extropy.org, where you can volunteer to test new technology, possibly allowing for radical human enhancement by the middle of this century.

IN a sense human flesh is made of stardust.

Every atom in the human body, excluding only the primordial hydrogen atoms, was fashioned in stars that formed, grew old and exploded most violently before the Sun and the Earth came into being. The explosions scattered the heavier elements as a fine dust through space. By the time it made the Sun, the primordial gas of the Milky Way was sufficiently enriched with heavier elements for rocky planets like the Earth to form. And from the rocks atoms escaped for eventual incorporation in living things: carbon, nitrogen, oxygen, phosphorus and sulphur for all living tissue; calcium for bones and teeth; sodium and potassium, indispensable for the workings of nerves and brains; the iron colouring blood red … and so on.

NIGEL CALDER, British writer, *The Key to the Universe*, 1977

NO one is born hating another person because of the colour of his skin, or his background, or his religion. People must learn to hate, and if they can learn to hate, they can be taught to love, for love comes more naturally to the human heart than its opposite.

NELSON MANDELA, *Long Walk to Freedom*, 1994

AH, but a man's reach should exceed his grasp, or what's a heaven for?

ROBERT BROWNING, 'Andrea del Sarto', 1855

MAN is naturally good, and only through institutions is he made bad.

JEAN-JACQUES ROUSSEAU, philosopher of the Enlightenment, 1712–78

For Mercy has a human heart
Pity a human face:
And Love, the human form divine,
And Peace, the human dress.

WILLIAM BLAKE, 1757–1827, 'The Divine Image'

CONTRARY to what clergymen and policemen believe, gentleness is biological and aggression is cultural.

STEFAN THEMERSON, writer and publisher, 1910–88

IF the cells and fibres in one human brain were all stretched out end to end, they would certainly reach to the moon and back. Yet the fact that they are not arranged end to end enabled man to go there himself. The astonishing tangle within our heads makes us what we are.

COLIN BLAKEMORE, British academic, Listener, 1976

THE inclination to goodness is imprinted deeply in the nature of man: insomuch, that if it issue not towards men, it will take unto other living creatures.

FRANCIS BACON, 1561–1626

Here men from the Planet Earth
First set foot upon the Moon.
July, 1969 AD
We came in peace for all mankind.

Plaque on the moon

MAN, unlike any other thing organic or inorganic in the universe, grows beyond his work, walks up the stairs of his concepts, emerges ahead of his accomplishments.

JOHN STEINBECK, The Grapes of Wrath, 1939

BUT we were born of risen apes, not fallen angels, and the apes were armed killers besides. And so what shall we wonder at? Our murders and massacres and missiles, and our irreconcilable regiments? Or our treaties whatever they may be worth; our symphonies, however seldom they may be played; our peaceful acres, however frequently they may be converted into battlefields; our dreams, however rarely they may be accomplished. The

miracle of man is not how far he has sunk but how magnificently he has risen. We are known among the stars by our poems, not our corpses.

ROBERT ARDREY, US anthropologist, *African Genesis*, 1961

THE Bible suggests seven Heavenly Virtues for us to strive towards: Faith • Hope • Charity • Fortitude • Justice • Temperance • Prudence

Prudentius (348–c. 413) wrote an epic poem in which he defined the Contrary Virtues:

Humility • Kindness • Abstinence • Chastity • Patience • Liberality • Diligence

And the Catechisms of the medieval Church stipulated the seven Corporal Works of Mercy:

Feed the hungry • Give drink to the thirsty • Give shelter to strangers • Clothe the naked • Visit the sick • Minister to prisoners • Bury the dead

The Golden Rule: 'As ye would that men should do to you, do ye to them likewise' is all very well, but philosopher Karl Popper (1902–94) pointed out that an even better maxim is, 'Do unto others as they would have you do unto them.'

According to US psychologist Abraham Maslow, humans are instinctively driven towards 'self-actualization' – that is, the striving to be the best they possibly can be. According to his famous 'Hierarchy of Needs', a human being cannot get that far unless his basic Physiological, Safety, Love/Belonging and Esteem needs are met. Once these are satisfied, however, he will then be filled with a desire to realize his true potential as a human being. 'What a man can be, he must be,' is how Maslow expresses it.

Happy the man, and happy he alone,
He, who can call to-day his own:
He who, secure within, can say,
To-morrow do thy worst, for I have
    lived to-day.

JOHN DRYDEN, translation of Horace, III, xxix

… the growing good of the world is partly dependent on unhistoric acts; and that things are not so ill with you and me as they might have been, is half owing to the number who lived faithfully a hidden life, and rest in unvisited tombs.

GEORGE ELIOT, *Middlemarch*, 1871–2

Law and Lawyers

THE people should fight for the law as for their city wall.

HERACLITUS

THE good of the people is the chief law.

CICERO, Roman statesman, 106–43 BC

NO freeman is to be taken or imprisoned or disseised [dispossessed] of his free tenement or of his liberties or free customs, or outlawed or exiled or in any way ruined, nor will we go against such a man or send against him save by lawful judgement of his peers or by the law of the land. To no-one will we sell or deny or delay right or justice.

Clause 29 of the Magna Carta, 1215

REASON is the life of the law, nay the common law itself is nothing else but reason ... The law, which is the perfection of reason.

SIR EDWARD COKE, English jurist, 1552–1634

WE hold these truths to be self-evident, that all men are created equal, that they are endowed by their Creator with certain unalienable rights, that among these are life, liberty and the pursuit of happiness.

Preamble to US Declaration of Independence, 1776

THE English constitution has in fact arrived at the point of excellence, in consequence of which all men are restored to those natural rights of which in nearly all monarchies they are deprived. These rights are: total liberty of person and property; freedom of the press; the right of trial in all criminal cases by an independent jury; the right of being tried only according to the strict letter of the law; and the right of each man to profess any religion he desires.

VOLTAIRE, Dictionnaire Philosophique, 1764

PRESSURE of opinion a hundred years ago brought about the emancipation of the slaves. It is now for man to insist upon the same freedom for his mind as he has won for his body.

PETER BENENSON, lawyer, article in the *Observer*, 28 May 1961, launching Appeal for Amnesty, later known as Amnesty International

JUDGE: But, Mr Smith, your client is no doubt aware of *vigilantibus, et non dormientibus, jura subveniunt?*

LAWYER: Indeed, my lord, in Barnsley they talk of little else.

Exchange in a court case involving a Yorkshire miner

Let me not be understood as saying that there are no bad laws, nor that grievances may not arise for the redress of which no legal provisions have been made. I mean to say no such thing. But I do mean to say that although bad laws, if they exist, should be repealed as soon as possible, still, while they continue in force, for the sake of example they should be religiously observed.

ABRAHAM LINCOLN

cannot remember the ten commandments? then try this:

I) Have thou no other gods but me,

II) And to no image bow thy knee.

III) Take not the name of God in vain:

IV) The Sabbath day do not profane.

V) Honour thy father and mother too;

VI) And see that thou no murder do.

VII) Abstain from words and deeds unclean;

VIII) Nor steal, though thou art poor and mean.

IX) Bear not false witness, shun that blot;

X) What is thy neighbor's covet not.

ANON, 1731, in *The Writer's Almanac*

IT may be true that the law cannot make a man love me, but it can keep him from lynching me, and I think that's pretty important.

MARTIN LUTHER KING

LiFe

THERE is no wealth but life.

JOHN RUSKIN

THERE'S night and day, brother, both sweet things; sun, moon, and stars, brother, all sweet things; there's likewise a wind on the heath. Life is very sweet, brother; who would wish to die?

GEORGE BORROW, English author, *Lavengro*, 1851

I slept and dreamed that life
    was joy,
I awoke and saw that life was duty,
I acted, and behold duty was joy.

RABINDRANATH TAGORE, Winner of the Nobel Prize for Literature, 1861–1941

IF you feel that life is one of God's jokes, there is still no reason why we shouldn't make it a *good* joke.

KENNETH WILLIAMS, British actor, 1926–88

THE mere sense of living is joy enough.

EMILY DICKINSON, US poet, 1830–86

22 December 1912

PALAEONTOLOGY has its comfortable words too. I have revelled in my littleness and irresponsibility. It has relieved me of the harassing desire to live, I feel content to live dangerously, indifferent to my fate; I have discovered I am a fly, that we are all flies, that nothing matters. It's a great load off my life, for I don't mind being such a micro-organism – to me the honour is sufficient of belonging to the universe – such a great universe, so grand a scheme of things. Not even Death can rob me of that honour. For nothing can alter the fact that I have lived; I have been I, if for ever so short a time.

W. N. P. BARBELLION, *Journal of a Disappointed Man*, 1919

The Bright Field

I have seen the sun break through
to illuminate a small field
for a while, and gone my way
and forgotten it. But that was
    the pearl
of great price, the one field that had
treasure in it. I realize now
that I must give all that I have
to possess it. Life is not hurrying

on to a receding future, nor
    hankering after
an imagined past. It is the turning
aside like Moses to the miracle
of the lit bush, to a brightness
that seemed as transitory as
    your youth
once, but is the eternity that
    awaits you.

R. S. THOMAS, Welsh poet, 1913–2000

… I DELIGHT in many Dutch paintings, which lofty-minded people despise. I find a source of delicious sympathy in these faithful pictures of a monotonous homely existence, which has been the fate of so many more among my fellow-mortals than a life of pomp or of absolute indigence, of tragic suffering or of world-stirring actions. I turn, without shrinking, from cloud-borne angels, from prophets, sibyls, and heroic warriors, to an old woman bending over her flower-pot, or eating her solitary dinner, while the noonday light, softened perhaps by a screen of leaves, falls on her mob-cap, and just touches the rim of her spinning-wheel, and her stone jug, and all those cheap common things which are the precious necessaries of life to her …

GEORGE ELIOT, *Adam Bede*, 1859

O EXCELLENT! I love long life better than figs.

WILLIAM SHAKESPEARE, *Antony and Cleopatra*, 1606

LIFE'S …

… a pure flame, and we live by an invisible Sun within us.
SIR THOMAS BROWNE

… the art of drawing sufficient conclusions from insufficient premises.
SAMUEL BUTLER

… colour and warmth and light
And a striving evermore for these …
JULIAN GRENFELL, 1888–1915, 'Into Battle'

Thanks a Lot

Appreciate your life. Experiments by positive psychologists have shown that the benefits of actually sitting down and counting your blessings are substantial. Getting into the daily habit – even for a couple of minutes – of being consciously grateful for what you have makes you healthier, kinder, more successful, more appreciative, more optimistic – happier, in a word. Try it for a month and feel the difference!

Question not, but live and labour
Till yon goal be won,
Helping every feeble neighbour,
Seeking help from none;
Life is mostly froth and bubble,
Two things stand like stone
Kindness in another's trouble
Courage in your own.

ADAM LINDSAY GORDON, Australian writer, 1833–70; this stanza is inscribed on his headstone

PLEASURE is the beginning and the goal of a happy life.

EPICURUS, Greek philosopher, 341–270 BC

Can't have too much of a good thing?

At birth, prehistoric man had a life expectancy of 18 years; in the developed world, by the beginning of the twentieth century, you could expect to live into your high 40s; by the end of the century, into your mid- to late 70s. And the figure keeps rising; some believe that, thanks to advances in medical technology, the first human to live a thousand years has already been born. Others believe that living for ever is achievable. If you wouldn't say no to an unlimited lifespan, go to www.imminst.org, the website of the Immortality Institute, an organization dedicated to the latest technologies and philosophies in the mission to 'conquer the blight of involuntary death'.

Is it so small a thing to have enjoyed the sun,
To have lived light in the spring,
To have loved,
To have thought,
To have done?

MATTHEW ARNOLD, 'The Hymn of Empedocles', 1852

Love

THERE is only one happiness in life, to love and be loved.

GEORGE SAND, French author, 1804–76

MAN has bought brains, but all the millions in the world have failed to buy love. Man has subdued bodies, but all the power on earth has been unable to subdue love. Man has conquered whole nations, but all his armies could not conquer love. Man has chained and fettered the spirit, but he has been utterly helpless before love. High on a throne, with all the splendor and pomp his gold can command, man is yet poor and desolate, if love passes him by. And if it stays, the poorest hovel is radiant with warmth, with life and color. Thus love has the magic power to make of a beggar a king.

EMMA GOLDMAN, *Anarchism and Other Essays*, 'Marriage and Love', 1911

HE who wants to do good knocks at the gate; he who loves finds the door open.

RABINDRANATH TAGORE, *Stray Birds*, 1916

I CAN neither Eat or Sleep for thinking of You my dearest love, I never touch even pudding You know the reason. No I would Starve sooner … last night I did nothing but dream of You altho' woke 20 times in the Night. In one of my dreams I thought I was at a large Table You was not present, Sitting between a Princess who I detest and another. They both tried to Seduce Me and the first wanted to take those liberties with Me which no Woman in this World but Yourself ever did. The consequence was I knocked her down and in the moment of bustle You came in and taking Me in Your embrace whispered I love nothing but You My Nelson. I kissed You fervently And we enjoy'd the height of love … Just 138 Miles distant, and I trust to find You like myself. For no love is like Mine towards You.

From a letter to Lady Hamilton from LORD NELSON, 29 January–2 February 1800

The Styles of Love

Those four letters, L-O-V-E, contain multitudes. The Ancient Greeks used three different words in place of our catch-all one: **Agape**, *the love that people have for God, duty or family;* **Philia**, *which denotes the love we feel for friends; and* **Eros**, *love for a lover. More recently, sociology professor John Alan Lee's Theory of Love Styles identified six basic 'colours' of love between lovers. They are:*

- *Eros*   *(passionate love)*
- *Ludus*   *(love as conquest, a game)*
- *Storge*   *(love that begins with friendship; between soulmates)*
- *Pragma* *(love from the head, not the heart)*
- *Mania*   *(volatile, obsessional, often teenage love)*
- *Agape*   *(selfless, altruistic, spiritual love)*

Opposites may attract, but relationships that are based on similar love styles last longer.

THE simple act of falling in love is as beneficial as it is astonishing.

ROBERT LOUIS STEVENSON

I SHALL show you a love philtre compounded without drug or herb or witches' spell. It is this: if you wish to be loved, love.

HECATO, Stoic philosopher, c. 100 BC

How do I love thee? Let me count
    the ways.
I Love thee to the depth and
    breadth and height
My soul can reach, when feeling
    out of sight
For the ends of Being and
    ideal Grace.
I love thee to the level of everyday's
Most quiet need, by sun and
    candlelight.
I love thee freely, as men strive
    for Right;
I love thee purely, as they turn from
    Praise.
I love thee with a passion put to use
In my old griefs, and with my
    childhood's faith.
I love thee with a love I seemed
    to lose
With my lost saints, – I love thee
    with the breath,
Smiles, tears, of all my life! – and,
    if God choose,
I shall but love thee better
    after death.

ELIZABETH BARRETT BROWNING, *Sonnets from the Portuguese*, 1850

From St Paul's Letter to the Corinthians

LUVE is patientfu; luve is couthie an kind; luve is nane jailous; nane sprosie; nane bowdent wi pride; nane mislaired; nane hame-drauchtit; nane toustie. Luve keeps nae nickstick o the wrangs it drees; finds nae pleisur i the ill wark o ithers; is ey liftit uyp whan truith dings lies; kens ey tae keep a caum souch; is ey sweired tae misdout; ey howps the best; ey bides the warst …

In smaa: there is three things bides for ey: faith, howp, luve. But the grytest o the three is luve.

From *The New Testament in Scots*, translated by William Laughton Lorimer, 1983

Love seeketh not itself to please,
Nor for itself hath any care;
But for another gives its ease,
And builds a Heaven in Hell's
    despair.

WILLIAM BLAKE, 'The Clod and the Pebble', 1794

IF I can't love Hitler, I can't love at all.

The Revd A. J. MUSTE, US pacifist, at a Quaker meeting, 1940

ACCORDING TO PROVERBIAL WISDOM FROM ALL AROUND THE WORLD, LOVE …

… makes the world go round; will find a way; teaches even donkeys to dance; sees roses without thorns; pays no attention to dignity; makes the impossible possible; rules without rules; makes labour light; laughs at locksmiths; can be neither bought nor sold; rules his kingdom without a sword; understands all languages; conquers all; is as strong as death.

O western wind, when wilt
    thou blow
That the small rain down can rain?
Christ, that my love were in
    my arms
And I in my bed again!

ANON, 16th century

LOVE, and do what you will.

ST AUGUSTINE

LOVE is a fruit in season at all times, and within reach of every hand.

MOTHER THERESA, Catholic missionary, 1910–97

Marriage

... FOR better, for worse, for richer, for poorer, in sickness and in health, to love, cherish, and obey, till death us do part, according to God's holy law.

Marriage vow, Council of the Church of England

Who said Iranian women were oppressed? The daily paper Etemad *reported that a wife in Iran has managed to have her husband condemned for his avarice in a court of law. The stingy husband was ordered to buy 124,000 red roses for his wife. The court seized the man's apartment until all the roses appeared.*

BUT from the beginning of creation, God made them male and female. Therefore a man shall leave his father and mother and hold fast to his wife, and they shall become one flesh. So they are no longer two but one flesh.

The Bible, Mark 10:6

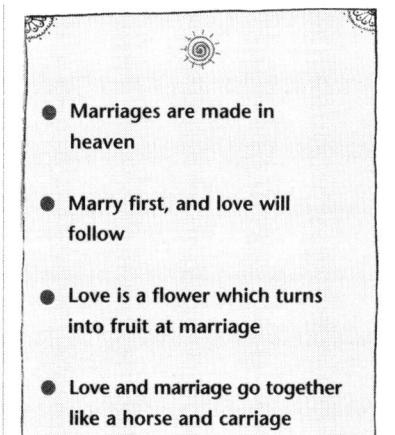

- Marriages are made in heaven

- Marry first, and love will follow

- Love is a flower which turns into fruit at marriage

- Love and marriage go together like a horse and carriage

IT is better to marry than to burn.

The Bible, I Corinthians 7: 8–9

The joys of marriage are the heaven
   on earth,
Life's paradise, great princess, the
   soul's quiet,
Sinews of concord, earthly
   immortality,
Eternity of pleasures ...

JOHN FORD, 1586–1639,
The Broken Heart

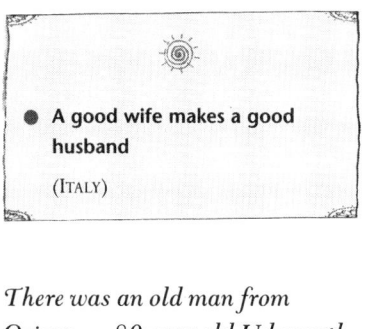

● **A good wife makes a good husband**

(ITALY)

There was an old man from Orissa … 80-year-old Udaynath Dakshiniray, from India, has had 90 wives and 29 children. All his 90 wives were from impoverished families and, before tying the knot, he presented each one with at least five acres of land. The **Asian Age** *reports that when asked why he had married so often, Dakshiniray said he was on a social mission to help women overcome social stigma and harassment. He had started out in life with over 400 acres of land and others weren't as fortunate as him. Udaynath Dakshiniray intends to carry on marrying. In fact, he claims to have recently received nine offers of marriage from abroad, from the US, Japan, Hungary and Germany. Serial monogamy as social service – could it catch on?*

… in what stupid age or nation
Was marriage ever out of fashion?

SAMUEL BUTLER, 1835–1902, 'Hudibras'

It must be love. The **Harian Metro** *newspaper in Malaysia recently reported that a 33-year-old man from the north of the country has married a 104-year-old woman. It is the man's first marriage and the bride's 21st. Muhamad, an ex-army serviceman, declared that he had found peace and a strong sense of belonging after meeting Wook Kundor. The groom went on to say that he couldn't be accused of going after his wife's money as she had none.*

THERE is no more lovely, friendly and charming relationship, communion or company than a good marriage.

MARTIN LUTHER, 1483–1546

Marriage is good for you. According to Professor Andrew Oswald, of Warwick University, 'the singleton life is seriously bad for your health and can be almost as bad as smoking,' while the wedded life boosts the immune system. If that's a bit too vague, research presented to the American Psychosomatic Society shows that, if you're happily married, cuts and grazes are likely to heal more quickly. Researchers monitored 42 couples and found that their (medically induced) minor wounds healed

almost twice as fast among those happily married than among those less so. But, in an extraordinary testimony to the power of wedlock, the research concluded that even those living in unhappy marriages still have one up on singletons and cohabitees, as they are less likely to develop arthritis, stomach ulcers, back problems, diabetes and certain cancers. Furthermore, married people are far less likely to die during surgery in hospital. Marriage – in sickness, and (but much more likely) … in health.

MARRIAGE is the result of the longing for the deep, deep peace of the double bed after the hurly-burly of the chaise-longue.

MRS PATRICK CAMPBELL, 1865–1940

Sir Temulji Bhicaji Nariman and Lady Nariman, from India, and Lazarus Rowe and Molly Webber, from the USA, share the world record for the longest marriage: 86 years. According to records, the oldest couple ever to wed were François Fernandez, aged 96, and Madeleine Francineau, aged 94, in 2002.

MAN'S best possession is a sympathetic wife.

EURIPIDES, 480–406 BC, Antigone

To My Dear and Loving Husband

If ever two were one, then
    surely we.
If ever man were loved by wife,
    then thee;
If ever wife was happy in a man,
Compare with me, ye women, if
    you can.
I prize thy love more than whole
    mines of gold,
Or all the riches that the East doth
    hold.
My love is such that rivers cannot
    quench,
Nor aught but love from thee give
    recompense.
Thy love is such I can no way
    repay;
The heavens reward thee manifold,
    I pray.
Then while we live, in love let's so
    persever,
That when we live no more we may
    live ever.

ANNE BRADSTREET, 1612–72

- A man without a wife is but half a man

- A cheerful wife is the joy of life

- A good wife and health is a man's best wealth

Men

EACH man is the smith of his own fortune.

APPIUS CLAUDIUS CAECUS, builder of the Appian Way, c. 340–273 BC

ONE machine can do the work of fifty ordinary men. No machine can do the work of one extraordinary man.

ELBERT HUBBARD, US writer and philosopher, 1856–1915

MEN are like wine. Some turn to vinegar, but the best improve with age.

POPE JOHN XXIII (The Good Pope), 1881–1963

In 1974, Janet Saltzman Chafetz, a sociology professor at the University of Houston, pinpointed the following Seven Areas of Masculinity:
1. *Physical – virile, athletic, strong, brave. Unconcerned about appearance and ageing*
2. *Functional – breadwinner, provider for family as much as mate*
3. *Sexual – sexually aggressive, experienced. Single status acceptable*
4. *Emotional – unemotional, stoic, the proverb says* **Boys don't cry**
5. *Intellectual – logical, intellectual, rational, objective, practical*
6. *Interpersonal – leader, dominating; disciplinarian; independent, free, individualistic; demanding*
7. *Other personal characteristics – success-oriented, ambitious, aggressive, proud, egotistical; moral, trustworthy; decisive, competitive, uninhibited, adventurous*

MEN build bridges and throw railroads across deserts, and yet they contend successfully that the job of sewing on a button is beyond them. Accordingly, they don't have to sew buttons.

HEYWOOD BROUN, US journalist, 'Seeing Things at Night', 1921

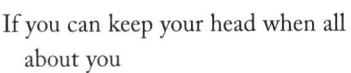

If

If you can keep your head when all
  about you
Are losing theirs and blaming it
  on you,
If you trust yourself when all men
  doubt you
But make allowance for their
  doubting too,
If you can wait and not be tired
  by waiting,
Or being lied about, don't deal in lies,
Or being hated, don't give way to
  hating,
And yet don't look too good, nor
  talk too wise:

If you can dream – and not make
  dreams your master,
If you can think – and not make
  thoughts your aim;
If you can meet with Triumph and
  Disaster
And treat those two impostors just
  the same;
If you can bear to hear the truth
  you've spoken
Twisted by knaves to be a trap for
  fools,
Or watch the things you gave your
  life to, broken,
And stoop and build 'em up with
  worn-out tools:

If you can make one heap of all
  your winnings
And risk it on one turn of pitch-
  and-toss,
And lose, and start again at your
  beginnings
And never breathe a word about
  your loss;
If you can force your heart and
  nerve and sinew
To serve your turn long after they
  are gone,
And so hold on when there is
  nothing in you
Except the Will which says to
  them: 'Hold on!'

If you can talk with crowds and
  keep your virtue,
Or walk with Kings – nor lose the
  common touch,
If neither foes nor loving friends
  can hurt you;
If all men count with you, but none
  too much,
If you can fill the unforgiving
  minute
With sixty seconds' worth of
  distance run,
Yours is the Earth and everything
  that's in it,
And – which is more – you'll be a
  Man, my son!

RUDYARD KIPLING, 1865–1936

What's Left for Men?

LOOK upon the achievements
of our fathers, O ye men, and
rejoice! It was men – yes, my
friends, MEN – who built such
memorable monuments as the

Step-Pyramid of King Djoser, the Baths of Caracalla, the Woolworth Building and the first Wal-Mart. MEN composed Pachelbel's Canon and all of Beethoven's string quartets. It was a MAN who penned the immortal lines, 'Hail to thee blithe spirit, Bird thou never wert!' MEN wrote the popular songs 'Massa's in de Cold, Cold Ground' and 'Yes, We Have No Bananas'. A MAN invented the lightning rod, bifocals and the Franklin stove. The Battle of Hastings was fought primarily by MEN ... MEN have discovered and named many fine places, like Hispaniola and the Bay of Fundy. We're more proficient than women at arm-wrestling, fresco-painting, ice hockey and particle physics. We make better cabinets, sun decks and booster rockets. We know how to read a map. In the movies, most Westerns and martial arts films would be poorer without our presence ... So let's renew our male mission and wear our antlers high on our heads. Let's stand up straight, aim well, and exercise our prerogative to leave the seat up. After all, we're MEN, and we hold a proud heritage in our hands.

RICK BAYAN, at the Cynic's Sanctuary, www.i-cynic.com, January 1999

ADVERSITY introduces a man to himself.

VISCOUNT HALIFAX, English political writer and statesman, 1633–9

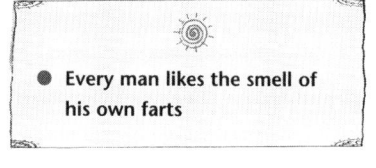

● **Every man likes the smell of his own farts**

The ManKind Project

For those who have lost or are still looking for their masculinity, the ManKind Project promotes 'accountability and integrity; connection to feelings; leadership; fatherhood; and the blessing of elders'. Join more than 40,000 men worldwide who have participated in its primary training, the New Warrior Training Adventure, at www.mkp.org.

WHAT a piece of work is a man! How noble in reason! how infinite in faculty! in form, how moving, how express and admirable! in action how like an angel! in apprehension how like a god! the beauty of the world! the paragon of animals!

WILLIAM SHAKESPEARE, *Hamlet*

A TABLE, a chair, a bowl of fruit and a violin; what else does a man need to be happy?

ALBERT EINSTEIN

MIDDLE AGE

YOU don't understand life any better at forty than twenty, but you know it and you admit it.

JULES RENARD, 1864–1910

AT twenty years of age, the will reigns, at thirty, the wit; at forty, the judgement.

BENJAMIN FRANKLIN, *Poor Richard's Almanac*, 1758

Defying age and science, record-breaking numbers of 40-plus women in the UK are giving birth. Figures out of the Office for National Statistics show 1,091 women gave birth over the age of 45 in 2005 compared to just 540 in 1995.

Life begins at 50. The number of new British businesses set up by middle-aged people has grown by 55 per cent in recent years.

I WANT to retire at 50. I want to play cricket in the summer and geriatric football in the winter, and sing in the choir.

NEIL KINNOCK, b. 1942, *The Times*, 28 July 1980

THIRTY-FIVE is a very attractive age. London society is full of women of the very highest birth who have, of their own free choice, remained thirty-five for years.

OSCAR WILDE, *The Importance of Being Earnest*, 1895

FORTY is the old age of youth, fifty is the youth of old age.

VICTOR HUGO, 1802–85

WOMEN are most fascinating between the ages of thirty-five and forty, after they have won a few races and know how to pace themselves. Since few women ever pass forty, maximum fascination can continue indefinitely.

Attributed to CHRISTIAN DIOR, 1905–57

Monarchy

WHAT a family is without a steward, a ship without a pilot, a flock without a shepherd, a body without a head, the same, I think, is a kingdom without the health and safety of a good monarch.

ELIZABETH I, 1533–1603

THE best reason why Monarchy is a strong government is, that it is an intelligible government. The mass of mankind understand it, and they hardly anywhere in the world understand any other.

WALTER BAGEHOT, English essayist, 1825–77

I SHALL be an autocrat, that's my trade; and the good Lord will forgive me, that's his.

CATHERINE THE GREAT of Russia, 1729–96

RUSSIA under Nicholas II, with all the survivals of feudalism, had opposition political parties, independent trade unions and newspapers, a rather radical parliament and a modern legal system. Its agriculture was on the level of the USA, with industry rapidly approaching the West European level. In the USSR there was total tyranny, no political liberties and practically no human rights. Its economy was not viable; agriculture was destroyed. The terror against the population reached a scope unprecedented in history. No wonder many Russians look back at Tsarist Russia as a paradise lost.

OLEG GORDIEVSKY, KGB officer who defected to the British, letter to the *Independent*, July 1998

THAT the king can do no wrong, is a necessary and fundamental principle of the English constitution.

SIR WILLIAM BLACKSTONE, English jurist, 1723–80

YOU are a member of the British royal family. We are never tired, and we all love hospitals.

QUEEN MARY, wife of George V, correcting a junior royal

MY people and I have come to an agreement which satisfies us both. They are to say what they please, and I am to do what I please.

FREDERICK THE GREAT of Prussia, 1712–86

THAT man is deceived who thinks it slavery to live under an excellent prince. Never does liberty appear in a more gracious form than under a pious king.

CLAUDIAN, 4th-century court poet to Roman emperors

I'D like to be a queen in people's hearts.

DIANA, PRINCESS OF WALES, 1961–97

THE British love their Queen, their Queen Mother, Prince Charles, and the comforting security of their hereditary constitutional monarchy, an institution of which the characters are beyond the manipulation of man, an institution guaranteeing continuity, overriding the dissensions of politics. The best governments are constitutional monarchies, and we may yet see some restored in eastern Europe.

LORD MENUHIN, Daily Telegraph, 1998

I SHALL take up dominoes again in my spare time.

TSAR NICHOLAS II, after his abdication in March 1917, four months before his execution

PARLIAMENTS and Ministers pass, but she [Queen Victoria] abides in lifelong duty, and she is to them as the oak in the forest is to the annual harvest in the field.

WILLIAM GLADSTONE, British prime minister, 1809–98

Not all the water in the rough rude sea
Can wash the balm off from an anointed king;

WILLIAM SHAKESPEARE, Richard II

I CANNOT lead you into battle, I do not give you laws or administer justice but I can do something else, I can give you my heart and my devotion to these old islands and to all the peoples of our brotherhood of nations.

QUEEN ELIZABETH II, first televised Christmas address, 1957

THOSE who imagine that a politician would make a better figurehead than a hereditary monarch might perhaps make the acquaintance of more politicians.

BARONESS THATCHER, British prime minister, 1995

MONTHS

EVERY man should be born again on the first day of **January**. Start with a fresh page. Take up one hole more in the buckle if necessary, or let down one, according to circumstances; but on the first of January let every man gird himself once more, with his face to the front, and take no interest in the things that were and are past.

HENRY WARD BEECHER, US abolitionist, 1813–87

In tangled wreath, in clustered
  gleaming stars,
In floating, curling sprays,
The golden flower comes shining
  through the woods
These **February** days …

CONSTANCE FENIMORE WOOLSON, 1840–94, 'Yellow Jessamine'

March is the month of expectation –

EMILY DICKINSON, 'XLVIII'

Oh, to be in England
Now that **April**'s there,
And whoever wakes in England
Sees, some morning, unaware,
That the lowest boughs and the
  brushwood sheaf
Round the elm-tree bole are in tiny
  leaf,
While the chaffinch sings on the
  orchard bough
In England – now!

ROBERT BROWNING, 'Home-Thoughts, from Abroad', 1845

OH, what will this beloved month bring?

KATHARINE MANSFIELD, New Zealand author, diary, 1 **May** 1922

The Romans tended to wed in the month of **June**, *which was named after Jupiter's wife Juno, the goddess of marriage, and the tradition has held strong ever since. According to the old rhyme:*

Married in the month of roses – **June**,
Life will be one long honeymoon.

*The first of **July** is International Joke Day. In 2002, Dr Richard Wiseman undertook the largest study of humour ever, in an experiment for LaughLab. Two million people voted for the world's funniest joke:*

'Two hunters are out in the woods when one of them collapses. He doesn't seem to be breathing and his eyes are glazed.

'The other guy whips out his phone and calls the emergency services. He gasps: "My friend is dead! What can I do?" The operator says: "Calm down, I can help. First, let's make sure he's dead."

'There is a silence, then a shot is heard. Back on the phone, the guy says: "OK, now what?"'

August! August! If thou starvest, Fret thou not: here comes the harvest.

ADAM FERGUSON, Scottish writer, 1723–1816

HAPPY we who can bask in this warm **September** sun, which illumines all creatures, as well when they rest as when they toil, not without a feeling of gratitude.

HENRY DAVID THOREAU, *A Week on the Concord and Merrimack Rivers*, 1849

ALL things on earth point home in old **October**: sailors to sea, travellers to walls and fences, hunters to field and hollow and the long voice of the hounds, the lover to the love he has forsaken.

THOMAS WOLFE, US novelist, 1908–38

Than these **November** skies
Is no sky lovelier. The clouds
   are deep;
Into their grey the subtle spies
Of colour creep,
Changing their high austerity
   to delight,
Till ev'n the leaden interfolds are
   bright.

JOHN FREEMAN, English poet, 1880–1929, 'November Skies'

'We are nearer to Spring
Than we were in September,'
I heard a bird sing
In the dark of **December**.

OLIVER HERFORD, US writer, 1863–1935, 'I Heard a Bird Sing'

MUSIC

MUSIC is Love in search of a word.

SIDNEY LANIER, 'The Symphony', 1875

———•———

In early 2008, The Beatles' song 'Across the Universe' was broadcast in space by NASA towards the star Polari and became the first music sent into orbit. As well as aiming to connect with aliens, the purpose was to mark NASA's fiftieth anniversary.

———•———

THE exercise of singing is delightful to nature and good to preserve the health of Man.

WILLIAM BYRD, *Psalmes, Sonets and Songs*, 1588

IF the king loves music, there is little wrong in the land.

MENG-TZU, Chinese sage, c. 371–c. 289 BC

———•———

The term 'Mozart effect' was first used to depict a supposed increase in brain activity and development that occurs when young children hear Mozart. It has entered common usage to describe the beneficial effects of music on all ages, from education to relaxation. Practitioners of music therapy believe, in fact, that music helps people with sensory and learning difficulties, neurological disabilities and/or mental health problems. It can be effective, it is further believed, in addressing behavioural and emotional issues, by focusing the body on motor functions, awareness, expression and memory mechanisms. Studies at the American Association for the Advancement of Science, at Brown University, certainly back the belief that music can help construct emotional and intellectual abilities and reinforce children's academic skills.

———•———

The West-Eastern Divan was created by Daniel Barenboim and the late Edward Said. It brings together musicians from Israel, Palestine and various Arab states.

It uses music as enjoyment and fulfilment, but also as a way to bridge gaps between cultures and peoples, sharing knowledge and group work. In a similar way and, in an effort to ease tense relations with a country identified by George W. Bush as belonging to the Axis of Evil, America's oldest orchestra, the New York Philharmonic, stayed two days in North Korea, playing to packed audiences and standing ovations. Among the pieces they played were Dvořák's 'New World' Symphony and Gershwin's 'American in Paris'.

MY idea is that there is music in the air, music all around us, the world is full of it and you simply take as much as you require.

Sir Edward Elgar, 1857–1934

MUSIC is a higher revelation than all wisdom and philosophy.

Ludwig van Beethoven

THERE is no feeling, except the extremes of fear and grief, that does not find relief in music.

George Eliot

THERE is nothing more futile than theorizing about music. No doubt there are laws, mathematically strict laws, but these laws are not music; they are only its conditions. The essence of music is revelation.

Heinrich Heine, *Letters on the French Stage*, 1837

'A Very Silent Night' hit New Zealand's music stores shortly before Christmas 2007 and became a bestseller. The song, aimed solely at dogs and completely inaudible to human beings, was sold for charity.

TOP OPTIMISTIC SONGS!

'I Will Survive'

'Reasons To Be Cheerful, Part III'

'All You Need Is Love'

'Don't Worry, Be Happy'

'Singin' In The Rain'

'Keep On The Sunny Side'

'Imagine'

'You'll Never Walk Alone'

'Somewhere Over The Rainbow

'On The Sunny Side Of The Street'

WITHOUT music, life would be a mistake.

Friedrich Nietzsche

Newspapers and other media

I BELIEVE it has been said that one copy of *The Times* contains more useful information than the whole of the historical works of Thucydides.

RICHARD COBDEN, 1804–65

LET me make the newspapers, and I care not what is preached in the pulpit or what is enacted in Congress.

WENDELL PHILLIPS, US abolitionist and orator, 1811–62

I THINK it's fair to say that personal computers have become the most empowering tool we've ever created. They're tools of communication, they're tools of creativity, and they can be shaped by their user.

BILL GATES, b.1955

THE BBC World Service is perhaps Britain's greatest gift to the world this century.

KOFI ANNAN, UN Secretary-General, 1999

THE printing press is the greatest weapon in the armoury of the modern commander.

COLONEL T. E. LAWRENCE 'of Arabia', 1888–1935

IT'S not that the world has got much worse, just that the news coverage has got so much better.

Attributed to G. K. CHESTERTON

HERE is the living disproof of the old adage that nothing is as dead as yesterday's newspaper … This is what really happened, reported by a free press to a free people. It is the raw material of history; it is the story of our own times.

HENRY STEELE COMMAGER, American historian, 1951

HOW beautiful upon the mountains are the feet of him that bringeth good tidings.

The Bible, Isaiah 52:7

NEWSPAPERS are to the body politic what arteries are to the human body, their function being to carry blood and sustenance and repair to every part of the body.

Henry Ward Beecher

IN these times we fight for ideas, and newspapers are our fortresses.

Heinrich Heine, 1797–1856

FOUR hostile newspapers were more to be feared than a thousand bayonets.

Napoleon, 1769–1821

WE may be scum, but at least we're la crème de la scum.

Member of the 'ratpack' of reporters assigned to cover the British royal family

MOST of us probably feel we couldn't be free without newspapers, and that is the real reason we want the newspapers to be free.

Edward Murrow, US broadcast journalist, 1958

If you're fed up with the veritable torrent of depressing news pouring out from various media outlets, then log on to www.positivenews.org.uk, where you can subscribe to the newspaper that reports on 'the people, events and influences that are helping to create a more positive future for the world and its people'.

THE pen is mightier than the sword.

Edward Bulwer-Lytton, English writer and politician, 1803–73

WERE it left to me to decide whether we should have a government without newspapers, or newspapers without a government, I should not hesitate a moment to prefer the latter.

Thomas Jefferson, 1743–1826

Every time a newspaper dies, even a bad one, the country moves a little closer to authoritarianism; when a great one goes, like the *New York Herald Tribune*, history itself is denied a devoted witness.

Richard Kluger, Pulitzer Prize winner

THERE is so much media now with the Internet and people, and it's so easy and so cheap to start a newspaper or start a magazine, there's just millions of voices and people want to be heard.

Rupert Murdoch, media tycoon, b. 1931

OLD AGE

AS I grow older, I constantly learn more.

SOLON, Athenian statesman, c. 640–c. 559 BC

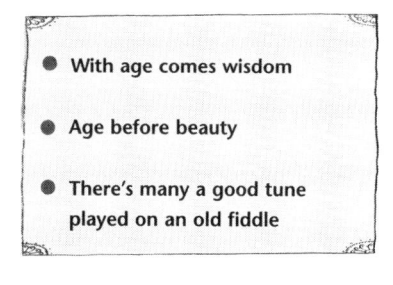

- With age comes wisdom

- Age before beauty

- There's many a good tune played on an old fiddle

Strength and beauty are the
    blessings of youth;
Temperance, however, is the flower
    of old age.

DEMOCRITUS, c. 460–c. 370 BC

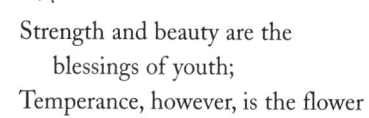

We are apparently not necessarily our calendar or birth age, but are all ageing in different ways. Some of us, in fact, may not be that old at all! You might be eighty years old and in fact be sixty-five biologically. To find out how to test your real age, go to www.realage.com.

WELL, there's no help for it. Ageing seems to be the only available way to live a long time.

DANIEL-FRANÇOIS-ESPRIT AUBER, 1782–1871

Paris Solidaire is an innovative concept taking root in Paris. It started with the observation that many old people in need of care and help live in large flats in which they feel lonely. Paris Solidaire is an association which vets young students looking for a place to stay in the French capital. It then pairs young people with old people and signs an agreement that exchanges a spare room for help and company: www.leparisolidaire.fr.

TO me old age is always fifteen years older than I am.

BERNARD MANNES BARUCH, *Newsweek*, 29 August 1955

A MAN's only as old as the woman he feels.

GROUCHO MARX

Britain's first playground especially designed for old people has opened near Manchester. The playground is in Dam Head Park, Blackley, and was set up by local residents. It has old-age-friendly equipment for taking exercise as well as play features. It is accessible for those in wheelchairs. You're never too old to fight over who goes down the slide first.

I do not think seventy years is the
time of a man or woman,
Nor that seventy millions of years is
the time of a man or woman,
Nor that years will ever stop the
existence of me, or any one else.

WALT WHITMAN, 'Who Learns My Lesson
Complete?', 1855

Certain ancient peoples are almost legendary in their longevity. Among the Abkhasia, a people who live in the Caucasus, it is claimed that elders regularly live up to 150 years. It is certainly true that people remain remarkably agile into old age and free from disease. Their secret: a lot of exercise (mountain climbing) and raw food such as nuts. The Hunza live in North Pakistan and also have mythical status for eternal youth. Their secret: fresh mountain air,

exercise and a diet based almost exclusively on fresh vegetables and, all-importantly, apricots, plums and peaches which they grow themselves. See if you can get your hands on some Hunza apricots.

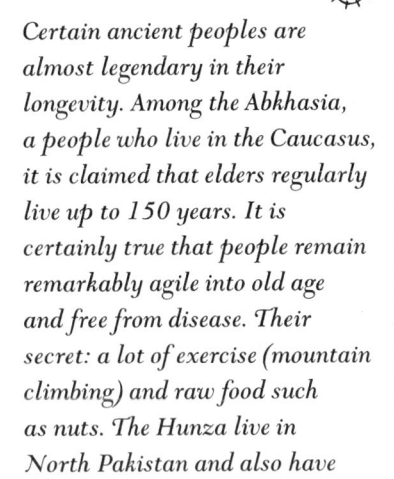

- I may be getting older, but I refuse to grow up!

- I may be old, but I'm ahead of you.

(US BUMPER STICKERS)

According to UK government statistics, 50,000 retired Britons now receive their state pension in Spain, 28,000 in Italy, 21,000 in France, and 4,700 in Portugal. The days of spending your retirement in slippers and reading a paper by the fire are over. It is time for flip-flops and sun.

NO man loves life like him that's growing old.

SOPHOCLES

I was a convent girl and didn't lose my virginity until I was 21 so I had no knowledge of sex at 20, at 30 it was getting better, 50 good and 60 terrific. In fact, I might even do a sex video.

ANNE ROBINSON, TV presenter, b. 1944

Various foods stave off the ageing process. Eating raw vegetables and fruit, for example, is key to neutralizing free radicals and regenerating cells. Blueberries, broccoli and red peppers are age-busters. Some other so-called superfoods or age suppressants are bee pollen, hempseed, spirulina, maca root, algae and goji berries. Do drink a lot of water too. And sleep well.

Grey power: term used to designate the elderly vote, purchasing weight and pressure. In fact, for the first time ever, Britain now has more pensioners than young people. According to the Office for National Statistics there are 11.58 million people over 60 compared to 11.52 million people under 16.

In 1895, Count Leo Tolstoy had his first-ever go on a bicycle and, using one which he'd just been given by the Moscow Society of Velocipede-Lovers, he soon became an enthusiastic cyclist. He was 67 years old.

Sunshine can cause cancer, we know, but it can also make you live longer. Researchers at King's College London, studying 2,160 women, found that women with higher levels of vitamin D had better protection against age-related diseases and their DNA aged at a slower pace.

Jeanne Calment from Arles, South of France, survived the longest of any documented person. She died in 1997 at the ripe old age of 122. She was riding a bicycle at 100 and met Vincent van Gogh when she was 14. She went to Victor Hugo's funeral in 1885. She once famously remarked: 'I have but one wrinkle and I'm sitting on it.'

> ● Old age is winter for the ignorant and harvest time for the wise

Although from about 50 I have often published my pictorial works, before 70 none is of much value. At the age of 73, I was able to fathom slightly the structure of birds, animals, insects and fish, the growth of grasses and trees. Thus perhaps at 80 my art may improve greatly; at 90, it may reach real depth, and at 100 it may become divinely inspired. At 110, every dot and every line may be as if living. I hope all good men of great age will feel that what I have said is not absurd.

KATSUSHIKA HOKUSAI, Japanese print-maker, 1760–1849

order

A PLACE for everything and everything in its place.

Mrs Beeton, *The Book of Household Management*, 1861

YOU'RE free. And freedom is beautiful. And, you know, it'll take time to restore chaos and order – order out of chaos. But we will.

George W. Bush, 2003

WE can form a precise idea of order, but not of disorder. Beauty, virtue, happiness, all have their proportions; ugliness, vice and unhappiness have none.

Jacques-Henri Bernardin de Saint-Pierre, *Paul et Virginie*, 1788

All things shall begin in order, so they end, and so shall they begin again; according to the ordainer of order, and mystical mathematics of the city of heaven.

Sir Thomas Browne, 1605-82

THE sacred formula of positivism: love as a principle, order as foundation, progress as goal.

Auguste Comte, 1798–1857

BE regular and orderly in your life, so that you may be violent and original in your work.

Gustave Flaubert, 1821–80

Man is all symmetry
Full of proportions, one limb to
    another

George Herbert, *The Temple: Sacred Poems and Private Ejaculations*, 1633

I HAVE been a rock of order.

Prince Metternich

PARENTHOOD

TRUST yourself. You know more than you think you do.

DR BENJAMIN SPOCK, opening words, *Baby and Child Care*, 1955

For the hand that rocks the cradle
Is the hand that rules the world.

WILLIAM ROSS WALLACE, US poet,
1819–81

THE mother's yearning, that completest type of the life in another life which is the essence of real human love, feels the presence of the cherished child even in the debased, degraded man.

GEORGE ELIOT, *Adam Bede*, 1859

If I were damned of body and soul,
I know whose prayers would make
    me whole,
Mother o' mine, O mother o' mine.

RUDYARD KIPLING, 'The Light that Failed',
1891

PARENTS learn a lot from their children about coping with life.

MURIEL SPARK, Scottish writer, *The Comforters*, 1957

I WROTE several letters to announce my son's birth. I indulged some imaginations that he might perhaps be a great man.

JAMES BOSWELL, *Diary*, 9 October 1775

Hush, little baby, don't say a word,
Papa's going to buy you a
    mocking-bird.
If the mocking-bird won't sing,
Papa's going to buy you a
    diamond ring.
If the diamond ring turns to brass,
Papa's going to buy you a
    looking-glass.
If the looking-glass gets broke,
Papa's going to buy you a billy-goat.
If that billy-goat runs away,
Papa's going to buy you another
    today.

And a woman who held a babe against her bosom said, 'Speak to us of Children.'
And he said:
Your children are not your children.
They are the sons and daughters of Life's longing for itself.
They come through you but not from you,
And though they are with you yet they belong not to you.

You may give them your love but not your thoughts,
For they have their own thoughts.
You may house their bodies but not their souls,
For their souls dwell in the house of tomorrow,
Which you cannot visit, not even in your dreams.
You may strive to be like them,
But seek not to make them like you.
For life goes not backward nor tarries with yesterday.

You are the bows from which your children
As living arrows are sent forth.
The archer sees the mark upon the path of the infinite,
And He bends you with His might
That His arrows may go swift and far.
Let your bending in the archer's hand be for gladness;
For even as He loves the arrow that flies,

So he loves also the bow that is stable.

KHALIL GIBRAN, Lebanese-US writer, *The Prophet*, 1932

A **Time** *poll conducted in December 2004 asked participants: 'What one thing in life has brought you the greatest happiness?' Thirty-five per cent said it was their children or grandchildren or both.*

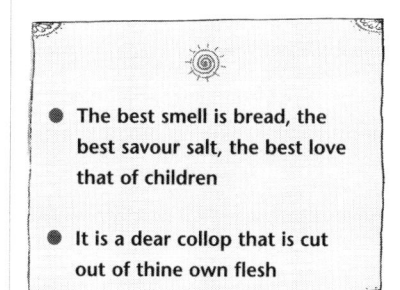

- The best smell is bread, the best savour salt, the best love that of children

- It is a dear collop that is cut out of thine own flesh

WHEN I was a boy of 14, my father was so ignorant I could hardly stand to have the old man around. But when I got to be 21, I was astonished at how much the old man had learned in seven years.

Attributed to MARK TWAIN

I have given you, forsooth, kisses in plenty and but few stripes ... if ever I have flogged you 'twas but with a peacock's tail.

THOMAS MORE, English statesman, writer, martyr and saint, 1478–1535

COLD, rainy. *Little Grobby's birthday.* Present from Wakefield. He can just stand by himself, but not walk. Speaks no syllable, but understands a few words, such as 'window', 'fire'. Only two teeth. On the whole in very good health, feeding exclusively on Allen & Hanbury's Malted Food. First thing in the morning, I crowned him with a wreath of ivy.

GEORGE GISSING, *Diary*, 10 December 1892

ABOUT three in the afternoon I went to my mother, and found her change was near. I sat down on the bed-side. She was in her last conflict; unable to speak, but I believe quite sensible. Her look was calm and serene, and her eyes fixed upward, while we commended her soul to God. From three to four the silver cord was loosing, and the wheel breaking at the cistern; and then without any struggle, or sigh, or groan, the soul was set at liberty. We stood round the bed, and fulfilled her last request, uttered a little before she lost her speech: 'Children, as soon as I am released, sing a psalm of praise to God.'

JOHN WESLEY, *Diary*, 23 August 1742

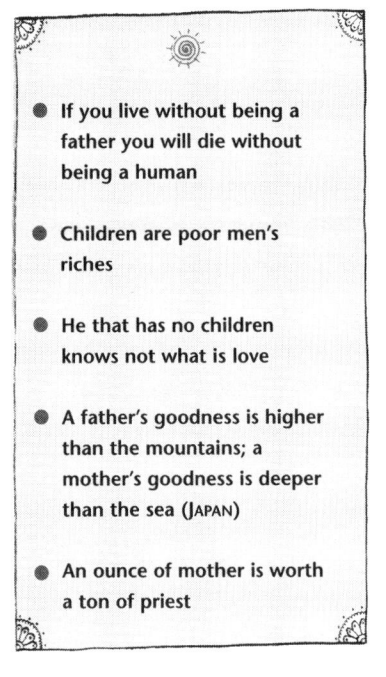

- If you live without being a father you will die without being a human

- Children are poor men's riches

- He that has no children knows not what is love

- A father's goodness is higher than the mountains; a mother's goodness is deeper than the sea (JAPAN)

- An ounce of mother is worth a ton of priest

ALLOW [children] to be happy their own way: for what better way will they ever find?

SAMUEL JOHNSON

My mother was the most beautiful woman I ever saw. All I am I owe to my mother. I attribute all my success in life to the moral, intellectual and physical education I received from her.

GEORGE WASHINGTON, 1732–99

The Fifth Commandment:

HONOUR thy father and thy mother.

The Bible, Exodus 20:12

patriotism

IS it an offence, is it a mistake, is it a crime to take a hopeful view of the prospects of your own country? Why should it be? Why should patriotism and pessimism be identical? Hope is the mainspring of patriotism.

DAVID LLOYD GEORGE, 1863–1945

HOW sweet and fitting it is to die for one's country.

HORACE

I ONLY regret that I have but one life to lose for my country.

NATHAN HALE, American patriot, prior to execution by the British for spying in 1776

A MOMENT comes, which comes but rarely in history, when we step out from the old to the new, when an age ends, and when the sound of a nation, long suppressed, finds utterance.

JAWAHARLAL NEHRU, Indian nationalist leader, 1889–1964

MEN who are infused with a faith, even a false one, will beat men who have no faith; only a good one can withstand the impact. Those who complain of the younger generation's lack of patriotism should, rather, reproach themselves for their failure to define and teach patriotism in higher terms than the mere preservation of a geographical area, its inhabitants, and their material interests. Such material appeal offers no adequate inspiration, nor cause for sacrifice to the young. Those who are concerned with practical questions of defence ought to realize the practical importance of ideals.

CAPTAIN SIR BASIL LIDDELL HART, *Thoughts on War*, 1944

STANDING as I do in the view of God and eternity, I realize that patriotism is not enough. I must have no hatred or bitterness towards anyone.

Nurse EDITH CAVELL to the chaplain before her execution by German firing squad in 1915

POLITICS

A SMALL body of determined spirits fired by an unquenchable faith in their mission can alter the course of history.

MAHATMA GANDHI

WE enter into a covenant that we shall build a society in which all South Africans, both black and white, will be able to walk tall, without any fear in their hearts, assured of their inalienable right to human dignity – a rainbow nation at peace with itself and the world.

NELSON MANDELA, South African president, inaugural address, 1994

WITH malice toward none; with charity for all; with firmness in the right, as God gives us to see the right, let us strive on to finish the work we are in.

ABRAHAM LINCOLN, 2nd inaugural address

WE have made it our guiding rule not to promise what we cannot deliver.

Labour Party manifesto, 1997

POLITICS is the art of the possible.

OTTO VON BISMARCK, German chancellor, 1815–98

THE Labour government will mean a fresh start for Britain ... It will mean greater freedom, security and opportunity. It will mean change for the better. It's time to make that change. It's time for Labour.

NEIL KINNOCK, party leader, 1992 election manifesto. Labour led in the opinion polls during the election campaign but slumped to a fourth defeat in a row on the day.

TOP FIVE OF A 2007 GALLUP POLL ASKING AMERICANS WHO THEY REGARDED AS THE COUNTRY'S GREATEST PRESIDENT

Abraham Lincoln (18%)

Ronald Reagan (16%)

John F. Kennedy (14%)

Bill Clinton (13%)

Franklin Roosevelt (9%)

ON 5 May you can let the sunshine of hope break through the clouds of disappointment. Twenty-first-century Britain should be a place of optimism, dynamism and unprecedented progress. It may not feel like that today but there's no reason it can't feel like that tomorrow.

MICHAEL HOWARD, party leader, launching the Conservative Party's unsuccessful 2005 election campaign

I AM not, and never have been, a man of the right. My position was on the left and now in the centre of politics.

SIR OSWALD MOSLEY, English fascist, 1896–1980

I JUST want you to know that, when we talk about war, we're really talking about peace.

GEORGE W. BUSH

WHEN I'm sitting on the Woolsack in the House of Lords I amuse myself by saying 'Bollocks!' sotto voce to the bishops.

LORD HAILSHAM, 1907–2001

WHAT are the Bolsheviki? They are the representatives of the most democratic government in Europe … Let us recognise the truest democracy in the world today.

WILLIAM RANDOLPH HEARST, US newspaper magnate, 1863–1951

5 OPTIMISTIC U.S. ELECTION PLEDGES

Woodrow Wilson vows to keep the US out of the First World War.

Franklin Roosevelt vows to keep the US out of the Second World War.

Lyndon B. Johnson promises to win the 'war on poverty'.

Richard Nixon promises to quickly resolve the Vietnam War.

George Bush Sr says, 'Read my lips: No new taxes.'

OUR country has accepted obligations that are difficult to fulfil, and would be dishonorable to abandon. Yet because we have acted in the great liberating tradition of this nation, tens of millions have achieved their freedom. And as hope kindles hope, millions more will find it. By our efforts, we have lit a fire as well – a fire in the minds of men. It warms those who feel its power, it burns those who fight its progress, and one day this untamed fire of freedom will reach the darkest corners of our world.

GEORGE W. BUSH, 2nd inaugural address, 2005

FIRST they ignore you, then they laugh at you, then they fight you, then you win.

MAHATMA GANDHI

Religion

THIS most beautiful System of the Sun, Planets and Comets, could only proceed from the counsel and dominion of an intelligent and powerful being.

ISAAC NEWTON, *Philosophiae Naturalis Principia Mathematica*, 1687

AND then, into this tasteless heap of gold and marble [Rome], He came, light and clothed in an aura, emphatically human, deliberately provincial, Galilean, and at that moment gods and nations ceased to be and man came into being – man the carpenter, man the ploughman, man the shepherd with his flock of sheep at sunset, man who does not sound in the least proud, man thankfully celebrated in all the cradle songs of mothers and in all the picture galleries the world over.

BORIS PASTERNAK, 1890–1960, *Dr Zhivago*

I CANNOT imagine how the clockwork of the universe can exist without a clockmaker.

VOLTAIRE

TRUE religion is real living; living with all one's soul, with all one's goodness and righteousness.

ALBERT EINSTEIN

ONLY barbarians are not curious about where they come from, how they came to be where they are, where they appear to be going, whether they wish to go there, and if so, why, and if not, why not.

ISAIAH BERLIN, British philosopher, 1909–97

THEY are for religion when in rags and contempt; but I am for him when he walks in his golden slippers, in the sunshine and with applause.

JOHN BUNYAN, *The Pilgrim's Progress*, 1678

I DO not feel obliged to believe that the same God who has endowed us with sense, reason, and intellect has intended us to forgo their use.

GALILEO GALILEI

THIS is my simple religion. There is no need for temples; no need for complicated philosophy. Our own brain, our own heart is our temple; the philosophy is kindness.

DALAI LAMA, Tibetan spiritual leader, b. 1935

———

According to research, those in the US who believe in God give, on average, over 50 per cent more to human-welfare charities than non-religious people do.

———

In 1991, former goalkeeper and TV presenter David Icke appeared at a press conference, wearing a shiny turquoise robe, to announce to hacks: 'I am a channel for the Christ spirit. The title was given to me very recently by the Godhead.' Days later, he chose **The Terry Wogan Show** *to expand on his revelation, telling a startled British public that he was, in fact, 'the son of God', and that Britain would soon be destroyed by tidal waves and earthquakes. In 1999, he relieved the British people of the silly idea that much of the population, including Tony Blair, the royal family and all prison warders, are human beings. They are, of course, hybrid reptilian humanoids, he explained. Icke now lives in Ryde on the Isle of Wight.*

———

THE best remedy for those who are afraid, lonely or unhappy is to go outside, somewhere where they can be quiet, alone with the heavens, nature and God. Because only then does one feel that all is as it should be and that God wishes to see people happy, amidst the simple beauty of nature.

ANNE FRANK, 1929–45

> ● **Some are atheists only in fair weather**

I WANT nothing to do with any religion concerned with keeping the masses satisfied to live in hunger, filth, and ignorance. I want nothing to do with any order, religious or otherwise, which does not teach people that they are capable of becoming happier and more civilized, on this earth, capable of becoming true man, 'master of his fate and captain of his soul'.

JAWAHARLAL NEHRU

'What parable do you like best?' the Sunday School teacher asked her class. One pupil replied, 'The one about the multitude what loafs and fishes.'

Reader's Digest, September 1981

Reviews and Critics

HE writes so well he makes me feel like putting the quill back in the goose.

FRED ALLEN, American comedian, 1894–1956

ONE always tends to overpraise a long book, because one has got through it.

E. M. FORSTER, 1879–1970

ALL my shows are great. Some of them are bad. But they are all great.

LEW GRADE, British impresario, 1906–98

IN the first serious literary work on the subject, Nicolas Rouvière's *Astérix ou les lumières de la civilisation* proposes an intellectually ambitious response to the claim of Asterixian chauvinism. Its central postulate is that the stories reject ethnocentrism altogether, and are rooted in the Enlightenment ideal of a common civilisation.

The Times Literary Supplement, 2007

UNLESS the bastards have the courage to give you unqualified praise, I say ignore them.

JOHN STEINBECK, US novelist, 1902–68, on critics

A BOOK is a version of the world. If you do not like it, ignore it; or offer your own version in return.

SALMAN RUSHDIE, British novelist, b. 1947

Shakespeare's stuff is different from mine, but that's not to say it is inferior.

P. G. WODEHOUSE, 1881–1975

Although written many years ago, *Lady Chatterley's Lover* has just been reissued by Grove Press, and this fictional account of the day-by-day life of an English gamekeeper is still of considerable interest to outdoor-minded readers, as it contains many passages on pheasant-raising, the apprehending of poachers, ways to control vermin, and other chores and duties of the professional gamekeeper.

Review in the American outdoors magazine *Field & Stream*, 1959

SCHOOL REPORTS

Queen Elizabeth I
(1533–1603)

IF she be no more educated than she now appeareth to me, she will prove of no less honour and womanhood, than shall beseem her father's daughter.

THOMAS WRIOTHESLEY, report on the home-tutored six-year-old princess

George Gordon, Lord Byron
(1788–1824)

HE has talents, my Lord, which will add lustre to his rank.

To Byron's guardian, Lord Carlisle, from Harrow School

John Maynard Keynes
(1883–1946)

I HAVE rarely known any boy so clever, and yet so far removed from any trace of priggishness ... I fear it may be long before I have again a pupil who will combine ability and industry so well; of his character I will only say that I think he is a boy on whom one can depend entirely.

Eton College

Lewis Carroll
(1832–98)

HE is ... marvellously ingenious in replacing the ordinary inflexions of nouns and verbs, as detailed in our grammars, by more exact analogies, or convenient forms of his own devising. You may fairly anticipate for him a bright career ... You must not entrust your son with a full knowledge of his superiority over other boys.

Headmaster's letter, Richmond Grammar School

Albert Einstein
(1879–1955)

ONE student, by the name of Einstein, even sparkled by rendering an adagio from a Beethoven sonata with deep understanding.

Violin teacher, Aarau village school

Eleanor Roosevelt
(1884–1962)

AS a pupil she is very satisfactory, but even that is of small account when you compare it with the perfect quality of her soul.

Letter from the Headmistress, Allenswood, London

Daphne du Maurier
(1907–89)

DAPHNE has written the best story but with the worst handwriting and the worst spelling.

Oak Hill Park School, Hampstead, London

Saul Bellow
(b. 1915)

WIT and humour abound in him.

Sabin Junior High School, Chicago

Spike Milligan
(1918–2002)

HE has a very good appearance and is keen, energetic and reliable. He made steady progress in all subjects. I recommend him for employment with complete confidence.

Woolwich and Greenwich Day Continuation School, London

Jenni Murray, radio presenter
(b. 1950)

JENNIFER tells a good story, but is somewhat cavalier with the facts – could do well in journalism.

History report, Barnsley High School for Girls

Carol Vorderman
(b. 1960)

AN EXCELLENT result in every way. Carol has a masterly hold over mathematical computation which should prove profitable later on.

Ysgol Mair, Rhyl

science

On the Scientific Method

The scientific method – as opposed to the method of tenacity (believing what one is inclined to think); or the method of authority (believing what you're told); or the method of congruity (believing what makes sense but what's not necessarily true) – has been practised in various forms for thousands of years, not least by Ancient Egyptians, Arabs and Greeks, and is itself one of mankind's greatest and yet most consistently humble achievements. The modern scientific method, which was crystallized (more or less) in the 17th century via Bacon and Descartes, does not rest on belief, or culture; its techniques of observation and experimentation are genuinely accessible to all mankind; it is eternally open to correction – it never assumes that it has 'proof' but deals in 'hypotheses' and 'theories' which may be overturned in the light of new knowledge; and nobody has any special, priest-like authority, because peer review, in which other scientists may reproduce and verify the results of their colleagues, as well as building on their knowledge, is a vital part of the process. Yet the technique is never cut-and-dried; the roles of creativity and inspiration cannot be understated. This genuinely global social enterprise, whose goal is Truth, no more or less, is essentially the most optimistic of human endeavours.

ONE of the greatest gifts science has brought to the world is continuing elimination of the supernatural, and it was a lesson that my father passed on to me, that knowledge liberates mankind from superstition. We can live our lives without the constant fear that we have offended this or that deity who must be placated by incantation or sacrifice, or that we are at the mercy of devils or the Fates.

JAMES D. WATSON, co-discoverer of the structure of DNA, b. 1928

SCIENCE

... is simply commonsense at its best.

T. H. HUXLEY, 1825–95

... is the great antidote to the poison of enthusiasm and superstition.

ADAM SMITH, 1723–90

... is the poetry of reality.

RICHARD DAWKINS, b. 1941

... knows no country, because knowledge belongs to humanity, and is the torch which illuminates the world.

LOUIS PASTEUR, French chemist, 1822–95

... alone can solve the problems of hunger and poverty, of insanitation and illiteracy, of superstition and deadening of custom and tradition, of vast resources running to waste, or a rich country inhabited by starving poor ... Who indeed could afford to ignore science today? At every turn we have to seek its aid ... The future belongs to science and those who make friends with science.

JAWAHARLAL NEHRU

ALL men by nature desire to know.

ARISTOTLE, *Metaphysics*

————

Without Science, and its handmaiden Technology, where would we be? Could the freeing of slaves have occurred without the industrial processes that made them replaceable? It is clear that the political process follows the scientific. As for Women's Liberation, would women everywhere not be confined to a life of domestic drudgery – the hard daily grind of finding water, food, cooking, washing and keeping the house clean and warm – without technological assistance? Since the invention of the wheel some 5,000 years ago, via proper sanitation and antibiotics, humans have consistently used their wit and skills to improve their lot. Below is the US National Academy of Engineering's list of the top twenty greatest engineering achievements of the twentieth century:

1 Electrification

2 Cars

3 Aeroplanes

4 Water supply and distribution

5 Electronics

6 Radio and TV

7 Agricultural mechanization

8 Computers

9 Telephones

10 Air conditioning and refrigeration

11 Highways

12 Spacecraft

13 Internet

14 Imaging

15 Household appliances

16 Health technologies

17 Petroleum and petrochemical technologies

18 Laser and fibre optics

19 Nuclear technologies

20 High-performance materials

This remarkable list is merely the tip of the iceberg; and meanwhile we are inventing technologies with the ability to make even a cornucopian's wildest dreams come true.

THE most beautiful thing we can experience is the mysterious. It is the source of all true art and science.

ALBERT EINSTEIN

The visionary and innovator R. Buckminster Fuller's challenge – 'to make the world work for 100% of humanity in the shortest possible time through spontaneous cooperation without ecological offense or the disadvantage of anyone' – has been taken up by the Buckminster Fuller Institute. Go to http://challenge.bfi.org to find out more about the $100,000 annual prize for brilliant scientific solutions to humanity's most pressing problems.

In early 2008, the following fourteen challenges were laid down to scientists by the American Association for the Advancement of Science:

- **Make solar energy affordable**

- **Provide energy from fusion**

- **Develop carbon sequestration**

- **Manage the nitrogen cycle**

- **Provide access to clean water**

- **Reverse-engineer the brain (in order to better understand intelligence)**

- **Prevent nuclear terror**

- **Secure cyberspace**

- **Enhance virtual reality**

- **Improve urban infrastructure**

- **Advance health informatics (i.e. rationalize data on patients, etc.)**

- **Engineer better medicines**

- **Advance personalized learning**

- **Explore natural frontiers**

and just to take one example of how these challenges are already being met, water-harvesting technology – making water from thin air – is already a reality. A company called Aqua Sciences has created a 20-foot machine that can pump out 600 gallons of water a day, even in the desert, without using toxic materials or creating toxic waste.

WHAT one man can imagine, another can do.

JULES VERNE, French author, 1828–1905

HARDLY anyone seems to realize it, but we're on the threshold of an era of unbelievable abundance. Within a generation – sooner, if we want it enough – we will be able to make a self-replicating machine … Such a machine would absorb energy through solar cells, eat rock and use the energy and minerals to make copies of itself. Numbers would grow geometrically, and if we manage to design one with a reasonably short replication time – say six months – we could have trillions working for humanity in another generation. You might compare this process to a single cell of blue-green algae, which replicates over the summer until it covers the entire pond. But unlike algae, a self-replicating machine would be programmed and controlled by us. If it could make its own mechanical and electronic parts, it would also be able to make toasters, refrigerators, and Lamborghinis, as well as the electricity to power them. We could make the deserts bloom, put two cars in every pot, and end world poverty, while simultaneously fighting global warming. It's closer than you think, since the key technologies are already being developed for use in rapid prototyping and desktop manufacturing. Aristotle thought that slavery would end only when looms wove by themselves. We're almost there.

GREGORY COCHRAN, Professor of Anthropology, University of Utah, on www.edge.org, in response to the 2007 question, What Are You Optimistic About?

Why? What? When? Where? How?

In 2005, in celebration of its 125th anniversary, the world's largest science journal, Science, *published 125 questions that are still a puzzle. The full list is at www.sciencemag.org/sciext/125th and it includes such exciting and important conundrums as: What is the universe made of? Are we alone in the universe? Can the laws of physics be unified? Is morality hardwired into the brain? Why do we sleep? What causes schizophrenia? What causes autism? How much can the human lifespan be extended? How and where did life on Earth arise? What caused mass extinctions? What causes ice ages? What can replace cheap oil – and when? Questions which, surely, are well worth asking – and answering.*

sex

WHEN I glimpse the back of a woman's knees I seem to hear the first movement of Beethoven's Pastoral Symphony.

CHARLES GREVILLE, British diarist, 1794–1865

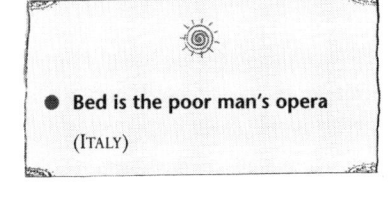

● **Bed is the poor man's opera**

(ITALY)

IT doesn't matter what you do in the bedroom as long as you don't do it in the street and frighten the horses.

MRS PATRICK CAMPBELL, English actress, 1865–1940

12 January 1763

I CAME softly into the room, and in a sweet delirium slipped into bed and was immediately clasped in her snowy arms and pressed to her milk-white bosom. Good heavens, what a loose did we give to amorous dalliance! The friendly curtain of darkness concealed our blushes. In a moment I felt myself animated with the strongest powers of love, and, from my dearest creature's kindness, had a most luscious feast. Proud of my godlike vigour, I soon resumed the noble game. I was in full glow of health. Sobriety had preserved me from effeminacy and weakness, and my bounding blood beat quick and high alarms. A more voluptuous night I never enjoyed. Five times was I fairly lost in supreme rapture. Louisa was madly fond of me; she declared I was a prodigy, and asked me if this was not extraordinary for human nature. I said twice as much might be, but this was not, although in my own mind I was somewhat proud of my performance.

JAMES BOSWELL, *Diary*

PROSTITUTES for pleasure, concubines for services, wives for breeding and a melon for ecstasy.

Attributed to SIR RICHARD BURTON, English explorer, 1821–90

From the Song of Solomon, Ch. 2

I am the rose of Sharon, and the
　　lily of the valleys.
As the lily among thorns, so is my
　　love among the daughters.
As the apple tree among the trees
　　of the wood, so is my beloved
　　among the sons. I sat
　　down under his shadow with
　　great delight, and his fruit was
　　sweet to my taste.
He brought me to the banqueting
　　house, and his banner over me
　　was love.
Stay me with flagons, comfort me
　　with apples: for I am sick of love.
His left hand is under my head, and
　　his right hand doth embrace me.
I charge you, O ye daughters of
　　Jerusalem, by the roes, and by
　　the hinds of the field, that ye
　　stir not up, nor awake my love,
　　till he please.

From the Authorised Version of
the Bible, 1611

Three ways to increase fertility if the drugs don't work:

1 Take a tip from the Ancient Europeans: drink potions made of powdered hare's womb, sparrow's brain or wolf's genitals.

2 Visit the 1,500-year-old 'Penis Shrine' in Komaki, Japan, and take part in the Hounen

Matsuri fertility festival, next to a building called the Shinmeisha which is filled with penis-shaped objects.

3 Go to sleep or make love on the 27-foot-long penis belonging to the 'Rude Man', aka the Cerne Abbas Giant, the vast figure carved into the chalk of a Dorset hill.

Fuck for the Future!

ADVERTISING slogan of BJÖRN BORG'S
Swedish fashion label

License my roving hands and let
　　them go,
Before, behind, between, above,
　　below.
O my America! My new-found
　　land,
My kingdom, safeliest when with
　　one man mann'd …

JOHN DONNE, 1572–1631, 'Elegy XIX, To
His Mistress Going to Bed'

Any Which Way

*In 1524, Renaissance author Pietro Aretino more or less invented Western pornography with his **Sixteen Postures**, sonnets written to accompany erotic drawings. (Casanova was to spend a New Year's Eve, almost exactly 200 years later, trying out*

Aretino's 'Straight Tree' position on a nun.) In the mid-20th century, Dr Alfred C. Kinsey categorized six basic positions in his reports on human sexual behaviour: man on top; woman on top; side by side; rear entrance; sitting; standing — but don't despair if you feel that this is too reductive; it has been estimated that there are at least four million possible sexual positions for a man and a woman.

Some of those 4,000,000 sexual positions:

The Kama Sutra, the ancient Hindu book of erotic love, describes sixty-four kinds of sexual acts, including the Windmill, the Crab, Splitting the Bamboo, the Mare's Trap and the Lotus Seat, and other examples from Arabic manuals and Chinese books on the art of the bedchamber include Cat and Mouse in the Same Hole, Old Man Pushing a Wheelbarrow, Phoenix Sporting in the Cinnabar Cleft, Congress of an Ass, The Donkeys of Late Spring, Fixing a Nail, Hovering Butterflies, Swinging Monkey, The Rooster Perches on a Stick, The Unicorn's Horn and The Toothpick in the Vulva.

Finally, one from Aristophanes' Lysistrata (411 BC), which might make you want to reconsider the missionary position. It requires a woman to crouch with her buttocks in the air, and it's called the Lioness on the Cheese Grater.

From pent-up aching rivers,
From that of myself without which
    I were nothing,
From what I am determin'd to
    make illustrious, even if I stand
    sole among men,
From my own voice resonant,
    singing the phallus,
Singing the song of procreation,
Singing the need of superb children
    and therein superb grown people,
Singing the muscular urge and the
    blending,
Singing the bedfellow's song,
(O resistless yearning!
O for any and each the body
    correlative attracting!
O for you whoever you are your
    correlative body! O it, more
    than all else, you delighting!) …

WALT WHITMAN, 'From Pent-up Aching Rivers'

Automatic response

It was Woody Allen who pointed out that being bisexual doubles your chances of a date on a Saturday night; but soon your sex appeal — or lack of — will no longer be an issue. In 2006, Dr Henrik Christensen, director of the Center for Robotics and Intelligent Machines at Georgia Tech, predicted that people will be having sex with robots by 2011.

The aged Sophocles may have welcomed impotence as an escape from a 'mad and savage master', but most people certainly do not. Here is a small selection of aphrodisiacs and performance-enhancers which have all been hopefully promoted, with varying degrees of success, at some time or place:

- **Artichokes** (an old French street cry was 'Artichokes! Artichokes! Heats the body and the spirit! Heats the genitals!')

- **Avocados** (hang in pairs from the 'testicle tree', and were once considered so powerful that they were forbidden to virgins)

- **Bald Chicken Drug** (in Ancient China, a potent concoction allowing a man to easily satisfy 40 women)

- **Chocolate** (packed with potent chemicals and used enthusiastically by the Aztecs)

- **Damiana** (a South American aphrodisiac which makes the nether regions throb)

- **Deer blood,** human semen and hawk excrement mixed together (in Ancient China)

- **Ginger** (made into a paste and rubbed on the stomach, scrotum and anus, according to Pliny the Elder, AD 23–79)

- **Kneading bread with your naked buttocks** (in Germany)

- **Pearls dissolved in vinegar** (a speciality of Cleopatra's)

- **Powdered frog bones** (in Ancient Rome)

- **Ram testicle boiled in milk** (in India, c. 1,000 BC)

- **Seafood** (mussels and crabs, according to the Ancient Greeks; caviar; Casanova ate about fifty zinc-rich oysters a day)

- **Truffles** (fungi which give off chemicals similar to human sex hormones and praised by Rabelais, Napoleon and Mme de Pompadour)

- **Vanilla** (from the Latin for vagina; sex psychologist Henry Havelock Ellis once visited a vanilla-processing factory and found that all the men had permanent erections)

- **Viagra** (cleared for sale by the FDA in 1998, as the first effective oral treatment for impotence. Even though it may provoke abnormal hair growth, burping and hiccups, it works.)

Also worth a dishonourable mention: asses' milk, asparagus, bananas, basil, broad beans, beetroot, carrots, cinnamon, crushed rubies, cucumbers, doves' brains, ginseng, guinea fowl tongues, honey, jackal bile, kava kava, gold dust, lions' testicles, powdered rhino horn, saffron, snails, Spanish fly, whale vomit (the ultimate triumph of hope over experience?).

GIVE me chastity and continence – but not yet!

ST AUGUSTINE, 354–430, *Confessions*

sleep

The average person spends a third of their life asleep.

IN the Land of Nod at last.

ROBERT LOUIS STEVENSON, *A Child's Garden of Verses*, 1885

Come sleep, O sleep, the certain
   knot of peace,
The baiting place of wit, the balm
   of woe,
The poor man's wealth, the
   prisoner's release,
The indifferent judge between the
   high and low

SIR PHILIP SIDNEY, *Astrophel and Stella*, 1591

Nothing like a good night's sleep! Since caveman days, and the night-time scramble for the softest mammoth skins, the search for the most comfortable bedding has been a battle. Nowadays mattresses are feats of engineering with technologically advanced visco-elastic features, water-latex substances and memory foam elements. Forget duck or goose feathers, you can now buy shiatsu massage bases, silicon moulds to support your neck and spiral hollow-fibre pillows ... If it's time to change your all-important mattress, you might want to buy from a mattress company which believes that a perfect night's sleep isn't just an optimistic fantasy but a technological certainty.

BLESSINGS on him who invented sleep, the mantle that covers all human thoughts, the food that satisfies hunger, the drink that slakes thirst, the fire that warms cold, the cold that moderates heat, and, lastly, the common currency that buys all things, the balance and weight that equalizes the shepherd and the king, the simpleton and the sage.

CERVANTES, *Don Quixote*, 1605

WHILE we are asleep in this world, we are awake in another one; in this way, every man is two men.

Attributed to JORGE LUIS BORGES, 1899–1986

Many early childhood specialists believe that lullabies should, ideally, be part of putting any baby or child to bed. Lullabies simultaneously encourage sleep, language and musical development. Johannes Brahms's lullaby is said to be particularly effective:

Lullaby and good night, with roses bedight,
With lilies o'er spread is baby's wee bed.
Lay thee down now and rest, may thy slumber be blessed,
Lay thee down now and rest, may thy slumber be blessed.

GOOD night, sweet prince, and flights of angels sing thee to thy rest.

WILLIAM SHAKESPEARE, *Hamlet*

Wakeful children are the bane of parents' nights. If you feel you have exhausted all options and yourself, placed your baby's dummy in thirty different positions, installed a mattress on the floor by the cot to catch five minutes' sleep and even contemplated jumping out of the window, then do know that specialists are at hand. www.mill-pond.co.uk is there to help for children's sleep problems.

For adults, Sleepwise, www.sleepwise.co.uk, runs professional sleep clinics. Instead of tossing and turning at night, think positive. You can also contact the Insomnia Helpline: www.insomniahelpline.com.

Care-charmer Sleep, son of the sable Night,
Brother to Death, in silent darkness born,
Relieve my languish and restore the light …

SAMUEL DANIEL, *Delia*, 1592

Sleep isn't just lying flat and dead to the world. It is an active process, part light, part deep. When we enter REM, or Rapid-Eye Movement sleep, scientists believe our bodies are undergoing an all-important repairing process for enhancing memories. Non-REM sleep appears to be key for restoring energy and concentration.

WHATEVER we may say, the happiest moment of the happy man is that of his falling asleep, just as the unhappiest moment of the unhappy man is that of his awakening.

ARTHUR SCHOPENHAUER, *The World as Will and Representation*, 1844

great sleepers of all time

RIP VAN WINKLE fell asleep in the Catskill Mountains and returned home 20 years later to find things had changed somewhat in his absence

EPIMENIDES, the Greek poet, fell asleep for 57 years, according to Pliny's Natural History. When he awoke, he was possessed of all wisdom, and lived until he was 299

THE SLEEPING BEAUTY, a rose among thorns, slept for a century, to be awoken by a complete stranger kissing her

FREDERICK I BARBAROSSA, 11th-century King of Germany and Holy Roman Emperor, sleeps at a table, which his red beard has grown through, in a Bavarian cave. When the ravens stop flying around the mountain, he will awaken and make Germany great again

KING ARTHUR is fast asleep, possibly on the island of Avalon or under some hill or mound, awaiting the moment when England is in dire need of leadership. (It's perhaps surprising that he and Barbarossa didn't come to blows during the last century)

THE SEVEN SLEEPERS (of Ephesus) – Constantius, Dionysius, Joannes, Maximianus, Malchus, Martinianus and Serapion fled from their religious persecutors to a cave where they were walled up. Some 200 years later, they awoke for breakfast, and then fell back to sleep to await the resurrection

An AUSTRALIAN EASTERN PYGMY POSSUM once slept for 367 days in a New South Wales lab. Beat that!

Medical researchers have pinpointed some very clear steps to ensuring a good night's sleep. 1) Clear your mind of stressful thoughts, 2) Reduce alcohol consumption, caffeine and meal sizes, 3) Stick to a routine and go to bed at the same time, 4) Cut out noise as much as possible, as well as excessive heat, 5) Avoid medicines that are stimulants, 6) Do not watch TV or use a computer prior to sleep, 7) Use thick curtains or shutters to block out early light.

To maximize your chances of a good night, examine the Feng Shui of your bedroom too. It may be that objects like mirrors, computers, artificial lights, electric clocks or the position of the bed are disrupting the harmony of the room.

Now I lay me down to sleep,
I pray the Lord my soul to keep;
Angels guard me through the night
And wake me with the morning
    light.

Bedtime prayer

smoking

WHAT a blessing this smoking is! Perhaps the greatest that we owe to the discovery of America.

SIR ARTHUR HELPS, British writer, 1813–75

The number of smokers is falling in developed nations. Around 10 million adults smoke cigarettes in the UK today, roughly one sixth of the population. In 1974, just under half the adult population smoked. In the late 1940s nearly 70 per cent of British grown-ups smoked cigarettes. In the US, smoking rates shrank by nearly half from the mid-1960s to the mid-1990s, falling to 23 per cent of adults by 1997 and 21 per cent by 2007.

LASTLY (and this is, perhaps, the golden rule) no woman should marry a teetotaller, or a man who does not smoke.

ROBERT LOUIS STEVENSON, *Virginibus Puerisque*, 1881

20TH-CENTURY TOBACCO ADS CLAIMING HEALTH BENEFITS

Not a cough in a carload. (Chesterfield)

Not one single case of chest irritation. (Camel)

Why risk sore throats? (Old Gold)

I light a Lucky and go light on the sweets. That's how I keep in shape and always look peppy. To stay slender reach for a Lucky! A most effective way of retaining a trim figure. (Lucky Strike)

Guard against throat scratch. (Pall Mall)

Many prominent athletes smoke Luckies all day long with no harmful effects. (Lucky Strike)

Smoke as many as you want. They never get on your nerves. (Camel)

MY mother smoked religiously all her life. She is now 90 with clear lungs, unfurred arteries, and pale, unmottled skin, marooned in a nursing home because her legs gave out on her. We used to take her big packs of cheap cigarettes called Holiday, and she would wheel herself to the designated smoking area and chain-smoke, lighting one cigarette off the other with such eagerness that she sometimes had two going at once.

BERYL BAINBRIDGE, *Guardian*, 2007

YOU ask me what we need to win this war. I answer tobacco as much as bullets. Tobacco is as indispensable as the daily ration; we must have thousands of tons without delay.

GENERAL JOHN J. PERSHING, 1860–1948, during the First World War

Sublime tobacco! ...
Divine in hookas, glorious in a pipe,
When tipped with amber, mellow, rich, and ripe;
Like other charmers, wooing the caress
More dazzlingly when daring in full dress;
Yet thy true lovers more admire by far
Thy naked beauties – Give me a cigar!

LORD BYRON, 'The Island', 1823

THOSE who smoke outnumber those who do not by a hundred to one ... so non-smokers must learn to adapt themselves to existing conditions ... and when they come into contact with smokers, it is scarcely fair that the few should be allowed to prohibit the many from the pursuit of their comforts and their pleasures.

Good Housekeeping, 1940

OH! I like smoking, I do. I smoke for my health, my mental health. Tobacco gives you little pauses, a rest from life. I don't suppose anyone smoking a pipe would have road rage, would they?

DAVID HOCKNEY, artist, *Daily Telegraph*, 1999

IS THE noble Lord aware that, at the age of 80, there are very few pleasures left to me, but one of them is passive smoking?

BARONESS TRUMPINGTON, former Tory minister and ex-smoker, House of Lords, 2003

● Smoke your pipe and be silent; there's only wind and smoke in the world

(IRELAND)

SPORT

WERE cricket and football abolished, it would bring upon the masses nothing but misery, depression, sloth, indiscipline and disorder.

F. E. SMITH, 1st Earl of Birkenhead, British lawyer and politician, 1872–1930

THE noble science of boxing is all our own. Foreigners can scarcely understand how we can squeeze pleasure out of this pastime; the luxury of hard blows given or received; the joy of the ring; nor the perseverance of the combatants.

WILLIAM HAZLITT, *Merry England*, 1825

The ancient Olympic Games were held every four years for nearly 1,200 years until AD 393; about 1,500 years later, a young aristocrat called Baron Pierre de Coubertin, who was only seven at the time of the Franco-Prussian War, proposed that they be reinstated as a means of promoting peace. The first modern Olympic Games took place in Athens in 1896, and about 300 athletes, representing 13 countries, took part. Today we can expect to see around 10,000 athletes from 200 countries.

CRICKET civilizes people and creates good gentlemen. I want everyone to play cricket in Zimbabwe; I want ours to be a nation of gentlemen.

ROBERT MUGABE, president of Zimbabwe

BIGGEST RAID EVER – SCORE 78 to 26 – ENGLAND STILL BATTING.

Newspaper placard, summer 1940, during the Battle of Britain

I TEND to believe that cricket is the greatest thing that God ever created on Earth … certainly better than sex although sex isn't too bad either. But everyone knows which comes first when it's a question of cricket or sex.

HAROLD PINTER, b. 1930

IT was a very happy fight. I was enjoying hitting him and he enjoyed getting hit.

LENNOX LEWIS, British boxer, b.1965

GAZZA is a fantastic player when he isn't drunk.

BRIAN LAUDRUP, Denmark and Rangers footballer, b.1969

WE didn't lose the game; we just ran out of time.

VINCE LOMBARDI, American football coach, 1913–70

ONE was presented with a small, hairy individual and, out of general curiosity, one climbed on.

THE PRINCESS ROYAL, b.1950, on her first horse ride

THE three stumps are the triplefold muse or three fates – which must be held in balance. The two bails, as a man and a woman, are balanced on their fates to make up the fivefold wicket which must be defended against the fiery red sun.

From a petition presented in 1995 by TIM SEBASTIAN, Arch Druid of Wiltshire, Bard of the Gorsedd of Caer Abiri (Avebury) and frustrated village cricketer, for Stonehenge Cricket Club to be given back its ground at the ancient site. Cricket was played at Stonehenge until the 1920s.

THERE is plenty of time to win this game, and thrash the Spaniards too.

SIR FRANCIS DRAKE, c. 1540–1595, on hearing news of the Armada while playing bowls on Plymouth Hoe

Crossing the finishing line in a half-marathon in Essex in 2007, 101-year-old Buster Martin demanded: 'Where's my beer?' The working plumber, who has 17 children, finished the 13-mile race in five hours 13 minutes and downed a tankard of his favourite ale.

When asked why he and his colleague had dragged an ironing board 5,440 metres up Mount Everest in order to press the creases from a Union Jack, Ben Gibbon replied: 'Why not?' Extreme ironing is a new danger sport that, in the words of its British founder Phil 'Steam' Shaw, 'combines the thrills of an extreme outdoor activity with the satisfaction of a well-pressed shirt'. The first World Extreme Ironing Championship was held in Munich, Germany, in September 2002, with 13 nations taking part in various disciplines including ironing in the back of a car, while climbing a wall, up trees and under water. The enthusiasts have pressed shirts at exotic and inhospitable locations all round the globe, including Antarctica, as well as in challenging conditions such as while trampolining and standing naked in a fast-flowing river.

LIFE is a gamble. You can get hurt, but people die in plane crashes, lose their arms and legs in car accidents; people die every day. Same with fighters: some die, some get hurt, some go on. You just don't let yourself believe it will happen to you.

MUHAMMAD ALI

It's estimated that more than 700 million people (a ninth of the planet's population) watched the last World Cup final, while over 4 billion of us are said to have tuned in to the opening ceremony of the Beijing Olympic games. Couch potatoes have never had it so good …

Travel

MAKE voyages! – Attempt them! there's nothing else.

TENNESSEE WILLIAMS, 1911–83, *Camino Real*

FOR my part, I travel not to go anywhere, but to go. I travel for travel's sake. The great affair is to move; to feel the needs and hitches of our life more nearly; to come down off this feather-bed of civilisation, and find the globe granite underfoot and strewn with cutting flints.

ROBERT LOUIS STEVENSON

Toad of Toad Hall on the Motorcar:

THE poetry of motion! The *real* way to travel! The *only* way to travel! Here today – in next week tomorrow! Villages skipped, towns and cities jumped – always somebody else's horizon! O bliss! O poop-poop! O my! O my!

KENNETH GRAHAME, *The Wind in the Willows*, 1908

Adlestrop

Yes, I remember Adlestrop –
The name, because one afternoon
Of heat the express-train drew
    up there
Unwontedly. It was late June.

The steam hissed. Someone cleared
    his throat.
No one left and no one came
On the bare platform. What I saw
Was Adlestrop – only the name

And willows, willow-herb,
    and grass,
And meadowsweet, and
    haycocks dry,
No whit less still and lonely fair
Than the high cloudlets in the sky.

And for that minute a
    blackbird sang
Close by, and round him, mistier,
Farther and farther, all the birds
Of Oxfordshire and
    Gloucestershire.

EDWARD THOMAS

I ALWAYS love to begin a journey on Sundays, because I shall have the prayers of the church, to preserve all that travel by land, or by water.

JONATHAN SWIFT

You're Warped

In 2007, the British Interplanetary Society hosted a conference of physicists entitled Faster than Light: Breaking the Interstellar Distance Barrier. While there's little chance of any of us travelling at warp speed in the very near future, it's reckoned that humankind is on the way to learning the secret of warp speed, which would involve bending the very fabric of space and time in order to travel faster than the speed of light. To infinity and beyond …!

THE mere animal pleasure of travelling in a wild unexplored country is also great … The effect of travel on a man whose heart is in the right place is that the mind is made more self-reliant: it becomes more confident of its own resources – there is greater presence of mind.

DR DAVID LIVINGSTONE, Scottish explorer, 1813–73

I will drink
Life to the lees: all times I have
  enjoy'd
Greatly, have suffer'd greatly, both
  with those
That loved me, and alone; on shore,
  and when
Thro' scudding drifts the rainy
  Hyades
Vext the dim sea: I am become a
  name;
For always roaming with a hungry
  heart
Much have I seen and known; cities
  of men
And manners, climates, councils,
  governments,
Myself not least, but honour'd of
  them all;
And drunk delight of battle with
  my peers,
Far on the ringing plains of windy
  Troy.
I am a part of all that I have met;
Yet all experience is an arch
  wherethro'
Gleams that untravell'd world,
  whose margin fades
For ever and for ever when I move.
How dull it is to pause, to make an
  end,
To rust unburnish'd, not to shine in
  use!
As tho' to breathe were life.

ALFRED, LORD TENNYSON, 'Ulysses', 1842

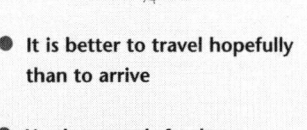

- **It is better to travel hopefully than to arrive**
- **He that travels far, knows much**
- **Travel broadens the mind**

THIS being my birth-day, the first day of my seventy-second year, I was considering, How is this, that I find just the same strength as I did thirty years ago? That my sight is considerably better now, and my nerves firmer, than they were then? That I have none of the infirmities of old age, and have lost several I had in my youth? The grand cause is, the good pleasure of God, who doeth whatsoever pleaseth Him. The chief means are,

1 My constantly rising at four, for about fifty years.

2 My generally preaching at five in the morning; one of the most healthy exercises in the world.

3 My never travelling less, by sea or land, than four thousand five hundred miles in a year.

JOHN WESLEY, 28 June 1774

At the moment, flying only accounts for 2 per cent of the world's carbon emissions but, with the aviation industry expanding at 5 per cent a year, aeroplanes need to clean up their act. Researchers are looking at four ways of doing this:

1 Build planes of lightweight materials as strong as metal but as light as plastic, thereby cutting fuel use dramatically;

2 Replace turbojet engines with much lighter, contra-rotating fans;

3 Rationalize international air-traffic control, so that planes fly from A to B rather than dithering around wasting fuel;

4 Discover and use environmentally friendly fuel – which is still the Holy Grail: one idea, which is a far-off but apparently realistic prospect, is to fit micro-organisms with artificial chromosomes, so that they can convert sunshine into fuel; hydrogen-powered aircraft are also a possibility.

THE world is a book, and those who do not travel, read only a page.

ST AUGUSTINE, *City of God*

TRUTH

FOR a human, truth is what makes him or her a human being.

ANTOINE DE SAINT-EXUPÉRY, 1900–44

TRUTH is tough. It will not break, like a bubble, at a touch; nay, you may kick it about all day like a football, and it will be round and full at evening.

OLIVER WENDELL HOLMES

I'M for truth, no matter who tells it. I'm for justice, no matter who it's for or against.

MALCOLM X, 1925–65

THREE things cannot long be hidden: the sun, the moon, and the truth.

CONFUCIUS, 551–471 BC

FOR who knows not that Truth is strong next to the Almighty? She needs no policies, no stratagems, nor licensings to make her victorious.

JOHN MILTON, *Areopagitica: a speech for the liberty of unlicensed printing*, 1644

SIT down before fact as a little child, be prepared to give up every preconceived notion…

T. H. HUXLEY, letter to Charles Kingsley, 1860

———

America for Truth is an organization that attempts to hold politicians and leaders accountable. It works in a grassroots way with local groups or by direct action in trying to pin down the truth. Their motto: **Politicians + Truth = Better America!** *see* http://truthinthenews.com.

———

I MAINTAIN that Truth is a pathless land, and you cannot approach it by any path whatsoever, by any religion, by any sect.

J. KRISHNAMURTI, speech in Holland, 3 August 1929

TRUTH exists; only lies are invented.

GEORGES BRAQUE, French artist, 1882–1963

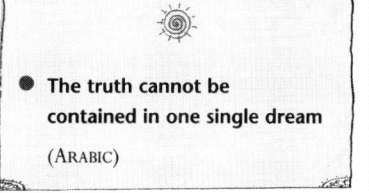

> ● **The truth cannot be contained in one single dream**
>
> (Arabic)

WHEN will women begin to have the first glimmer that above all other loyalties is the loyalty to Truth, i.e., to yourself, that husband, children, friends and country are as nothing to that.

Alice James, *Diary*, 19 November 1889

I SWEAR to tell the truth, the whole truth and nothing but the truth, so help me God.

Courtroom oath

TRUTH is the glue that holds governments together. Compromise is the oil that makes governments go.

Gerald Ford, US president, 1913–2006

AND ye shall know the truth, and the truth shall make you free.

The Bible, John 8:32

ABOVE all, tell the truth.

Stephen Grover Cleveland, US president, 1837–1908

ON the mountains of truth you can never climb in vain: either you will reach a point higher up today, or you will be training your powers so that you will be able to climb higher tomorrow.

Friedrich Nietzsche

I BELIEVE that unarmed truth and unconditional love will have the final word in reality. This is why right, temporarily defeated, is stronger than evil triumphant.

Martin Luther King

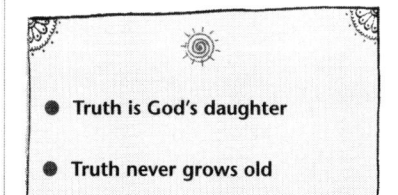

> ● **Truth is God's daughter**
>
> ● **Truth never grows old**
>
> ● **Truth is mighty and will prevail**
>
> ● **Truth will out**
>
> ● **Many a true word is spoken in jest**
>
> ● *In vino veritas*
>
> ● **Truth comes from the mouth of children**
>
> ● **Truth fears no trial**

united states

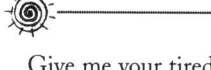

Give me your tired, your poor,
Your huddled masses yearning to
breathe free.

Inscription on the Statue of Liberty

YOUNG man, there is America –
which at this day serves for little
more than to amuse you with
stories of savage men and
uncouth manners; yet shall,
before you taste of death, show
itself equal to the whole of that
commerce which now attracts
the envy of the world.

EDMUND BURKE, speech, 1775

THE one being abhorrent to the
powers above the earth and
under them is the hyphenated
American – the German-
American, the Irish-American, or
the native-American. Be
Americans, pure and simple!

THEODORE ROOSEVELT, US president, 1895

NOW, I say to you today my
friends, even though we face
the difficulties of today and
tomorrow, I still have a dream.
It is a dream deeply rooted in
the American dream. I have a
dream that one day this nation
will rise up and live out the true
meaning of its creed: we hold
these truths to be self-evident,
that all men are created equal.

MARTIN LUTHER KING

I ALWAYS consider the
settlement of America with
reverence and wonder, as the
opening of a grand scene and
design in providence, for the
illumination of the ignorant and
the emancipation of the slavish
part of mankind all over the
earth.

JOHN ADAMS, US president, 1735–1826

WE must be the great arsenal of
democracy.

FRANKLIN D. ROOSEVELT, US president,
1882–1945

HUSBAND TO WIFE: The egg timer is pinging. The toaster is popping. The coffee pot is perking. Is this it, Alice? Is this the great American dream?

HENRY MARTIN, cartoon in the *New Yorker*

———

Citizens of the United States have been awarded a total of 304 Nobel prizes, almost three times more than Britain, the second most decorated country. There have been 20 Peace Prize winners including Al Gore (2007), Jimmy Carter (2002), Martin Luther King, Jr (1964), George C. Marshall (1953), the Quakers (1947), Frank B. Kellogg (1929), Woodrow Wilson (1919) and Theodore Roosevelt (1906).

———

YOU cannot spill a drop of American blood without spilling the blood of the whole world … We are not a nation, so much as a world.

HERMAN MELVILLE, American novelist, 1819–91

SOMETIMES people call me an idealist. Well, that is the way I know I am an American. America is the only idealistic nation in the world.

WOODROW WILSON, US president

FOR we must consider that we shall be as a city upon a hill. The eyes of all people are upon us. So that if we shall deal falsely with our God in this work we have undertaken … we shall be made a story and a by-word throughout the world. We shall open the mouths of enemies to speak evil of the ways of God … We shall shame the faces of many of God's worthy servants, and cause their prayers to be turned into curses upon us til we be consumed out of the good land whither we are a-going.

GOVERNOR JOHN WINTHROP to Puritan settlers of New England, 1630

THE American, by nature, is optimistic. He is experimental, an inventor and a builder who builds best when called upon to build greatly.

JOHN F. KENNEDY, US president, 1917–63

THERE is nothing wrong with America that cannot be cured by what is right with America.

BILL CLINTON, US president, first inaugural address, 1993

THE United States themselves are essentially the greatest poem.

WALT WHITMAN, preface to *Leaves of Grass*, 1855

war

AT eleven o'clock this morning came to an end the cruellest and most terrible War that has ever scourged mankind. I hope we may say that thus, this fateful morning, came to an end all wars.

DAVID LLOYD GEORGE, British prime minister, 11 November 1918

YOU will be home before the leaves have fallen from the trees.

KAISER WILHELM, to the German troops, August 1914

THERE are poets and writers who see naught in war but carrion, filth, savagery, and horror … they refuse war the credit of being the only exercise in devotion on the large scale existing in this world. The superb moral victory over death leaves them cold. Each one to his taste. To me this is no valley of death – it is a valley brim full of life at its highest power.

GENERAL SIR IAN HAMILTON, diary entry at Gallipoli, 30 May 1915

 ————————————————

When you go home
Tell them of us and say,
For their tomorrow
We gave our today.

Inscription on the British monument commemorating 17,587 casualties at the Battle of Kohima, India, against the Japanese in 1944

————————————————

WHILE war is terribly destructive, monstrously cruel, and horrible beyond expression, it nevertheless causes the divine spark in men to glow, to kindle, and to burst into a living flame, and enables them to attain heights of devotion to duty, sheer heroism, and sublime unselfishness that in all probability they would never have reached in the prosecution of peaceful pursuits.

MAJOR-GENERAL JOHN A. LEJEUNE, *Reminiscences of a Marine*, 1929

BY every canon of military science the British Expeditionary Force has been doomed for the last four or five days. Completely outnumbered, out-gunned, out-planed, all but surrounded, it had seemed certain to be cut off from its last channel of escape. Yet for several hours this morning we saw ship after ship come into harbour and discharge thousands of British soldiers safe and sound on British soil.

Guardian, from Dunkirk, 1 June 1940

OH, my dear fellow, the noise! ... Uh, and the people!

Unknown GUARDS OFFICER on his experiences in the Second World War

I'M glad we've been bombed. It makes me feel I can look the East End in the face.

Queen Elizabeth, the QUEEN MOTHER, after German bombs landed on Buckingham Palace, 1940

I TELL you Wellington is a bad general, the English are bad soldiers; we will settle the matter by lunchtime.

NAPOLEON at Waterloo, 8.30 a.m., 18 June 1815. Come dusk, the French army was in full flight.

Progress of sorts. It has been conservatively estimated that over 100 million people died from war and related causes, including disease and famine, in the 20th century. In War before Civilisation, *anthropologist Lawrence Keeley estimates that the total would have been two billion if we'd continued killing each other at the same rate as in our primeval period.*

THERE is no immediate prospect of an invasion.

FIELD MARSHAL GERD VON RUNDSTEDT, evening, 5 June 1944, to German forces he commanded in France. The D-Day landings began the following morning.

THOSE heroes that shed their blood and lost their lives ... You are now lying in the soil of a friendly country. Therefore rest in peace. There is no difference between the Johnnies and the Mehmets to us where they lie side by side here in this country of ours ... You the mothers who sent their sons from far away countries wipe away your tears. Your sons are now living in our bosom and are in peace. Having lost their lives on this land they have become our sons as well.

ATATÜRK, founder of the Turkish Republic, on a plaque erected to fallen Australians and New Zealanders at ANZAC Cove, Gallipoli

WEALTH

TRAMP: I haven't eaten for three days.

PASSER-BY: My dear chap – you must *force* yourself!

'Gross National Happiness' is a concept created by the king of Bhutan, His Majesty Jigme Singye Wangchuck, in 1972 as an alternative measure for gauging the development and condition of countries. Rooted in the Buddhist idea that inner peace and happiness is more important than material wealth, GNH encourages people to look beyond dry economic measurements such as GNP to assess the value of their lives.

In Britain, the New Economics Foundation has developed its own audit of success, the Happy Planet Index, which also includes environmental factors. Go to www.neweconomics.org for more.

WE believe that once the peoples, including their corporations and labour and other organizations of the world, understand the benefits of a single global currency, they will demand it from their governments. The single global currency is what the peoples of the world need, and it is what they want.

Single Global Currency Association

I'M off to my mansion and 300-acre farm, you lot can bugger off to your council houses.

KEN BATES, b. 1931, former chairman of Chelsea FC, as he swept out of the club in his Jaguar pursued by a pack of reporters

---

- Better to go to Heaven in rags than Hell in embroidery

- A heavy purse makes a light heart

- Money is the ace of trumps

- No one is poor but he thinks himself so

10 RICHEST PEOPLE IN THE WORLD IN $ BILLIONS

Warren Buffett (US, stocks): 62

Carlos Slim Helú (Mexico, telecommunications): 60

Bill Gates (US, software): 58

Lakshmi Mittal (India, steel): 45

Mukesh Ambani (India, various): 43

Anil Ambani (India, various): 42

Ingvar Kamprad (Sweden, flat-pack furniture): 31

K. P. Singh (US, property): 30

Oleg Deripaska (Russia, natural resources): 28

Karl Albrecht (Germany, supermarkets): 27

Forbes, 2008

You can loathe the City as much as you want, but its importance to the wealth of Britain as a whole is indisputable. The business generated there and in associated organizations across London amounts to 10 per cent of GDP, contributing roughly £90 billion to government revenues, roughly the annual amount needed to run the NHS.

Eight of the 10 most severe stock market crashes happened in the early part of the 20th century, indicating either that economies have developed better self-defence mechanisms or that governments have learned to manage economies better.

Britain became the largest donor to the World Bank's main fund for assistance to poor countries when it overtook the United States in 2007. The total of $25.1 billion pledged by the world's richest countries was a record sum, up 41 per cent from the bank's previous fundraising campaign in 2005. The sum included donations by China and Egypt, countries that were once recipients of such aid.

TEN RICHEST COUNTRIES BY GNP PER CAPITA

Luxembourg $56,380

Norway $51,810

Switzerland $49,600

United States $41,440

Denmark $40,750

Iceland $37,920

Japan $37,050

Sweden $35,840

Ireland $34,310

United Kingdom $33,630

World Bank, 2006

Rich parents have started to enrol their children in 'philanthropy' workshops designed to teach them how to apply their wealth to good causes and use their money responsibly. New Philanthropy Capital, the first charity in the UK to advise donors on effective ways to give money, set up their offices on the fringes of the City, providing seminars for the families of super-rich bankers and brokers.

It is not having a lot of money that makes people happy, but spending it on others, according to research by the University of British Columbia published in Science magazine in 2008. Staff who spent some of their bonuses on others were happier than those who spent their bonuses on themselves, the survey found.

MONEY is not an end in itself. It enables one to live the kind of life of one's own choosing. Some will prefer to put a large amount to raising material standards, others will pursue music, the arts, the cultures, others will use their money to help those here and overseas about whose needs they feel strongly, and do not let us underestimate the amount of hard-earned cash that this nation gives voluntarily to worthy causes. The point is that even the Good Samaritan had to have the money to help, otherwise he too would have had to pass by on the other side.

MARGARET THATCHER, speech, 'What's Wrong with Politics?', 1968

WORLD'S MOST GENEROUS PHILANTHROPISTS IN 2007 AND THEIR DONATIONS IN $ MILLIONS

1 Warren Buffett, 40,650

2 Bill and Melinda Gates, 3,519

3 George Kaiser, 2,271

4 George Soros, 2,109

5 Gordon and Betty Moore, 2,067

6 Walton (Wal-Mart) family, 1,475

7 Herbert and Marion Sandler, 1,368

8 Eli and Edythe Broad, 1,216

9 Donald Bren, 915

10 Jon Huntsman, 800

(*Forbes*)

ALL I ask is the chance to prove that money can't make me happy.

ANON

weaTHer

CIVIL SERVANT: Prime Minister, I have to report that a minister was found half-naked with a guardsman in Hyde Park last night.

WINSTON CHURCHILL: Last night? Coldest night of the year? Makes you proud to be British.

Two Russian scientists who believe the threat of global warming is overstated have bet a British climate expert $10,000 that the Earth will cool over the next decade.

Solar physicists Galina Mashnich and Vladimir Bashkirtsev, who agreed the wager with climate expert James Annan in 2005, believe that global temperatures are driven more by changes in the sun's activity than by the emission of greenhouse gases.

IT was a gloriously beautiful Scotch morning. The rain fell softly and quietly.

STEPHEN LEACOCK, Canadian writer, 1869–1944

SUNSHINE is delicious, rain is refreshing, wind braces us up, snow is exhilarating; there is really no such thing as bad weather, only different kinds of good weather.

JOHN RUSKIN

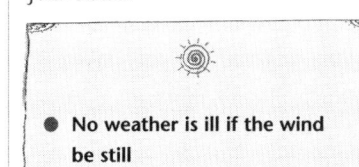

No weather is ill if the wind be still

From the man who once announced 'Harry Commentator is your carpenter':

I'M glad to say that this is the first Saturday in four weeks that sport will be weather-free.

DAVID COLEMAN, sports presenter

IN the depths of winter I finally learned there was in me an invincible summer.

ALBERT CAMUS, French writer, 1913–60

IT is the umbrella that has made Englishmen what they are.

SIR MAX BEERBOHM, English writer, 1872–1956

A PICNIC is the Englishman's grand gesture, his final defiance flung in the face of fate. No climate in the world is less propitious than the climate of England, yet with a recklessness which is almost sublime the English rush out of doors to eat a meal on every possible and impossible occasion.

GEORGINA BATTISCOMBE, *English Picnics*, 1951

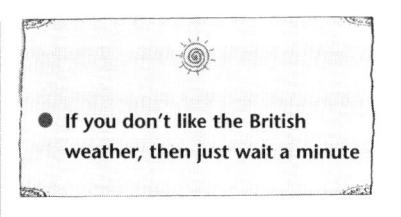

● **If you don't like the British weather, then just wait a minute**

A WOMAN rang to say she heard a hurricane was on the way. Well don't worry, there isn't.

MICHAEL FISH, BBC weather forecaster, 15 October 1987, on the eve of Britain's worst storm for 284 years

women

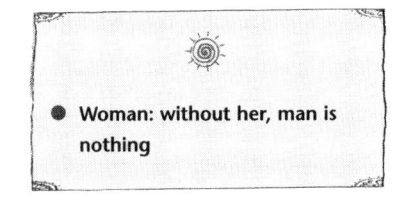

● **Woman: without her, man is nothing**

THE surest remedy for the male disease of self-contempt is the love of a sensible woman.

FRIEDRICH NIETZSCHE, *Human, All-Too-Human*, 1878

AND what is bettre than wisedoom?

Womman.

And what is bettre than a good womman?

Nothyng.

GEOFFREY CHAUCER, 'The Tale of Melibee'

THAT is the great distinction between the sexes. Men see objects, women see the relationship between objects. Whether the objects need each other, love each other, match each other. It is an extra dimension of feeling we men are without and one that makes war abhorrent to all real women – and absurd.

JOHN FOWLES, 1926–2005, *The French Lieutenant's Woman*

A Date for Your Diary

The eighth of March is International Women's Day (www.un.org/events/women/iwd), but it is also the day when the Global Women's Strike is held each year to highlight just how much of the world's work is done by women, and the difference it makes when their contribution is withdrawn. Other issues pointed out on the website at www.globalwomenstrike.net include the fact that a mere 10 per cent of the world's annual one-trillion-dollar military budget would provide everyone in the world with basic healthcare, enough food and drinkable water, proper sanitation, literacy, and a minimum income.

Make Love, Not War

Some 2,500 years ago, the great Greek playwright Aristophanes wrote Lysistrata, *the story of a woman who, during the Peloponnesian War, persuades her fellow wives to go on a sex strike in order to force their husbands to vote for peace with Sparta. Her reasoning is as follows: 'We need only sit indoors with painted cheeks, and meet our mates lightly clad in transparent gowns of Amorgos silk, and perfectly depilated; they will get their tools up and be wild to lie with us. That will be the time to refuse, and they will hasten to make peace, I am convinced of that.'*

In real life, sex strikes have been used by women: in Sudan, to protest against the civil war; in Colombia to protest against drug wars; in Poland to fight for legal abortion; and in Turkey to fight for the rights of communities against poisonous cyanide-based gold-mining.

The Lysistrata Project, www.lysistrataproject.org, is an ever-growing movement dedicated to the pursuit of peace and to encouraging women to take positive action in one way or another.

WOMAN seems to differ from man in mental disposition, chiefly in her greater tenderness and less selfishness.

CHARLES DARWIN, *The Descent of Man*, 1871

EVERY man who is high up likes to feel that he has done it all himself; and the wife smiles, and lets it go at that. It's our only joke. Every woman knows that.

SIR JAMES BARRIE, *What Every Woman Knows*, 1908

WOMEN are the real architects of society.

HARRIET BEECHER STOWE, US author, 1811–96

THE cocks may crow, but it's the hen that lays the egg.

BARONESS THATCHER, British prime minister, b. 1925

Sure, Fred Astaire was great, but don't forget that Ginger Rogers did everything he did, backwards … and in high heels.

BOB THAVES, US cartoonist, 1924–2006, *Frank and Ernest*

WE have to free half of the human race, the women, so that they can help to free the other half.

EMMELINE PANKHURST, suffragist, 1858–1928

Universal Suffrage

After years of struggle and suffering, women in America were finally given the vote in 1920, and in the UK in 1928. New Zealand was the first self-governing country in the world where women could vote, in 1893, but Switzerland did not give women the right to vote in every election until 1990. Womankind Worldwide (see www.womankind.org.uk) is among the organizations working on practical solutions, such as the introduction of separate polling booths, to encourage the civil and political participation of women worldwide.

WOULD men but generously snap our chains, and be content with rational fellowship instead of slavish obedience, they would find us more observant daughters, more affectionate sisters, more faithful wives, more reasonable mothers – in a word, better citizens.

MARY WOLLSTONECRAFT, British feminist, 1759–97

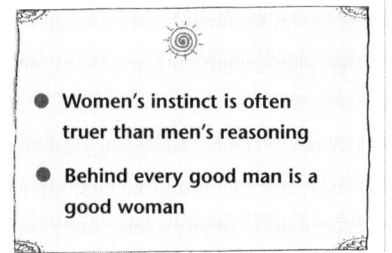

- Women's instinct is often truer than men's reasoning
- Behind every good man is a good woman

WE are not asking for superiority for we have always had that; all we ask is equality.

NANCY ASTOR, first female MP, 1879–1964

Ourstory

Let us now praise women
with feet glass slippers wouldn't fit;

not the patient, nor even the
   embittered
ones who kept their place,

but awkward women, tenacious
   with truth,
whose elbows disposed of the
   impossible;

who split seams, who wouldn't wait,
take no, take sedatives;

who sang their own numbers,
   went uninsured,
knew best what they were missing.

Our misfit foremothers are
   joining forces
underground, their dusts mingling

breast-bone with scapula, forehead
with forehead. Their steady mass

bursts locks; lends a springing foot
to our vaulting into enormous
   rooms.

CAROLE SATYAMURTI, English poet, b. 1939

Tiresias, the transsexual blind prophet of Thebes

When Tiresias displeased Hera, Queen of the Gods, she punished him by turning him into a woman. Years later, when Hera and her husband, Zeus, were arguing over which gender received more sexual pleasure – each of them insisting it was the other – they came to Tiresias to ask his/her opinion, since s/he had experienced both. Tiresias revealed that, by a ratio of ten to one, women have far more sexual pleasure than men. Hera was so angry that she instantly struck Tiresias blind, but Zeus made compensation with another gift of sight – that of prophecy.

THE great question that has never been answered, and which I have not yet been able to answer, despite my 30 years of research into the feminine soul, is 'What does a woman want?'

SIGMUND FREUD, 1856–1939

What women want

Look, for example, at www.guerillagirls.com, where discrimination is fought with 'facts, humor, and fake fur', or stay one step ahead at www.global-sisterhood-network.org, on the lookout for developments which may affect women adversely.

WHAT the woman who labours wants is the right to live, not simply exist – the right to life as the rich woman has it; the right to life, and the sun, and music, and art … The worker must have bread, but she must have roses, too.

ROSE SCHNEIDERMAN, US socialist, 1882–1972

The Weaker Sex?

According to Thomas Perls of the Boston University School of Medicine, women, evolutionarily speaking, are more fit than men – evolution naturally selects the genes of women who live long and age slowly (because they can bear and raise more children) over those who die young. Women outlive men in all developed and most undeveloped countries, sometimes by as much as ten years, and they've been out-surviving men since at least the 1500s, in spite of the sizeable risk of childbirth. Remarkably, this gender gap is most pronounced in the really old: among centenarians worldwide, women outnumber men nine to one.

WORDS OF WISDOM

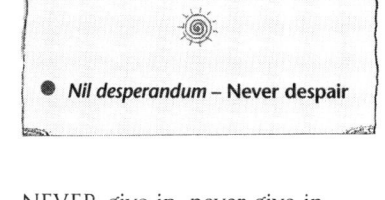

● *Nil desperandum* – **Never despair**

NEVER give in, never give in, never, never, never, never — in nothing, great or small, large or petty – never give in except to convictions of honour and good sense.

WINSTON CHURCHILL, speech at Harrow School, 29 October 1941

Beware of desperate steps. The
    darkest day
(Live till tomorrow) will have passed
    away.

WILLIAM COWPER, 'The Needless Alarm', 1790

HITCH your wagon to a star.

RALPH WALDO EMERSON, 'Society and Solitude'

LET us all be happy, and live within our means, even if we have to borrer the money to do it with.

ARTEMUS WARD, US humorist, 1834–67

YOU never enjoy the world aright, till the Sea itself floweth in your veins, till you are clothed with the heavens, and crowned with the stars: and perceive yourself to be the sole heir of the whole world, and more than so, because men are in it who are every one sole heirs as well as you ...

THOMAS TRAHERNE, English mystic, 1636–74, *Centuries of Meditation*

● **Worse things happen at sea**

● **Look on the bright side**

● **Better light a candle than curse the darkness**

● **Every cloud has a silver lining**

Whatever you can do, or dream you
    can, begin it.
Boldness has genius, power and
    magic in it.
Only engage!

JOHANN WOLFGANG VON GOETHE

EVER tried. Ever failed. No
matter. Try again. Fail again. Fail
better.

SAMUEL BECKETT, 1906–89, *Worstward Ho*

- **Bear with evil and expect good**

- **Nothing so bad but it might have been worse**

- **The darkest hour is just before dawn**

IT is the greatest of all mistakes
to do nothing because you can
only do a little. Do what you
can.

SYDNEY SMITH

YOU should make a point of
trying every experience once —
excepting incest and folk-
dancing.

ANON

ALWAYS fornicate between
clean sheets and spit on a well-
scrubbed floor.

CHRISTOPHER FRY, 1907–2005, *The Lady's
Not for Burning*

Self-help from the Bible:

A MAN hath no better thing
under the sun, than to eat, and
to drink, and to be merry.

Ecclesiastes 8:15

THE Kingdom of God is within
you.

Luke 17:21

BE joyful in hope, patient in
affliction, patient in prayer.

Romans 12:12

RESIST not evil: but whosoever
shall smite thee on thy right
cheek, turn to him the other
also.

Matthew 5:39

CAST thy bread upon the
waters: for thou shalt find it
after many days.

Ecclesiastes 11:1

Huckleberry Finn's motto:

- **Trust in the unexpected**

- That the birds of care and worry fly above your head, this you can't help
- That they nest in your hair, this you can

(CHINA)

IT is worth a thousand pounds a year to have the habit of looking on the bright side of things.

SAMUEL JOHNSON

MY message to you is: Be courageous! Be as brave as your fathers before you. Have faith! Go forward.

THOMAS EDISON

IF you are going through hell, *keep going.*

WINSTON CHURCHILL

- When God closes a door, he opens a window

- When life throws lemons at you, make lemonade

(JEWISH)

- Even a clock that is not going is right twice a day

(POLAND)

ANGELS can fly because they take themselves lightly.

G. K. CHESTERTON, 1874–1936

Sin is behovely, but all shall be well and all shall be well and all manner of thing shall be well.

JULIAN OF NORWICH, woman mystic, c. 1342–c. 1416, *Revelations of Divine Love*

IT is a little embarrassing that, after 45 years of research and study, the best advice I can give to people is to be a little kinder to each other.

ALDOUS HUXLEY

CARPE diem – Seize the day!

HORACE, *Odes*

LIFE is short. Live it up.

NIKITA KHRUSHCHEV, Soviet president, 1894–1971

LIVE all you can; it's a mistake not to.

HENRY JAMES, 1843–1916, *The Ambassadors*

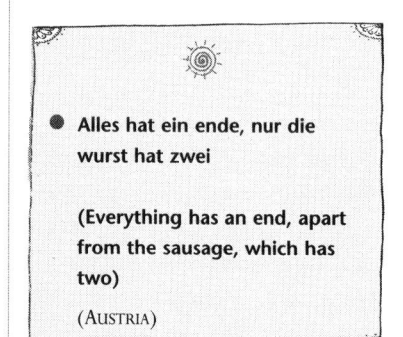

- Alles hat ein ende, nur die wurst hat zwei

(Everything has an end, apart from the sausage, which has two)

(AUSTRIA)

work

- **Many hands make light work**
- **Hard work never hurt anyone**

LABOUR is the Father and active principle of Wealth.

Sir William Petty, *Treatise of Taxes*, 1662

WORK earnestly at anything, you will by degrees learn to work at all things.

Thomas Carlyle, *Past and Present*, 1843

WORK banishes those three great evils, boredom, vice, and poverty.

Voltaire, *Candide*

Most people questioned in opinion polls on job satisfaction give 'respect from their boss' as the biggest source of work happiness.

IN all labour there is profit.

The Bible, Proverbs 14:23

TO secure for the workers by hand or by brain the full fruits of their industry and the most equitable distribution thereof that may be possible upon the basis of the common ownership of the means of production, distribution, and exchange, and the best obtainable system of popular administration and control of each industry or service.

British Labour Party constitution, Clause IV, 1918–96

Researchers studying Shell Oil employees found that people who retire at 55 are 89 per cent more likely to die within ten years of retiring than those who left work at 65.

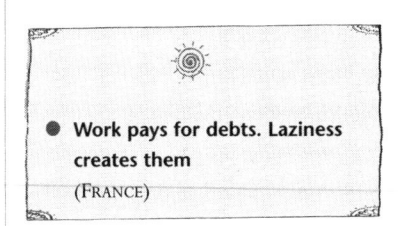

- **Work pays for debts. Laziness creates them**
  (France)

THERE is no success without hard work.

SOPHOCLES, *Electra*

FAR and away the best prize that life has to offer is the chance to work hard at work worth doing.

THEODORE ROOSEVELT

According to figures from the Office for National Statistics, over 3.4 million people, or 12 per cent of the British workforce, now regularly work from home and this phenomenon is increasing thanks to the explosive growth of new technologies such as emailing, webcams, video-conferencing, mobile phones and the internet.

Whistle While You Work!

A survey undertaken to discover who were Britain's happiest employees revealed, in the following order:
1st Hairdressers
2nd Clergy
3rd Chefs/cooks
4th Beauticians
5th Plumbers, Mechanics, Builders
6th Electricians, Florists, Fitness Instructors

City & Guilds, 2005

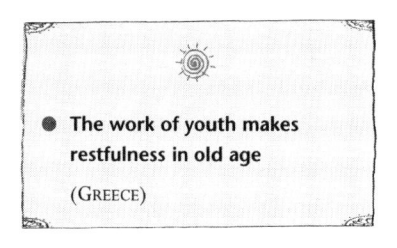

● The work of youth makes restfulness in old age
(GREECE)

In every rank, or great or small,
'Tis industry supports us all.

JOHN GAY, 'Man, Cat, Dog, and Fly'

I LIKE work; it fascinates me. I can sit and look at it for hours. I love to keep it by me: the idea of getting rid of it nearly breaks my heart.

JEROME K. JEROME, *Three Men in a Boat*, 1889

PERSISTENT work triumphs.

VIRGIL

YOUTH AND CHILDHOOD

IF help and salvation are to come, they can only come from the children, for the children are the makers of men.

MARIA MONTESSORI

LET our children grow tall, and some taller than others if they have it in them to do so.

MARGARET THATCHER, speech, October 1975

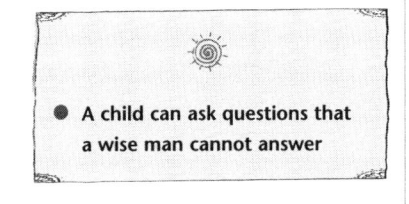

● A child can ask questions that a wise man cannot answer

ADOLESCENCE is the only time when we can learn something.

MARCEL PROUST, *A la Recherche du temps perdu*, 1919

IF you want to be creative, stay in part a child, with the creativity and invention that characterizes children before they are deformed by adult society.

JEAN PIAGET, 1896–1980

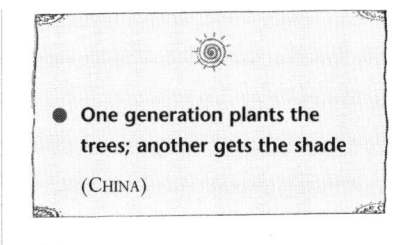

● One generation plants the trees; another gets the shade

(CHINA)

When all the world is young, lad
And all the trees are green;
And every goose a swan, lad,
And every lass a queen;
Then hey for the boot and horse,
    lad,
And round the world away:
Young blood must have its course,
    lad,
And every dog his day.

CHARLES KINGSLEY, *The Water Babies*, 1863

CHILDREN have neither past nor future. They live in the present, something which rarely happens to us.

JEAN DE LA BRUYÈRE, *Les Caractères ou les moeurs de ce siècle*, 1688

THE child shall have the right to freedom of expression; this right shall include freedom to seek, receive and impart information and ideas of all kinds, regardless of frontiers, either orally, in writing or in print, in the form of art, or through any other media of the child's choice.

Article 13.1, Convention of the Rights of the Child, 1989

MAKING children happy now will make them happy twenty years hence.

SYDNEY SMITH

AND they brought unto him also infants, that he would touch them: but when his disciples saw it, they rebuked them. But Jesus called them unto him, and said, Suffer little children to come unto me, and forbid them not: for of such is the kingdom of God. Verily I say unto you, Whosoever shall not receive the kingdom of God as a little child shall no wise enter therein.

The Bible, Luke 18:15–17

There was a time when meadow, grove, and stream,
The earth, and every common sight
To me did seem
Apparelled in celestial light,
The glory and the freshness of a dream ...

... Our birth is but a sleep and a forgetting;
The Soul that rises with us, our life's Star,
Hath had elsewhere its setting
And cometh from afar;
Not in entire forgetfulness,
And not in utter nakedness,
But trailing clouds of glory do we come
From God, who is our home:
Heaven lies about us in our infancy!

WILLIAM WORDSWORTH, 'Ode on Intimations of Immortality', from *Recollections of Early Childhood*

LOVE children especially, for like the angels they too are sinless, and they live to soften and purify our hearts, and, as it were, to guide us. Woe to him who offends a child!

FYODOR DOSTOYEVSKY, *The Brothers Karamazov*

A child born in AD 1000 had a life expectancy of around 24 years. By the 1900s it was 49 years. Today, a child born in Europe can hope to live to over 80.

GOODBYE

May the road rise to meet you.
May the wind be always at your back.
May the sun shine warm upon your face,
And rains fall soft upon your fields.
And until we meet again,
May God hold you in the hollow of His hand.

(IRELAND)

WHEN we know the truth, we sit in the middle of the circle